DEBUNKING THE GRIT NARRATIVE IN HIGHER EDUCATION

Debunking the Grit Narrative in Higher Education examines pressing structural issues currently impacting African American, Asian American, Pacific Islander, Latinx, and Native American students accessing college and succeeding in U.S. postsecondary environments. Drawing from asset-based work of critical race education scholars such as Yosso, Ladson-Billings, and contributing author Solórzano, the authors interrogate how systems and structures shape definitions of academic merit and grit, how these systems constrain opportunities to attain access and equitable educational outcomes, and challenge widely held beliefs that Students of Color need grit to succeed in college. Dominant narratives of educational success and failure tend to focus mostly on individual student effort. Contributing authors explore the myriad ways that institutional structures can support Students of Color utilizing their strengths through critical perspectives, asset-based, anti-deficit perspectives to access postsecondary environments and experience success. Scholars, scholar-practitioners, student affairs professionals, and educational leaders will benefit from this timely edited book as they work to transform postsecondary institutions into entities that meet the needs of Students and Communities of Color.

Angela M. Locks is Executive Director for Diversity, Equity, and Inclusion for Academic Affairs and Professor of Educational Leadership and Student Development in Higher Education at California State University, Long Beach, USA.

Rocío Mendoza is Assistant Professor of Educational Leadership and Higher Education at the University of Redlands, USA.

Deborah Faye Carter is Associate Professor of Higher Education at Claremont Graduate University, USA.

DEBUNKING THE GRIT NARRATIVE IN HIGHER EDUCATION

Drawing on the Strengths of African American, Asian American, Pacific Islander, Latinx, and Native American Students

Edited by Angela M. Locks, Rocío Mendoza, and Deborah Faye Carter

NEW YORK AND LONDON

First published 2024
by Routledge
605 Third Avenue, New York, NY 10158

and by Routledge
4 Park Square, Milton Park, Abingdon, Oxon, OX14 4RN

Routledge is an imprint of the Taylor & Francis Group, an informa business

ISBN: 978-1-032-36523-7 (hbk)
ISBN: 978-1-032-35815-4 (pbk)
ISBN: 978-1-003-33249-7 (ebk)

DOI: 10.4324/9781003332497

Typeset in Galliard
by SPi Technologies India Pvt Ltd (Straive)

CONTENTS

PREFACE

Toni Morrison discussed historical legacies of racism, capitalism, and the responsibilities of Black artists and scholars:

> It's important ... to know who the real enemy is, and to know the function, the very serious function of racism, which is distraction. It keeps you from doing your work. It keeps you explaining, over and over again, your reason for being.
>
> *(Morrison, 1975)*

She urged Black creators to focus on their art and scholarly endeavors and not to engage with others acting in bad faith. Morrison described the continuing dilemma faced by many practitioners and researchers of color, including the editors of this book. What kinds of theories and research perspectives garner the most interest from funding agencies and foundations? What new understandings of education and society might we instead approach if we spent less time arguing for our basic human rights and working to challenge deficit views? How might our practices change as administrators in higher education if we were free to lead in ways that we believe would be best for students?

This book arose from the co-editors' questions and concerns about grit. The development of this book originates from a symposium we organized at the annual American Educational Research Association (AERA) meeting in April 2018. We sought to challenge the idea of grit in higher education while engaging in Ladson-Billings' (2015) call for more public scholarship to challenge grit. The symposium garnered frank dialogue and thoughtful critique of traditional notions of academic success, and participants in the session reflected on the ways researchers and practitioners, often despite our best intentions, may continue to reinforce deficit ideas by promoting grit as a lens to understand student success.

One of the arguments that has been driving this book is that, simply put, *grit is a tool of white supremacy*. Grit is widely discussed as a neutral concept, with benign intents; after all, "who would not want to be perseverant?" Yet grit is just one in a long line of concepts, all designed to categorize low-performing students as having individual deficits and poor character if they are not successful. Low-income children already display forms of grit in that they have survived challenging circumstances to be educated (Goodman & Fine, 2018). Conceptualizations of grit and how to be grittier seem to uphold traditional standards of whiteness and privilege (Ris, 2015).

We also consider grit during these years of crises and pandemic. We are now entering the fourth year of the COVID-19 pandemic, while living through the multiple transnational crises of creeping fascism, institutional racism, climate injustice, and economic injustice. These circumstances have profoundly shifted the ways we live, work, and interact with one another. In times that we need to pull together as societies, these crises have painfully highlighted the ways that we are indeed *not* "all in this together" nor are we all "beginning from the same starting line." Yet, legislators continue to propose policies that deny (a) appropriate resources to change structures and (b) support services that would allow students to understand society better, see themselves reflected in their courses, and experience overall well-being and academic success.

We collaborated on this edited book because we are motivated to reflect on the current moment and ways to move forward toward a better future in understanding student achievement. Our relationships to each other are an important starting point for the form and structure of this book. Deborah Carter served as Angela Locks' advisor, mentor, and dissertation chair; years (and an institution) later, Deborah also became Rocío Mendoza's advisor, mentor, and dissertation chair. Rocío later met Angela through an academic mentoring program. These intergenerational forms of mentorship and guidance as women of color and first-generation faculty of color (Buenavista et al., 2022) have shown us ways that we could support each other and navigate our professional and personal lives in and out of academia. Similarly, we consider the contributors of this book as esteemed colleagues and peers, some of whom recently completed degrees themselves and others who have been naming and interrogating systems of exclusion for many years.

Background and Context

Morrison (1975) cautioned writers and academics about how white supremacy can negatively affect their work:

... and I urge you to be careful. For there is a deadly prison: the prison that is erected when one spends one's life fighting phantoms, concentrating on myths, and explaining over and over to the conqueror your language, your lifestyle, your history, your habits.

(Morrison, 1975)

As editors of this book, we, too, carry that spirit of trying to ignore distraction as external forces bear down on us. We are deeply committed to this work and project: as scholars who work in the field of higher education, we often must engage with racism (institutional racism and personal prejudice lodged against us or our mutuals) and try to work through the distractions. We find Morrison's call to action—to avoid distraction—to be as urgent now as it was nearly 50 years ago. Currently, one such distraction is the systematic, political attempt to ban books and knowledge that have their foundation in the true history of what is now the United States of America. The bans and the exhortations against certain topics (like Critical Race Theory) is, as scholar Robin D. G. Kelley stated, "attacking the whole concept of racial justice and equity" (Taylor, 2023, para. 7). In recent years, several states have passed legislation to restrict the instruction of various topics, including issues concerning lesbian, gay, bisexual individuals, and transgender communities, and severely restricting classroom curriculum related to racial/ethnic minoritized communities (Shen-Berro & Darville, 2023).

Higher education institutions (and related organizations) have met this moment by seemingly capitulating to those who devalue the experiences of marginalized people, tacitly endorsing Right-wing attacks on higher education and on the fields and disciplines (and people!) most recently scrutinized. For example, leaders of K-12 and higher education systems have capitulated to requests to search faculty email messages, limit programs and services, and remove content from previously approved courses (Schwartz, 2023). To date, higher education systems in states such as Texas, Florida, Arizona, and North Carolina have edited their institutional websites to remove language referring to diversity initiatives, disallowed funding or statements related to diversity, equity and inclusion, or have asked faculty to remove courses that engage with Critical Race Theory (Lu et al., 2023).

These current events may be "new," but what is new is never new. Cobb (2023) notes a lineage of political actors who have tried to shape public understanding of the nation's history: "the late-nineteenth-century romanticization of the Confederacy was meant to justify the new regime of segregation then being implemented across the South" (para. 1). Scholarly research supports Cobb's point. Bailey (1991) investigated the role of Confederate Southern elites in promoting revisionist history in late-nineteenth century schools. Until mid-way through the twentieth century, several organized groups, in support of white supremacy, removed from schools and libraries materials they deemed unacceptable, fired teachers who disagreed with their orthodoxy, and "indoctrinated southern children with aristocratic social values unchanged since the antebellum epoch" (p. 508). As noted above, 140 years later, Southern elites are still promoting censorship.

The current political movement toward banning courses, curricula, and books aimed at discussing an accurate history of the United States relates to an American lack of general understanding of racial economic equality. Keeping children and adults ignorant of the past significantly hinders the degree to which we can collectively reduce inequality. Kraus et al. (2019) stated that "Americans vastly underestimate racial economic inequality, especially the racial wealth gap" (p. 899). The underestimation is rooted in the fact that adults in our society are committed to an "unyielding belief in a specific, optimistic narrative regarding racial progress" (p. 900). That so many people believe this false narrative is a critical problem in trying to increase equity between racial/ethnic groups. The underestimation and misunderstanding about inequality translate into a lack of support for policy measures to address inequality.

There are multiple reasons for this widespread belief, but Kraus et al. (2019) explained that "researchers in the social sciences are largely guilty of analyzing the impacts of inequality in ways that do not also consider its racial patterning" (p. 916). Not only have researchers not considered racial patterning, but we argue that there are longstanding examples of social science disciplines explaining inequality through the lens of biological, racial differences (Andoh, 2021; Zuberi & Bonilla-Silva, 2008). Eugenics has been the foundation of many inquiries in social science, and it also serves as the basis of disciplinary understanding of human differences. Winston (2004) described that in the past, "many psychologists [adopted] an empiricist language for the discussion of racial differences," which meant that they could not be described as racist "because no hostility or personal animus was evident" (p. 8). Since "overt hostility" was not part of the early psychologists' analyses, "oppression could be wrapped in a value-neutral cloak" (Winston, 2004, p. 8). Although early psychologists' work led to immigration bans, sterilization, and other significant harms, this work has long been deemed "value-neutral" (Andoh, 2021). Thirty years ago, *The Bell Curve*, co-written by a Harvard University psychology professor, argued that biological inferiority explained the lower IQ scores of African American people in comparison to white people (Williams, 2020). While widely criticized, the book was very popular and had a resurgence as recently as six years ago (Dickens et al., 1995; Siegel, 2017). The popularity of such regressive ideas is harmful to efforts to reduce inequality and stratification; our society's understandings of the source of inequality also have implications for what policies we prioritize and how countries respond to crises.

COVID-19 Pandemic, Racial Trauma, and Precarity

The year 2020 marked several generational events—across the globe and throughout the nation—that underscored for us the need for this specific book. Again, we are reminded how important it is to understand how the structure of societies affects us. For too many communities, racialized trauma in the United States continued in 2020, notably with the visible, filmed police killings of George Floyd and Andres Guardado. In addition, there have been significant incidents of violence toward Asian Americans in public spaces, state violence against immigrants, and disproportionate gendered violence of Native American women (Rosay, 2016). Political leaders who embrace authoritarianism (and fascism) have increased people's feelings of precarity. The continued, structurally based vulnerability of people of color in the United States makes the individual and collective voices of this book necessary and timely.

Communities of Color have disproportionately been impacted by the COVID-19 pandemic, either through infection and death rates, violence, or both. Perspectives centered around assumptions of grit minimize how social structures impact educational achievement, particularly in areas where families and communities have suffered from COVID-19 infections at incredibly high numbers. The personal, financial, and educational costs to Communities of Color in this pandemic have not been fully examined, nor have structural barriers, including institutionalized racism, been thoroughly documented or understood by the broader postsecondary education community or U.S. society.

As a result, the disproportionate personal losses experienced by Students of Color have only been partially documented. These losses have resulted in lower college enrollment and graduation rates (U.S. Department of Education, 2021). Communities of Color were also disproportionately impacted by financial and employment losses, and job losses were particularly acute for African Americans, with those employed in personal care services and leisure and hospitality industries the most negatively impacted. Further, while there are indications that African Americans have experienced some wage growth since the pandemic, it remains to be seen if such growth is permanent or sustainable (The White House, 2022). For Latinx communities, a similar pattern occurred with nearly 20% of the Latinx workforce reporting unemployment during the height of the pandemic (Galdámez & Carmona, 2022). In Native American communities, employment declines again were swift and sharp (Feir & Golding, 2020). Asian American communities were impacted in a myriad of ways; one data point is that AAPI women experienced the highest rates of Long-Term Unemployment directly related to the COVID-19 Pandemic (National Asian Pacific American Women's Forum, 2021). Through the beginning of 2023, the scarcity of opportunities to work remotely has constrained employment prospects for multiple communities (Mohr, 2023).

Grounding our Ideological Orientation

We write against a backdrop of societal stratification, increased authoritarianism, and current crises that inform this book and our overall ideological orientation to what educational achievement means, particularly for marginalized students. We are compelled to map our ideological orientations to this book and describe how we are making sense of the ideas and notions of grit, along with our orientations to the world. As critical educators, we bring multidisciplinary frameworks and draw from a number of fields in approaching our work, including sociology, psychology, ethnic studies, as well as Black Feminist Thought (Collins, 1986, 2000) and Chicana Feminist Epistemologies (Calderón et al., 2012; Delgado Bernal, 1998). These frameworks allow us to understand grit from multiple vantage points and understand the role and relevance of sociohistorical and sociopolitical contexts. We see the value in historicizing ideas and unearthing assumptions, beliefs, and values of current practices and fads in educational "interventions."

In his introduction to *On Critical Race Theory*, Victor Ray (2022) described the audience for his book to be those who "are genuinely committed to racial equality" (xvii) and who are committed to discussing related concepts in good faith. We share similar sentiments: we invite scholars, scholar-practitioners, student affairs professionals, policy makers, and educational leaders and administrators who believe in the academic potential of African American, Latinx, Asian American, Pacific Islander, Native American, and other marginalized students to engage with the ideas and recommendations presented in this book. This book contributes to the discourse on race and ethnicity in higher education by rethinking and reimagining theories, research, and practices that collectively debunk grit and deficit ways of thinking, interrogating how systems and structures shape definitions of grit that constrain opportunities to experience accessible and equitable educational outcomes in postsecondary contexts. We write this book for those who are committed to exploring how seemingly "objective" criteria can be harmful to students and limit how we understand research problems in higher education.

References

Andoh, E. (2021). Psychology's urgent need to dismantle racism. *Monitor on Psychology, 52*(3), 38.

Bailey, F. A. (1991). The textbooks of the "Lost Cause": Censorship and the creation of Southern state histories. *The Georgia Historical Quarterly, 75*(3), 507–533.

Buenavista, T. L., Jain, D., & Ledesma, M. C. (Eds.) (2022). *First-generation faculty of color: Reflections on research, teaching, and service*. Rutgers University Press.

Calderón, D., Bernal Delgado, D., Huber, L. P., Malagón, M., & Vélez, V. N. (2012). A Chicana feminist epistemology revisited: Cultivating ideas a generation later. *Harvard Educational Review, 82*(4), 513–539.

Cobb, J. (2023, January 29). Ron DeSantis battles the African American A.P. Course-and history. *The New Yorker.* https://www.newyorker.com/magazine/2023/02/06/ron-desantis-battles-the-african-american-ap-course-and-history

Collins, P. H. (1986). Learning from the outsider within: The sociological significance of Black feminist thought. *Social Problems, 33*(6), s14–s32.

Collins, P. H. (2000). *Black feminist thought: Knowledge, consciousness and the politics of empowerment* (2nd ed.). Routledge.

Delgado Bernal, D. (1998). Using a Chicana feminist epistemology in educational research. *Harvard Educational Review, 68*(4), 555–583. https://doi.org/10.17763/haer.68.4.5wv1034973g22q48

Dickens, W. T., Schultze, C. L., & Kane, T. J. (1995, June 1). *Does The Bell Curve ring true? A closer look at a grim portrait of American Society*. Brookings. From https://www.brookings.edu/articles/does-the-bell-curve-ring-true-a-closer-look-at-a-grim-portrait-of-american-society/

Feir, D. L., & Golding, C. (2020, August 5). Native employment during COVID-19: Hit hard in April but starting to rebound? *Federal Reserve Bank of Minneapolis.* https://www.minneapolisfed.org/article/2020/native-employment-during-covid-19-hit-hard-in-april-but-starting-to-rebound

Galdámez, M., & Carmona, G. N. (2022, September 8). All work and no pay: Unpaid Latina care work during the COVID-19 pandemic. *Latino Policy & Politics Institute, UCLA.* https://latino.ucla.edu/research/latina-care-work-covid19/

Goodman, S., & Fine, M. (2018). *It's not about grit: Trauma, inequity, and the power of transformative teaching*. Teachers College Press.

Kraus, M. W., Onyeador, I. N., Daumeyer, N. M., Rucker, J. M., & Richeson, J. A. (2019). The misperception of racial economic inequality. *Perspectives on Psychological Science, 14*(6), 899–921. https://doi.org/10.1177/1745691619863049

Ladson-Billings, G. (2015, April 22). Now I need to have grit. *Black and Smart Word Press.* https://blackandsmart.wordpress.com/2015/04/22/now-i-need-to-have-grit/

Lu, A., Elias, J., June, A. W., Marijolovic, K., Roberts-Grmela, J., & Surovell, E. (2023, March 29). DEI legislation tracker. *The Chronicle of Higher Education.* https://www.chronicle.com/article/here-are-the-states-where-lawmakers-are-seeking-to-ban-colleges-dei-efforts

Mohr, C. (2023, January 18). Native Americans have fewer opportunities to work remotely. *Federal Reserve Bank of Minneapolis.* https://www.minneapolisfed.org/article/2023/native-americans-have-fewer-opportunities-to-work-remotely

Morrison, T. (1975, May 30). *A humanist's view* [Speech audio recording]. Portland State University Library Collections. https://soundcloud.com/portland-state-library/portland-state-black-studies-1

National Asian Pacific American Women's Forum (NAPAF). (2021, June). *Long-term unemployment among Asian American and Pacific Islander women Fact Sheet.* https://www.napawf.org/s/Long-Term-Unemployment-Among-AAPI-Women.pdf

Ray, V. (2022). *On critical race theory: Why it matters & why you should care.* Random House.

Ris, E. W. (2015). Grit: A short history of a useful concept. *Journal of Educational Controversy, 10*(1), article 3.

Rosay, A. B. (2016). Violence against American Indian and Alaska Native women and men. *National Institute of Justice Journal,* (*277*), 38–45. https://www.ojp.gov/pdffiles1/nij/249822.pdf

Schwartz, S. (2023, March 23). Map: Where critical race theory is under attack. *Education Week.* https://www.edweek.org/policy-politics/map-where-critical-race-theory-is-under-attack/2021/06

Shen-Berro, J., & Darville, S. (2023, February 2). Advanced placement debate feels high-stakes for Teachers of African American history. *Chalkbeat.* https://www.chalkbeat.org/2023/2/2/23582771/advanced-placement-african-american-studies-black-history-college-board

Siegel, E. (2017, April 12). The real problem with Charles Murray and "The Bell Curve." *Scientific American.* https://blogs.scientificamerican.com/voices/the-real-problem-with-charles-murray-and-the-bell-curve/

Taylor, K.-Y. (2023, February 3). The meaning of African American studies. *The New Yorker.* https://www.newyorker.com/culture/q-and-a/the-meaning-of-african-american-studies

The White House. (2022, August 24). Pandemic shifts in Black employment and wages. https://www.whitehouse.gov/cea/written-materials/2022/08/24/pandemic-shifts-in-black-employment-and-wages/

U.S. Department of Education. (2021). *Education in a pandemic: The disparate impacts of COVID-19 on America's students.* https://www2.ed.gov/about/offices/list/ocr/docs/20210608-impacts-of-covid19.pdf

Williams, M. T. (2020, November 30). Psychology's hidden history: Racist roots and poison fruits. *Psychology Today.* https://www.psychologytoday.com/us/blog/culturally-speaking/202011/psychology-s-hidden-history-racist-roots-and-poison-fruits

Winston, A. S. (2004). Introduction: Histories of psychology and race. In A. S. Winston (Ed.), *Defining difference: Race and racism in the history of psychology* (pp. 3–18). American Psychological Association. https://doi.org/10.1037/10625-001

Zuberi, T., & Bonilla-Silva, E. (Eds.). (2008). *White logic, white methods: Racism and methodology.* Rowman & Littlefield Publishers.

ACKNOWLEDGMENTS

We are indebted to the brilliant contributing authors for their willingness to share their intellect and join this conversation about grit, whiteness, and white supremacy and more importantly highlight the strength, love, and joy in the communities that have shaped us and our collective voices.

Thanks go to Jordan Beltran Gonzales, Lethia Cobbs, and Patrice Bounds for their editorial support, engagement, and careful attention to our project. We could not have pulled this off without you!

Angela M Locks: Working on this book with Deborah and Rocío has been a great honor and a source of tremendous joy. In many ways this book is part of a broader conversation we have been having amongst ourselves as a trio for many years about how our lived experiences as women of color, culture, and brilliance are overlooked narratives, in and outside, of U.S. postsecondary education.

This project was partially supported by a sabbatical granted by the Office of the Provost (thank you Brian and Karyn!) and the College of Education at California State University, Long Beach.

My honey, I am so very grateful to and for you.

This is for LeAsia and Patrick Jr., and the newest inspiring ladies in my life, Asha, Kaavya, and Viviana. I am confident each of you will use your voice for good, wherever your path leads in the future.

Rocío Mendoza gives thanks to the University of Redlands for being a place that supports the intellectual pursuits of its faculty and for her students who would check-in and ask about the progress of the book. She is also grateful to her mentors and co-authors, Deborah and Angela. This project sustained her in many ways, and it was a model of writing collectively, centering love, humanity, and support. *Le doy gracias a Reynalda and Joel Mendoza, siempre, por su apoyo.* Rocío is also grateful to her spouse, Letty, who has been a source of love and encouragement through the development of this project. She especially thanks her for her patience, and gentle reminders to go outside, get some sun, and always take care.

Deborah Faye Carter: The pandemic has been a tough period for people of color in general, but also for faculty: hard to find time to write, think, and connect with each other in the midst of chaos! I am grateful for the connection the three of us have been able to maintain over the past years: co-creating, co-editing, and thinking together.

I would also like to acknowledge Claremont Graduate University, my main employer, for the research resources that enabled this project: travel funds to conferences, funds to pay an editor, and time in the form of a sabbatical. I know well that not all faculty have the benefit of these resources and I do not take that for granted.

Finally, I would like to thank my family. Their love sustains me. Lawrence, you have been my beloved for 24 years. Partners in crime. Always and forever. To my parents, Margaret and Clyde, thank you for everything. I would not be here without your love, guidance, and support.

CONTRIBUTORS

Nancy Acevedo is a full professor in Educational Leadership Doctoral Studies at California State University, San Bernardino. She serves as the Dean's Fellow for Inclusion and Equity and the Director of Faculty Development for the James R. Watson and Judy Rodriguez Watson College of Education. As a critical race Chicana feminist scholar, she examines the experiences of Students of Color as they prepare for and navigate key transitions along higher education pathways in order to interrupt deficit policies, practices, and ideologies that contribute to the marginalization of Communities of Color.

Elyzza M. Aparicio is the director of the Office of Undergraduate Research Services at California State University, Long Beach. Her research explores the role of undergraduate research on degree aspirations for minoritized and underrepresented racial/ethnic groups at an earlier time point in their academic pathway, as well as undergraduate research as a catalyst for retention, sense of belonging, habits of mind, and student self-efficacy.

Maenette K. P. Benham, a kānaka maoli scholar and teacher, currently serves as chancellor, University of Hawaiʻi West Oʻahu, and previously served as the inaugural dean of the Hawaiʻinuiākea School of Hawaiian Knowledge at UH Mānoa. While faculty in the College of Education at Michigan State University she strengthened her commitment to the praxis of social justice through engaged scholarship and the theme of "school/university in community and community in university." Her work on alternative cultural frames of educational leadership is nationally and internationally respected.

She is author, co-author, and editor of five books and numerous published articles, book chapters, monographs and technical reports.

Jorge Burmicky is an assistant professor of higher education leadership and policy studies at Howard University in Washington, D.C. His research explores leadership in higher education, racial equity, and social justice.

Deborah Faye Carter is an associate professor of higher education in the School of Educational Studies at Claremont Graduate University. Her scholarly work focuses on adjustment to college and how college experiences affect outcomes like students' major choices (especially in STEM fields), persistence to graduation, and students' graduate school choices. Recently, she has been engaged in projects studying students' sense of belonging in STEM majors, faculty perceptions of their mentoring roles, and institutional environments for instructional change.

Juanita E. Razo Dueñas has more than 20 years of experience supporting college access and success among underserved students. She serves as the director of Student Success Programs at the University of California San Diego that supports the matriculation, retention, and graduation of first-generation, military-connected, transfer, and undocumented and mixed-status students. Her scholarly work explores how college environments, policies, and practices in both curricular and cocurricular settings promote or impede access, retention, and educational outcomes for underserved Students of Color. She is a doctoral candidate at Claremont Graduate University studying higher education.

Julio Fregoso is a postdoctoral research fellow at the Research and Equity Scholarship Institute on Student Trajectories in Education (RESISTE) and is also connected to the NSF INCLUDES Alliance: ALRISE (NSF-HRD-2120021) – both of which are housed within the San Diego State University Research Foundation. His research is characterized by critical quantitative approaches to survey (re)design and analysis, aimed at accurately measuring the racialized experiences of community college and transfer students, and contingent faculty of color. As a first-generation college student who embarked on his academic journey at a local community college, he is passionately committed to advocating for equitable opportunities for all.

Su Jin Gatlin Jez serves as CEO of California Competes, an organization that develops nonpartisan and financially pragmatic recommendations for improved higher education and workforce policies and practices across California. Prior to joining California Competes, she served as an associate professor of public policy and administration at California State University, Sacramento. She is an accomplished researcher whose work appears in a variety of publications including *Teachers College Record*, *Education Policy Analysis Archives*, *Research in Higher Education*, *Community College Review*, and *Michigan Journal of Race & Law*. She has provided guidance to the California Community College Chancellor's Office, the California State University system, and California's Bureau for Private Postsecondary Education.

Angela M. Locks serves as the executive director for Diversity, Equity, and Inclusion for Academic Affairs at California State University, Long Beach and is a full professor in student development in higher education and educational leadership in the College of Education. Her scholarly work examines college access and experiences for diverse students with an emphasis on retention, institutional diversity praxis, and the relationships between college student interactions with diverse others and diversity program engagement.

Jacqueline Mac is a first-generation Chinese Vietnamese woman graduate and faculty. She is an assistant professor of higher education at Northern Illinois University. Her work is informed by her family's refugee journeys, heavily shaped by Asian American studies, and drawn from her experiences as an organizer and former student affairs professional. Jacqueline researches the racial realities of colleges and universities and uncovers the possibilities and limitations of these institutions to advance racial justice and equity. She primarily focuses on racially marginalized students, such as Southeast Asian Americans, and the institutions that serve them, also known as minority-serving institutions.

Melissa M. Mahoney is a student advocate and higher education technology expert. Her work aims to bridge the gap between institutional priorities and inclusive, holistic student services. She believes edtech can be used to create more equitable campuses where students of all backgrounds and abilities can achieve their academic, personal, and professional goals.

Rocío Mendoza (she/her/ella) is currently an assistant professor in the Department of Leadership and Higher Education at the University of Redlands. She teaches and writes about the logics and methods of marginalization in higher education, the assets, and epistemologies of Communities of Color, and the institutional structures and practices shaping Student of Color outcomes. She has over 15 years of experience working in academic support/training programs, including TRiO programs and Educational Opportunity Programs (EOP). Her approaches to teaching, research and mentorship are shaped by her personal experiences growing up as a Chicana in the city of La Puente, California, and as a proud daughter of immigrants from Mexico.

Anna M. Ortiz is a student development educator and researcher with over 30 years of experience in higher education. She is the Dean of the College of Education at California State University, Long Beach and is a full professor of Educational Leadership. Her research centers on ethnic identity of college students with additional streams of scholarship on Latinx students, multicultural issues in higher education, and career issues for faculty and student affairs professionals. She has conducted numerous external evaluations in Communities of Color.

Robert T. Palmer is chair and professor in the Department of Educational Leadership and Policy Studies in the School of Education at Howard University. He is also a faculty affiliate of the Center for Minority Serving Institutions at Rutgers University. His research examines issues of access, equity, retention, persistence, and the college experience of racial and ethnic minorities, particularly within the context of Historically Black Colleges and Universities.

Kathleen Rzucidlo is a Ph.D. student in the higher education leadership and policy studies program in the School of Education at Howard University. She is also a research graduate assistant for the Department of Educational Leadership and Policy Studies as well as an adjunct professor in the Department of Undergraduate Studies at American University. Her research examines accreditation and the relationship with Historically Black Colleges and Universities.

Sabrina K. Sanders is a thought leader, student success practitioner and equity leader. Her professional expertise encompasses a breadth of areas in and out of the classroom and at the system-wide level. She spearheads the reengagement efforts at California State University, Dominguez Hills (CSUDH) focused on identifying and supporting students with some college, no degree to degree completion. Prior to CSUDH, she was at the CSU Office of the Chancellor on the team supporting Graduation Initiative 2025 and was the lead administrator in launching the Basic Needs Initiative. She has served as an adjunct faculty in the College of Education at CSU Long Beach and student affairs roles in private, public, and community colleges.

Daniel G. Solórzano is a professor of education at the University of California, Los Angeles. His teaching and research interests include critical race theory in education and racial microaggressions and microaffirmations. He has authored more than 100 research articles, book chapters, and books on educational equity issues for underrepresented student populations and communities in the United States. In 2007, Professor Solórzano received the *UCLA Distinguished Teaching Award*. In 2012, Solórzano was also awarded the *Critical Race Studies in Education Association (CRSEA) Derrick A. Bell Legacy Award*. In 2014, he was elected a Fellow of the American Educational Research Association. In 2020, he was elected to the *National Academy of Education*. He recently received the 2022 *Spencer Foundation Mentorship Award*.

Stacey R. Speller is a Ph.D. student in the higher education leadership and policy studies program in the School of Education at Howard University. She is also a research graduate assistant for the Department of Educational Leadership and Policy Studies. Her research examines federal funding for dually designated Historically Black Colleges and Universities and Hispanic-serving Institutions from an organizational lens. In addition, she explores policies and practices at HBCUs that support the educational goals and outcomes of Latinx/a/o students.

Megan Trinh is a Teochew Vietnamese American and a first-generation doctoral student in the Social Science and Comparative Education division with a specialization in Race, Ethnic, and Cultural Studies at the University of California, Los Angeles. Her work draws on critical, creative, and collective approaches to challenge dominant ideologies and systems that impact Students of Color. Currently, her research focuses on understanding and disrupting racialized narratives facing Southeast Asian American students and centers students and their communities as knowledge producers and sites of resistance.

Rikka J. Venturanza is a doctoral candidate at UCLA's School of Education, specializing in Race, Ethnic, and Cultural Studies with a concentration in Asian American Studies. She currently serves as a research associate at UCLA's Institute for Immigration, Globalization, and Education. Her research agenda is focused on advancing equity and inclusion agendas to increase the success of immigrant-origin and immigration-impacted college student populations. Prior to UCLA, Rikka developed and coordinated student-centered programs and lectured ethnic studies courses at public four- and two-year institutions in California.

Stephanie J. Waterman, Onondaga, Turtle Clan, Associate Professor at the Ontario Institute for Studies in Education/University of Toronto, in Leadership, Higher & Adult Education, coordinates the higher education program and student development/student services in higher education program. Her research interests are Indigenous student college experiences, First Nations/Native American Student Affairs units, Indigenous methodologies/pedagogy, and critical race theories. She is a co-editor of (2013) *Beyond the Asterisk: Understanding Native Students in Higher Education* and (2018) *Beyond Access: Indigenizing Programs for Native American Student Success*, (Stylus).

Varaxy Yi is an assistant professor of higher education administration and leadership and a core faculty member in the Doctoral Program in Educational Leadership at California State University, Fresno. As a first-generation Khmer American graduate and faculty, she is committed to advancing knowledge to serve racially minoritized communities. She conducts research to advance equity, access, and opportunity for historically underserved communities, such as racially minoritized, Southeast Asian American, and refugee populations. Her work focuses on building capacity within higher education institutions to advance issues of racial justice and equity to serve diverse students.

1

INTRODUCTION

The Problem with Grit

Deborah Faye Carter, Rocío Mendoza, and
Angela M. Locks

The Problem with Grit

The problem with grit is that the concept, and people's application of it, focuses on students' individual talents and strategies of resilience without a more critical and sociohistorical lens for analyzing educational conditions: "Our existing systems distribute opportunity based on income, class status, race, and ethnicity rather than hard work and talent" (Carnevale et al., 2019, p. 2). As Carnevale et al. (2019) conclude, opportunity in U.S. society is not based on merit, but on socioeconomic and racial status. We argue that promoting and reinforcing a logic of grit is especially harmful and the solutions proposed to overcome such disparities continue to rest with individual students.

Much of the popularization of grit stems from studies by Duckworth (2016) and Duckworth and colleagues, where they defined the term as a combination of "perseverance and passion for long-term goals" (Duckworth et al., 2007, p. 1087). Duckworth and her collaborators were looking to understand why some highly intelligent people were high achievers while others were not. Duckworth and colleagues explored how personality characteristics may explain the reasons why some may be more accomplished than others. In the past 15 years, Duckworth has become renowned as a proponent of grit in education circles, a MacArthur Fellow "Genius" grant award recipient with millions of views of a Ted Talk on the subject (Duckworth, 2013). Our training in education and critical multidisciplinary frameworks allow us to examine and interrogate grit not only as a methodological construct, but the ideology undergirding the concept. While we are motivated by the critiques of grit in recent years (see, e.g., Credé et al., 2017;

DOI: 10.4324/9781003332497-1

Gorski, 2016; Ris, 2015), we are concerned that the underlying ideas of grit continue to proliferate in higher education policies and practices.

The idea of cultivating grit may seem harmless and not particularly provocative. Who wouldn't want to persevere? Who wouldn't want to believe that success is within their control? The problem arises; however, when we focus so much of our collective attention and policy goals on improving individual effort. A common goal of educational interventions that promote or apply the concept of grit is for students to "unleash" their success by learning to develop resilience and sustain their passion and commitment to their academic endeavors. Gonzales (2016) explains that this can be an understandable response from higher education institutions that hesitate to engage in deeper historical and relational analyses which would also require changes in a highly politicized environment. Students can be identified as "lacking grit" if they do not achieve their goals, thus creating deficit notions of students' efforts and abilities. Valencia (1997) argues that deficit theories can be protean, concepts that continue to morph and shift according to current contexts, "... and while the popularity of different revisions may change, it never ceases to be important in determining school policy and practice" (p. 2). Similarly, we see how the logic of grit continues to shape and inform common practices in higher education, even when grit is not explicitly mentioned.

Layers of structural inequities shape student opportunities, and none have to do with a lack of "grittiness." These layers include the now decades-long public disinvestment of higher education with the simultaneous rise of tuition and cost of college attendance; the increase of poverty rates and basic needs for students; hyper individualism, hostile disciplinary cultures and classroom environments; and other neoliberal practices (Crutchfield et al., 2020; Giroux, 2014; Hurtado et al., 2011). Combined, this is what Love (2019) refers to as the "education survival complex," which leaves students of color no other choice but to simply survive—just have grit!—as they are socialized in a system that reinforces and reproduces oppression.

Love (2019) argues that studying grit without addressing the structural barriers mentioned above creates an educational version of *The Hunger Games*. And yet, we continue to observe policies and research informed by ideas of grit, resiliency, and other interventions using similar assumptions. "At the heart of grit research, then, is the desire to 'fix' marginalized people so that they can participate in and replicate the system that they might have just narrowly survived" (p. 116). We, too, call for practices and research that work to dismantle these ideologies and practices.

As we name the structures that have caused barriers, challenges, pain, and trauma in our school systems, we also want to take care that "we are naming social problems but not defining our students by them" (Goodman & Fine,

2018, p. 9). Similarly, Tuck (2009) cautions not to center damage in our work; rather we hope to highlight the history and contexts that have created harmful environments that necessitate marginalized students displaying "resiliency" and "grit" to survive. We also do not present a discussion of systemic issues in such a way that we see no hope for change; we are reminded by Freire (1970) that just because we name issues does not mean that we are perpetually bound by these conditions. It is our intent to challenge, disrupt, and transform these conditions for everyone pursuing higher education.

Background

Gaps in educational achievement rates between racial/ethnic and socioeconomic groups have been the focus of a significant amount of research for decades. It is important to note disparities between groups for several reasons: college educational attainment leads to higher wages and other life outcomes that come from having higher wages (e.g., better health, more stability, better education conditions for their children, etc.) (Oreopoulos & Petronijevic, 2013; Schanzenbach et al., 2017). College graduates also earn about four times more than those who did not earn a high school diploma, further highlighting the critical role that higher education can play in the overall health and betterment of our communities (Tyson, 2013).

A frustrating thing about the persistent discussion of achievement gaps is that our society has not tried to address the gaps systemically by reducing opportunity gaps. Studies have shown that "the United States [has] among the lowest levels of intergenerational social mobility—and one of the highest levels of influence of parental socioeconomic status on students' achievement and later earnings" (Welner & Carter, 2013, pp. 1–2). Welner and Carter consider the problems of differential achievement as caused by opportunity gaps: students attend schools that are not funded equally and there are resource gaps within schools such that higher-achieving students receive better instruction than students categorized as lower-achieving. It is important to consider educational outcomes through the lens of opportunity gaps because it helps "highlight the causes" (2013, p. 3) of what produces inequality.

Students and educators teach and learn under the banner of "no excuses" for poor student performance, but policymakers have not been required to provide adequate resources to support equitable learning environments (Welner & Carter, 2013). Opportunity gap research offers a strong framing for trying to understand how social forces, which begin early in students' childhoods, affect their educational outcomes and learning. In addition, students' experiences in schools and colleges significantly impact their ability to enroll in and graduate with higher education degrees.

The Objectives of the Book

This edited book examines how the use of grit and other merit-based lenses shape and sustain systems and structures of white privilege and supremacy in the United States. Contributing authors of this book seek to elucidate how students of color navigate these opportunity structures to access equitable educational outcomes. Further, this book addresses the pervasive ways that grit appears in higher education and, through asset-based theories, models, and methodologies, debunks notions that African American/Asian American/Pacific Islander/Latinx/Indigenous students need "grit" to succeed in college.

Using critical standpoints with an emphasis on praxis (theory, research, methods, reflection, and practice), our overall objective is to look deeper at the conceptualizations of grit and how it has been applied to students of color. Contributing authors also explain the myriad ways that institutional structures can support students of color utilizing their strengths through asset-based, anti-deficit perspectives such as Community Cultural Wealth (CCW) (Yosso, 2005) to access postsecondary environments and experience success. By focusing on these areas, we seek for this edited book and each of its chapters to become an organizing tool to challenge the ways that grit and similar concepts maintain systems of oppression that exclude communities of color from positive achievement narratives in higher education.

The Organization of the Book

In this introductory chapter, we have shared our view of the U.S. societal landscape and its impact on students of color in postsecondary education, making explicit our critique of grit. We have organized this edited book in three parts. In Part I, *Contexts and Foundations: The Origins of Grit*, we discuss the larger backdrop of grit in higher education. In Part II, *College Structural Barriers and Research Studies*, authors examine alternative conceptualizations of educational achievement for different groups of students of color. Finally, Part III, *Educational Practices Supporting Achievement*, highlights contributing authors' experiences in conducting research and engaging in higher education practices that reduce barriers to achievement and show promise for supporting students.

Part I begins with Chapter 2, "Critiques of Grit as a Measure of Academic Achievement in STEM Higher Education," where Deborah Faye Carter, Juanita Razo Dueñas, and Rocío Mendoza analyze the underlying assumptions of grit as it relates to achievement narratives. The authors focus on the historical foundations of "grit" (and its connection to "academic merit"), the main methodological critiques of grit, and how notions of grit negatively affect students in STEM educational environments.

In Chapter 3, Daniel G. Solórzano's "Challenging Everyday Structural Racism: A Critical Race Analysis of Grit in STEM," applies Critical Race Theory (CRT) to grit. Solórzano shows how the concept of character education (i.e., improving a student's personality or motivation) must be examined within the historical context of institutionalized racism and white supremacy.

Stephanie J. Waterman's "The Grit Narrative: Shifting the Gaze and the Danger" is Chapter 4. As an Indigenous faculty member in the Western, settler colonial academy, she interrogates the foundational assumptions of grit. Waterman also shares examples of how grit narratives mask the structural role of settler colonialism and continue to feed majoritarian stories (Stein, 2018) that deflect the responsibility of higher education systems to marginalized students.

Chapter 5, "Sometimes You're Gritty, and Sometimes You're Not: The Racialization of Grit for Asian Americans," authored by Jacqueline Mac, Rikka J. Venturanza, Megan Trinh, and Varaxy Yi, juxtaposes the "model minority myth" with the deviant minority myth. They argue that grit reinforces stereotypes of Asian Americans, which renders Asian Americans' educational needs invisible.

Part II features three chapters where authors offer critiques of grit through research studies that center the voices and experiences of students of color, specifically Latina and African American students. Chapter 6 is Nancy Acevedo's "More than Grit: Toward Critical Race College Retention and Persistence for Latina/o/x Students" which highlights the journey of Diana, a high school student transitioning to college, through the frameworks of the New Juan Crow in Education (Madrigal-Garcia & Acevedo-Gil, 2016) and Yosso's (2005) Community Cultural Wealth. Acevedo also challenges notions of grit by offering a "Depiction of College Retention and Persistence" model that can better explain the experiences of Latinx students who attend and graduate from college.

In Chapter 7, "Gritty Enough?: African American Science, Technology, Engineering, Mathematics (STEM) Student Success Factors," Melissa M. Mahoney investigates African American STEM degree completion using Harper's (2010) Anti-Deficit Achievement Framework. Findings from Mahoney's study identify how positive, sustained faculty-student interactions, holistic STEM success programming, and networks of social support influence student success. The final chapter in Part II is Chapter 8 by Julio Fregoso, "Beyond the Bootstraps Mentality: The Fallacy of Grit as a Measure of Success for Black and Latino Men in California Community Colleges." Fregoso uses Carter's (2002) model on degree aspirations of African Americans and Latina/os to study what affects the transfer aspirations of African American and Latino males in California community colleges. Fregoso suggests how institutional structures can support students in understanding their educational goals.

Part III of this book focuses on critical educational practices grounded in the experiences of scholars of color and the students they serve. In Chapter 9, Sabrina Sanders and Su Jin Gatlin Jez address a topic that is not previously well-researched: structural barriers for some college, no degree students (SCND) to return to campus to earn their baccalaureate degrees. In "Returning to Campus: Equity-Minded Approaches to Degree Completion" they challenge individualistic assumptions of grit by previewing promising practices of degree completion programs for working adults. Next, Chapter 10, "A Counternarrative to Grit through Scholarship on Latinx/a/o Students and HSIs: A Systematic Review of the Literature," is authored by Kathleen Rzucidlo, Stacey Speller, Jorge Burmicky, and Robert T. Palmer. The authors use Garcia et al.'s (2019) multidimensional conceptual framework of "servingness" to understand how Hispanic Serving Institutions (HSIs) can center Latinx/a/o student success. One strategy for centering student success focuses on asset-based conceptualizations of students in HSIs settings.

Anna M. Ortiz and Maenette K. P. Benham engage in scholarly conversation and reflection about the roles of evaluation and research when working with marginalized communities in Chapter 11, "Holo i ka 'Auwai, Flowing with the Power of the Stream: Empowerment-Based Evaluation and Research." The chapter offers evaluation and research models and practices that are grounded in Indigenous ways of knowing. Their reflection provides strategies to challenge white supremacy and traditional ways of conceptualizing achievement, empowering community members, and telling their stories in culturally relevant ways.

Finally, Rocío Mendoza, Elyzza Aparicio, Deborah Faye Carter, and Angela M. Locks focus on undergraduate research in Chapter 12, "Centering the Student in Undergraduate Research as a Retention Strategy." Drawing from their research and practice in this area, the authors examine how grit shapes who has access to opportunities to do research, and how success is defined in ways that constrain engagement for students of color. The chapter concludes with recommendations for how faculty, staff, and administrators can expand access to research opportunities and achieve greater racial equity in undergraduate research.

Summary

This book contributes to the discourse on race and ethnicity in higher education by offering alternative methods, theories, policies, and practices that help to debunk grit and deficit ways of thinking of students of color and their access to and success in postsecondary education. Moreover, the contributors present critical perspectives and methodological approaches to better address the educational conditions of college students of color using anti-deficit frameworks. Such conceptual, quantitative, and qualitative work may help inform the nature and structure of transforming and reimaging college access and university student support programs, policies, and practices for higher education professionals. This book holds promise for adding new layers of understanding and complexity regarding how students of color navigate systemic barriers to and through postsecondary education with an emphasis on such students' strengths and an interrogation of structures that impede their access and success.

We invite readers to reflect on the following questions as they read this book:

- How does grit uphold white supremacy and reinforce deficit and racist theories and research of minoritized students of color?
- What other models, frameworks, and understandings can we apply to challenge current applications of grit in higher education?
- How do we develop a critical awareness of concepts—current and those yet to come—that have similar foundational ideas as grit?

References

Carnevale, A. P., Fasules, M. L., Quinn, M. C., & Campbell, K. P. (2019). *Born to win, schooled to lose*. Georgetown University Center on Education and the Workforce.

Carter, D. F. (2002). College students' degree aspirations: A theoretical model and literature review with a focus on African American and Latino students. In J. C. Smart (Ed.), *Higher education: Handbook of theory and research* (pp. 129–171). Kluwer Academic Publishers.

Credé, M., Tynan, M. C., & Harms, P. D. (2017). Much ado about grit: A meta-analytic synthesis of the grit literature. *Journal of Personality and Social Psychology, 113*(3), 492–511. https://doi.org/10.1037/pspp0000102

Crutchfield, R. M., Carpena, A., McCloyn, T. N., & Maguire, J. (2020). The starving student narrative: How normalizing deprivation reinforces basic need insecurity in higher education. *Families in Society, 101*(3), 409–421. https://doi.org/10.1177/1044389419889525

Duckworth, A. L. (2013). *Grit: The power of passion and perseverance* [Video]. Ted Conferences. https://www.ted.com/talks/angela_lee_duckworth_grit_the_power_of_passion_and_perseverance/comments

Duckworth, A. L. (2016). *Grit: The power of passion and perseverance*. Scribner/Simon & Schuster.

Duckworth, A. L., Peterson, C., Matthews, M. D., & Kelly, D. R. (2007). Grit: Perseverance and passion for long term goals. *Journal of Personality and Social Psychology, 92*(6), 1087–1101. https://doi.org/10.1037/0022-3514.92.6.1087

Freire, P. (1970/2006). *Pedagogy of the oppressed* (30th Anniversary ed.). Continuum.

Garcia, G. A., Núñez, A.-M., & Sansone, V. A. (2019). Toward a multidimensional conceptual framework for understanding "Servingness" in Hispanic-Serving Institutions: A synthesis of the research. *Review of Educational Research, 89*(5), 745–784. https://doi.org/10.3102/0034654319864591

Giroux, H. A. (2014). *Neoliberalism's war on higher education.* Haymarket Books.

Gonzales, L. D. (2016). Revising the grounds for the study of grit: Critical qualitative inquiry in post-secondary education organizational research. In P. A. Pasque & V. M. Lechuga (Eds.), *Qualitative inquiry in higher education organization and policy research* (pp. 113–128). Routledge.

Goodman, S., & Fine, M. (2018). *It's not about grit: Trauma, inequity, and the power of transformative teaching.* Teachers College Press.

Gorski, P. C. (2016). *Reaching and teaching students in poverty: Strategies for erasing the opportunity gap.* Teachers College Press.

Harper, S. R. (2010). An anti-deficit achievement framework for research on students of color in STEM. *New Directions for Institutional Research, 2010*(148), 63–74.

Hurtado, S., Cuellar, M., & Wann, C. G. (2011). Quantitative measures of students' sense of validation: Advancing the study of diverse learning environments. *Enrollment Management Journal, 5*(2), 53–71.

Love, B. L. (2019). *We want to do more than survive: Abolitionist teaching and the pursuit of educational freedom.* Beacon Press.

Madrigal-Garcia, Y. I., & Acevedo-Gil, N. (2016). The new Juan Crow in education: Revealing panoptic measures and inequitable resources that hinder Latina/o postsecondary pathways. *Journal of Hispanic Higher Education, 15*(2), 154–181. https://doi.org/10.1177/1538192716629192

Oreopoulos, P., & Petronijevic, U. (2013, May). *Making college worth it: A review of research on the returns to higher education.* National Bureau of Economic Research. Working paper. https://www.nber.org/papers/w19053

Ris, E. W. (2015). Grit: A short history of a useful concept. *Journal of Educational Controversy, 10*(1), article 3.

Schanzenbach, D. W., Bauer, L., & Breitwieser, A. (2017). *Eight economic facts on higher education.* The Hamilton Project. Brookings Institute. https://www.brookings.edu/wp-content/uploads/2017/04/thp_20170426_eight_economic_facts_higher_education.pdf

Stein, S. (2018). Confronting the racial-colonial foundations of US higher education. *Journal for the Study of Postsecondary and Tertiary Education, 3*, 77–98. https://doi.org/10.28945/4105

Tuck, E. (2009). Suspending damage: A letter to communities. *Harvard Educational Review, 79*(3), 409–427. https://doi.org/10.17763/haer.79.3.n0016675661t3n15

Tyson, K. (2013). Tracking segregation, and the opportunity gap. In K. G. Welner & P. L. Carter (Eds.), *Closing the opportunity gap: What America must do to give every child an even chance* (pp. 169–180). Oxford University Press.

Valencia, R. (1997). *The evolution of deficit thinking: Educational thought and practice.* The Falmers Press.

Welner, K. G., & Carter, P. L. (2013). Achievement gaps arise from opportunity gaps. In K. G. Welner & P. L. Carter (Eds.), *Closing the opportunity gap: What America must do to give every child an even chance* (pp. 1–10). Oxford University Press.

Yosso, T. (2005). Whose culture has capital? A critical race theory discussion of community cultural wealth. *Race Ethnicity and Education, 8*(1), 69–91. https://doi.org/10.1080/1361332052000341006

PART I
Contexts and Foundations
The Origins of Grit

2

CRITIQUES OF GRIT AS A MEASURE OF ACADEMIC ACHIEVEMENT IN STEM HIGHER EDUCATION

Deborah Faye Carter, Juanita E. Razo Dueñas, and Rocío Mendoza

Will Smith described himself the following way in an interview years ago:

> The only thing that I see that is distinctly different about me is I'm not afraid to die on a treadmill. I will not be outworked, period. You might have more talent than me, you might be smarter than me, you might be sexier than me, you might be all of those things—you got it on me in nine categories. But if we get on the treadmill together, there's two things: you're getting off first, or I'm going to die. It's really that simple.
> *(Duckworth & Eskreis-Winkler, 2013)*

The above quote from the actor, made well before his well-publicized 2022 Academy Awards controversy, is one cited by Duckworth and Eskreis-Winkler (2013) as an example of the "gritty" personality. In the article that introduced and popularized the concept of grit, Duckworth et al. (2007) broadly define this concept as "perseverance and passion for long term goals" (p. 1087); it is a disposition in which individuals persist and overcome great obstacles to achieve success. Duckworth et al.'s characterization of the gritty individual, a person like Will Smith, who possesses a high level of perseverance and passion, forms the basis of the grit narrative which has been embraced by scholars, policymakers, and educators in K-12 and higher education.

Much of grit's appeal comes from the idea that it is a promising solution for reducing gaps in academic achievement, especially among low-income and/or students of color (Almeida, 2016; Credé et al., 2017). Further, grit has become a particular focus of Science, Technology, Engineering, and Mathematics (STEM) fields to promote degree completion among students

DOI: 10.4324/9781003332497-3

of color (McGee & Stovall, 2015). STEM disciplines value complementary ideals to grit, such as individualism and hard work and operate along meritocratic ideals (Carter et al., 2019). We argue that these ideals, along with grit, are counterproductive and harmful to supporting college student achievement and diversifying STEM fields. In light of widespread interest in grit, this chapter reviews the literature regarding definitions of "grit," examines and critiques the underlying conceptual and historical assumptions of grit, and describes alternatives to grit for supporting student achievement in STEM disciplines.

Grit and other non-cognitive personality traits such as motivation, self-efficacy, positive self-concept, and realistic self-appraisal have gained widespread attention as predictors and determinants of college success and achievement (Almeida, 2016; Credé et al., 2017; Thomas et al., 2007). Researchers and practitioners have had growing interest in the role of non-cognitive factors on academic outcomes as an alternative to cognitive measures of achievement for several reasons. First, while cognitive measures of college achievement (i.e., high school grade point average and SAT scores) are well-established predictors of student success, recent studies suggest that non-cognitive traits are equally strong measures of academic achievement and may even mediate the effects on cognitive ability (Almeida, 2016; Credé et al., 2017; Duckworth et al., 2007). Second, previous research suggests that non-cognitive traits are more malleable than cognitive traits and can be influenced by learning environments which lend themselves to a wider range of intervention strategies (Credé et al., 2017; Kwon, 2017). However, as we discuss later in the chapter, since Duckworth highlights that grit has innate features, this second reason seems less applicable. Third, the national assessment movement has encouraged measurement of educational outcomes, and the ability to measure these traits through psychometric means adds to the appeal of their use (Akos & Kretchmar, 2017; Bowman et al., 2015).

While researchers, practitioners, and policymakers have promoted grit as a driver of success for low-income and/or students of color, numerous researchers have raised serious methodological, conceptual, and philosophical concerns (Anderson et al., 2016; Credé et al., 2017; Kirchgasler, 2018; Kwon, 2017; Morell et al., 2021; Muenks et al., 2017; SRI International, 2018). The grit narrative persists as part of the discourse on academic achievement and degree completion that places the focus on students' personalities (mostly formed at birth) to facilitate persistence and success. This narrative diminishes or ignores the pervasive structural/environmental conditions that promote differential achievement outcomes (Akos & Kretchmar, 2017; Almeida, 2016; Bazelais et al., 2016; Bowman et al., 2015; McGee & Stovall, 2015).

Grit's focus on individualism and innate ability seems to particularly appeal to STEM disciplinary cultures where grit has salience because sustained interest and commitment are traditionally viewed as essential to STEM achievement (McGee & Stovall, 2015). Perhaps not coincidentally, STEM disciplines are sites of ongoing concerns regarding the underrepresentation of students of color as majors and graduates (Carter et al., 2019; McGee & Stovall, 2015). Students of color tend to be interested in pursuing STEM majors at college entry but are not retained in the major despite having histories of high academic achievement for admission into these fields (Chen, 2013; Lee & Ferrare, 2019). These phenomena lead some scholars to believe that the educational environments of STEM disciplines, more than individual characteristics of students, are what dissuades students of color from pursuing majors (Hurtado et al., 2010; Malone & Barabino, 2009; McGee & Martin, 2011). Moreover, these scholars argue that such environments can reduce sustained interest and effort in STEM (in other words, grit) and lead students to choose other majors and careers.

In reviewing previous research and conceptualizations of grit, we organize this review in the following way: first we discuss Duckworth's definition of grit, and we then discuss how Duckworth and team have measured grit, and grit's relationship to academic achievement. A section discussing major critiques of grit follows, and the chapter concludes with discussing STEM educational contexts and interventions for improving academic achievement. Throughout this chapter, we address the historical foundations of grit, how the concepts of grit and academic merit are connected particularly in STEM fields, and in what ways might grit have limited explanatory power in explaining the academic achievement of marginalized students in higher education.

What is Grit?

Duckworth et al. (2007) conceptualized grit through a series of qualitative and quantitative studies to determine what traits might help explain why some individuals are more successful than others in achieving their goals. They conducted exploratory interviews with a sample of professionals drawn from the fields of investment banking, painting, journalism, academia, medicine, and law to identify the personality characteristics that distinguish the most talented professionals from their less successful peers in these highly selective and challenging fields. Based on their research, they noted that "grit or a close synonym" (p. 1088) was a dominant trait that high-achieving professionals across the various professional fields possessed. A "trait," defined as a psychological term, is a personality characteristic (e.g., behavior, thoughts, and emotions) that is stable over time (Farrington et al., 2012); Duckworth and her colleagues considered grit an essential trait to success.

After identifying the relevant concepts through interviews, Duckworth et al. (2007) were interested in developing measures of grit and explored the psychometric structure of grit, which they conceptualized as a higher order trait consisting of two lower order facets: consistency of interest and perseverance of effort. Together, Duckworth et al. (2007) believe these two facets characterize an individual's ability to exert effort, show long-term stamina and commitment toward interests, and persist toward their goals despite adversity or obstacles.

Given this disposition, the gritty individual (a person who shows a high-level of grit) is often analogized as a person engaging in a footrace: no matter the obstacle, the gritty individual will stay on course to reach their goals in large part due to their sustained effort, interest, and drive. It is this emphasis on "long-term stamina rather than short-term intensity" that Duckworth and her colleagues claim distinguishes grit from other existing and well-researched psychological traits (Duckworth et al., 2007, p. 1089).

Research on the psychometric structure of the grit measure has led to some inconclusive findings regarding whether grit is in fact a unique trait or resembles other traits. Scholars have debated whether the grit survey items may instead be measuring the psychological trait of conscientiousness which captures impulse control, being goal directed, planning ahead, diligence in completing tasks, and delaying gratification (Bowman et al., 2015; Credé et al., 2017). Conscientiousness is a Big Five personality trait; the "Big Five" taxonomy of categorizing personality traits was designed to be broad and to organize the myriad of studies of human personality around a schema (John & Srivastava, 1999). Of the Big Five, only conscientiousness has been linked with academic performance (Farrington et al., 2012).

Duckworth and colleagues have acknowledged that conscientiousness does share some resemblance to grit, but also maintain it is distinct from this trait: "grit overlaps with achievement aspects of conscientiousness but differs in its emphasis on long-term stamina rather than short-term intensity. The gritty individual not only finishes tasks at hand but pursues a given aim over years" (Duckworth et al., 2007, p. 1089). Duckworth et al. also have maintained that their concept of grit is related to self-control and persistence—personality characteristics that seem important for sustained effort and interest.

One notable aspect of Duckworth and colleagues' conceptualization of grit is that grit was intended to be an explanation for why some high-IQ individuals do not achieve as well as other high-IQ individuals. A central question they pose is "Why do some individuals accomplish more than others of equal intelligence?", while a key hypothesis of their early work was "that grit is essential to high achievement" (Duckworth et al., 2007, pp. 1087–1088). Intelligence and IQ is conceptualized by psychological researchers as being influenced by genetics (Valencia, 1997). Similarly, Duckworth also conceptualizes grit as "largely influenced by genetic factors" (Park et al., 2020, p. 2), but does seem to acknowledge that it can be affected by learning environments. The process by which students gain grit is not clarified, which is an issue that we will discuss in more detail in later sections of the chapter.

How is Grit Measured?

A key focus of many psychometric studies of grit is to examine the nature of the structure of the grit measure to confirm if grit is a higher order trait that has two lower-order facets. The Grit Scale is a set of measures designed by Duckworth et al. (2007), revised by Duckworth and Quinn (2009), to assess perseverance of effort and consistency of interest. The scale currently comes in two forms: the original grit scale (Grit-O) is 12 items (Duckworth et al., 2007), and the second form is an 8-item short grit scale (Grit-S) (Duckworth & Quinn, 2009). Grit-S is based on the original Grit-O measure; Duckworth and her colleagues designed the Grit-O and Grit-S as self-reported, subjective measures, and respondents rate their perceptions on a 5-point scale ranging from 1 (not at all like me) to 5 (very much like me) on each item. Table 2.1 provides an overview of the items included on these measures.

TABLE 2.1 Grit Factor and Scale Item for Grit-O and Grit-S (Duckworth et al., 2007; Duckworth & Quinn, 2009)

Factor	Item
Consistency of Interest	*I often set a goal but later choose to pursue a different one.
	*I have been obsessed with a certain idea or project for a short time but later lost interest.
	*I have difficulty maintaining my focus on projects that take more than a few months to complete.
	*New ideas and projects sometimes distract me from previous ones.
	My Interests change from year to year.
	I become interested in new pursuits every few months.
Perseverance of Effort	*I finish whatever I begin.
	*Setbacks don't discourage me.
	*I am diligent.
	*I am a hard worker.
	I have achieved a goal that took years of work.
	I have overcome setbacks to conquer an important challenge.

Note: Items with an asterisk are included in the Grit-S scale.

Duckworth et al. (2007) present both Grit Scales as strong predictors of performance over and beyond traditional measures of achievement, including the SAT and high school GPA. Two years after the original grit scale article, Duckworth and Quinn (2009) tested the shorter version of the grit scale, Grit-S. They reevaluated data from the original study and analyzed new data from a group of high-achieving middle school students. Duckworth and Quinn replicated most of the findings of the original study and concluded that the Grit-S is "psychometrically stronger" (p. 174) than the Grit-O. They reached this conclusion after examining the results of a confirmatory factor analysis, finding that "the Grit-S fit the data better than did that of the Grit-O" (p. 174). Since this finding, many researchers have been trying to determine which scale seems to fit data better and what is the best structure of the grit construct.

What is Grit's Relationship to Academic Achievement?

As noted, Duckworth and her colleagues claim that grit is a strong predictor of future achievement across a variety of domains, and over and beyond traditional measures of talent (Duckworth et al., 2007; Duckworth & Quinn, 2009). In an interview with the *New York Times*, Duckworth stated unreservedly that the grit measure is a better predictor than other measures "to help us know in advance which individuals will be successful in some situations" (Scelfo, 2016). Early research by Duckworth et al. (2007) describes grit as related to achievement for West Point cadets and to grade point average (GPA) for Ivy League undergraduates. In analyzing grit and SAT scores for a sample of undergraduate students majoring in Psychology at an Ivy League institution, the authors found that grit was associated with higher GPA performance, a relationship that initially was modest but became stronger when controlling for SAT scores, which they used as a proxy for cognitive ability. Based on this, Duckworth et al. (2007) concluded that perseverance of effort and consistency of interest have greater impacts on achievement in comparison to talent, and that " ... among elite undergraduates, smarter students may be slightly less gritty than their peers" (p. 1093). It is unclear that grit *is* a better predictor of GPA, however, since the authors measured GPA and grit scores at the same time, and both were self-reported. Nevertheless, in Duckworth's estimation, the various studies she and her colleagues completed seem to bolster the claim that grit has a key role in students' academic achievement that is different from SAT or similar measures of academic ability.

Since Duckworth and her colleagues first introduced grit, more studies utilizing the concept of grit have been done in higher education settings. These research studies have focused primarily on exploring grit's links to core indicators of college success and academic achievement including academic performance, persistence, engagement, stress, and self-regulated learning (see Akos & Kretchmar, 2017; Bazelais et al., 2016; Bowman et al., 2015; Cross, 2014; Fosnacht et al., 2018; Muenks et al., 2017; Strayhorn, 2014; Wolters & Hussain, 2015). Our review of this research suggests that grit's relationship to academic achievement is not consistently strong. Some studies report a strong positive relationship between grit and indicators of college success (Bowman et al., 2015; Strayhorn, 2014), while others present mixed findings about the strength of the relationship (Akos & Kretchmar, 2017; Cross, 2014; Fosnacht et al., 2018).

Importantly, existing studies do not sufficiently help us understand how different contexts, such as institutional, socio-historical, and policy, influence students' individual persistence toward academic goals. These factors can facilitate or deter achievement and must be considered when employing and implementing practices and strategies to elevate success especially among historically marginalized students (Hurtado et al., 2012). While the studies referenced in this chapter have drawn data from diverse, multi-institutional samples of undergraduates attending different institutional contexts (e.g., predominantly white institutions, research extensive, minority-serving) future efforts are necessary to contextualize how college environments may encourage or dissuade students in their academic pursuits.

Critiques of Grit

The previous section covered how grit is defined and the claims Duckworth and colleagues make about its relationship to academic achievement. This section summarizes some of the major critiques of grit. First, we summarize key methodological critiques, then we delve into some theoretical and conceptual critiques.

Grit's Modest Predictive Power

Several researchers question Duckworth et al.'s (2007) claims that grit is a strong predictor of GPA. Credé (2018) and Credé et al. (2017) have been among the most critical. After completing a meta-analysis of several studies using grit measures, Credé et al. conclude that "overall grit exhibits relations with academic performance and retention that are only modest and that do not compare favorably with other well-known predictors of academic performance such as cognitive ability, study habits and skills, and academic adjustment" (2017, p. 502). While it is unclear to researchers what might be the reasons for the mixed results regarding the relationship between grit scales and academic achievement outcomes, Morell et al. (2021) posited a couple of reasons for the discrepancies. First, there are methodological weaknesses in Duckworth's conceptualization of grit. Morell et al. (2021) found that the two-factor structure of grit "is not only incorrect in a statistical sense given its mathematical equivalence to a correlated two-factor structure, but also an inappropriate conceptualization of grit as a construct made up of two distinct subfactors" (p. 1053). The authors did not find support for a super-order factor with two sub-factors structure of the grit concept. Instead, the authors believed that one factor seemed to fit their research findings better.

Credé et al. (2017) also found the structure of the grit scales as proposed by Duckworth et al. (2007) is not supported by other researchers' work. In their review of published studies, the weight of the evidence seems to indicate that perseverance (the sub-scale alone) is a better predictor of academic performance than consistency or consistency and perseverance together. This finding is significant according to Credé et al. in that "the practice of combining perseverance scores and consistency scores into an overall grit score appears to result in a significant loss in the ability to predict performance" (p. 502).

Furthermore, another complication in terms of seeing consistency in the results of studies of grit is that previous studies have neither used the grit scales consistently nor tested the structure of the grit construct. Some studies have focused their analysis on overall grit scores following the recommendation of Duckworth et al. (2007) (e.g., Bazelais et al., 2016; Cross, 2014; Strayhorn, 2014), while others have examined the facets/sub-factors (consistency and perseverance) separately (see Akos & Kretchmar, 2017; Bowman et al., 2015; Fosnacht et al., 2018; Wolters & Hussain, 2015). The lack of consistent measurement of grit may be an additional reason for the discrepant findings (Morell et al., 2021).

A second reason for unreliability of the construct's relationship to achievement in Morell et al.'s (2021) view is that the grit concept did not have similar predictability patterns across different cultural groups. They surveyed groups in the U.S. and South Korea at different grade levels and the construct's relationship to achievement was not the same across countries and grade groups. We echo questions raised about grit's external validity in terms of broader populations of people—especially those who are not "intellectually gifted." As noted earlier, Duckworth and her colleagues developed the grit scales to distinguish differences between intellectually gifted individuals and tested the scale on elite (and atypical) segments of the general population: Ivy League college students, West Point Cadets, National Spelling Bee participants, and more recently magnet middle school students. The standardization of the grit scales on narrow populations of people has led some researchers to question whether the scale would work as well with more diverse populations of people (Fosnacht et al., 2018;

Muenks et al., 2017). Duckworth et al. (2007) argue that the validation of the scales on highly selective populations of individuals contributes to its psychometric strength; others posit that the scales and conceptualization may better represent social stratification (Kwon, 2017; Ris, 2015).

For example, Kwon (2017) argued that the dispositions, knowledge, and skills the grit scale measure are reflective of the cultural capital of the economically and socially advantaged in society, suggesting that the Grit Scale, not unlike the SAT, may be highly correlated with socioeconomic status and is not an independent measure of achievement or perseverance. Cultural capital as conceptualized by Pierre Bourdieu described the knowledge and skills of the middle and upper classes as a form of capital that is valued in society (Bourdieu & Passeron, 1977). If grit is measuring cultural capital, it may be supporting established theories of social reproduction (Kwon, 2017). In other words, the measurement of grit may capture SES differences more than the qualities of traits that are meant to be independent of social stratification dynamics.

Conceptual Muddiness and Grit

Another major critique of grit is that it lacks conceptual clarity. While Duckworth and colleagues have provided a clear definition of "grit," some researchers believe that the concept of grit closely resembles other psychological concepts and ideas. For example, Credé et al. (2017) examined grit's relation to conscientiousness and conclude the psychometric similarities between grit and conscientiousness suggest that grit may be "old wine in new bottles" (p. 495). Credé et al. believe that because of grit's relationships with other variables and concepts—especially conscientiousness and self-control—the "incremental value of grit for the prediction of [academic] performance is likely to be limited" (p. 502). In other words, grit might be a redundant measure for conscientiousness.

Others have recommended more conceptual clarity around the concept of grit (Anderson et al., 2016; SRI, 2018). An SRI International (2018) report, *Promoting Grit, Tenacity, and Perseverance: Critical Factors for Success in the 21st Century* urged that future research bring more clarity and theoretical refinement to grit-related research. The report described "grit" as having a "jingle/jangle" problem: "jingle" occurs when the same term is used to refer to different concepts, and "jangle" occurs when different terms are used for the same concept (p. 88). A persistent problem with the concept of grit is jangle because grit may really be measuring perseverance and/or conscientiousness.

Duckworth's approach to studying grit may be what is at issue here: she drew upon conceptualizations of what might affect achievement among intellectually gifted people without grounding her conceptualizations in what is already known about links to student achievement by education and psychological researchers. Vazsonyi et al. (2019) discussed how Duckworth conceptualized the relationships between grit and self-control, stating, "There appears to have been insufficient clarity of the conceptual differences between self-control and grit, particularly in the original work by Duckworth and colleagues" (p. 223). Since they did not test many of the relationships between concepts empirically, it is unclear how the relationships might work theoretically and practically.

An additional problem in assessing how distinct "grit" is in comparison to related psychological concepts is that different psychological concepts that may seem similar have distinct theoretical traditions and unique meanings and connotations across communities of practice (Kwon, 2017; SRI, 2018). In referring to the conceptual antecedents of grit, Kwon (2017) stated that researchers, particularly in the field of psychology, "have not provided a clear explanation about how grit develops" (p. 6). If grit has utility in helping to conceptualize student achievement, it is important for researchers to have clarity about grit, its related concepts, and its development (Kwon, 2017; SRI, 2018). The next section discusses historical foundations of grit which adds to its limitations as a useful concept for educational practice.

Historical Origins: Debunking Grit as "Neutral" or "Universal"

Related to the conceptual "muddiness" of grit, researchers have also called into question grit's utility as a neutral, universal concept. Grit has its historical foundation in a settler colonial context of rugged individualism, white supremacy, and racism (Anderson, 2014; Anderson et al., 2016; Kirchgasler, 2018; McGee & Stovall, 2015). As such, the conceptual origins of grit may limit its usefulness when applied to the educational achievement processes of traditionally underrepresented and underserved students; students for whom improving grit has been viewed as a possible solution for reducing differences in achievement outcomes.

"Rugged individualism" has been a significant part of the U.S. societal culture since at least the eighteenth century (Kirchgasler, 2018; Bazzi et al., 2020). Bazzi et al. (2020) described individualism in part as "a view of the self as independent rather than interdependent [with] emphasis on self-reliance, primacy of self-interest . . ." (p. 2). This view of individualism is rooted in the rapid westward expansion of settler colonialism in the United States. President Herbert Hoover is popularly known for the term and included it as part of his campaign speech in 1928 before the onset of the Great Depression. However, the culture of individualism has been a feature of white United States society for decades prior to Hoover's speech (Bazzi et al., 2020).

Many politicians and scholars have promoted the concept of a "frontier thesis" for centuries in the United States (Kirchgasler, 2018). This thesis is related to rugged individualism and "argued that European-descended settlers' 'contact' with a geographical frontier was the source of American exceptionalism" (Kirchgasler, 2018, p. 698). Additionally, this thesis carries the belief that the United States and white Americans of European ancestry specifically are superior to other nations and peoples, and with that comes "innate qualities of a unique kind of individual" (p. 698). The "frontier"— which included land and people that were to be acquired and defeated—was to be conquered through will and it was through this violent struggle that immigrant white ethnic groups from Europe became "Americanized."

In justifying oppression and elimination, those who were considered "others" (i.e., Native Americans and African Americans) were defined as those who did not hold the kind of desired personal traits necessary for contributing to the country's social or economic growth (Omi & Winant, 2015; Smedley, 2013; Valencia, 1997). By extension, those who became white and were successful in their violent conquests displayed "rugged individualism" (Kirchgasler, 2018). The historical foundations of innate qualities such as "rugged individualism" and "grit" were inherently and exclusively coined to refer to white Americans and were never meant or created with people of color in mind.

Alongside historical notions of "American" moral character exemplified by rugged individualism, some influential nineteenth-century scholars were conceptualizing moral character explicitly through the lens of white supremacy. British scientist Francis Galton, who is the father of eugenics and whose ideas were embraced by American scholars at the turn of the twentieth century (Valencia, 1997; Zuberi & Bonilla-Silva, 2008), has been cited by Duckworth as being foundational to the concept of grit (see Duckworth et al., 2007; Duckworth & Gross, 2014).

Galton held biologically inferior and racist views of non-European individuals and groups and structured his beliefs about human capabilities through the logic of eugenics (Anderson, 2014; Valencia, 1997). In reviewing the writing and scholarship of Galton, Fancher (2004) concluded that "Galton's racial attitudes influenced his scientific theories" (pp. 71–72) and that he often described differences in character and intellect among and between races and ethnic groups as evidence for his main arguments. Galton felt that through evolution (i.e., sexual relationships with people of other races), inferior peoples could gain intellectual and moral character (Maxwell, 2008). It is puzzling that Duckworth and co-authors repeatedly linked grit to the work of early scholars such as Galton who held such disdain for groups and cultures that he did not consider genetically superior. The scientific practices and theories founded by Galton, for instance, are the underpinnings of deficit-thinking (Valencia, 1997). We wonder how a concept, built on the assumption that whole groups of people were not biologically equal with other groups, could hold widespread value for understanding human achievement. Similarly, we reflect on the contradictions of grit being advanced as an asset-based solution to help students from underrepresented groups academically thrive and flourish as suggested by Duckworth and her colleagues.

Grit in Higher Education: An Examination of Students of Color in STEM

The frontier thesis and rugged individualism were important in the modern structure of U.S. higher education systems. At the turn of the twentieth century, white Americans turned to educational institutions as a new "frontier" to structure competition for leaders to emerge (Kirchgasler, 2018). James Bryant Conant, a scientist and former president of Harvard University, drew from the "frontier thesis to explain the exceptional character of American democracy" (Kirchgasler, 2018, p. 700). In Conant's view, the frontier "was responsible for widening the concept of equality" and that "equality became … equality of opportunity [and] an equal start in a competitive struggle" (Conant, 1959, p. 5). Conant regarded higher education institutions as being critical to the economic development of the nation. It is ironic that Conant and others consider the U.S. frontier as widening the concept of equality when so much destruction was wrought in service to westward expansion. This irony remains a part of the core assumptions of grit.

While the actual term "grit" is not as commonly utilized in higher education literature as it has been in K-12, the underlying assumptions framing this construct seems to particularly appeal to STEM disciplinary cultures. On this point, McGee and Stovall (2015) wrote:

> … grit has been touted as the missing link for students trying to earn a degree in science, technology, engineering, and mathematics (STEM), as this pursuit requires traditional measures of success (for example, a high GPA) along with focused and sustained application over a long period of time.
>
> *(p. 493)*

STEM disciplines often have been described as academic areas that reinforce individualism and innate ability (Carter et al., 2019; Traweek, 1988). These disciplines are also sites of decades-long concerns regarding the underrepresentation of students of color among those who major and attain graduate degrees (Bazelais et al., 2016; McGee & Stovall, 2015). Despite national calls to diversify these fields, the lack of representation and equity of STEM degree holders across race/ethnicity, gender, and other marginalized identities continues to persist (McGee et al., 2022; Miriti, 2020; National Science Board, 2018).

The challenges students of color, and women of color in particular, experience attaining a STEM degree are well-documented by multiple research communities, including disciplinary-based STEM education researchers, and higher education scholars (Carlone & Johnson, 2007; Hurtado et al., 2008; McGee et al., 2022; Miriti, 2020; Núñez et al., 2020). Across disciplines and fields, these researchers have called attention to the significant underrepresentation of women and men of color in the sciences, highlighting the roles of racialized campus climates and gender-biased classrooms in underrepresented women and men of color persistence in science fields (Bejerano & Bartosh, 2015; Carter et al., 2019). These campus and classroom environments can dissuade interest in STEM and lead students to choose other majors and careers, which continue to drive the low numbers of diverse students in these fields (Hurtado et al., 2010; Malone & Barabino, 2009; McGee & Martin, 2011). Together, previous research shows the importance of supportive educational environments as factors in the production of STEM degree recipients from marginalized groups.

Grit as an Exclusionary Concept

Scholars who study students' experiences in STEM environments have found "grit" to not be representative of the experiences of students of color. For example, McGee and Stovall (2015) believe that the conceptualization of grit and related concepts mischaracterizes the educational experiences of Black students.

> … [C]urrent research on "grit" and "resilience," at least as these concepts are sometimes defined and operationalized, does not account for the toll societal racism takes on students who may be viewed as successful [and the research does not account for] how structural racism breeds the racial practices, policies, and ideologies that force black students to adopt a racial mental toughness.
>
> *(p. 492)*

McGee and Stovall question whether comparatively lower academic performance of African American students in K-12 and higher education settings is due to lack of grit (or perseverance or conscientiousness) *or* whether the stress associated with learning in educationally hostile environments may be a better explanation for achievement gaps. They further discuss the negative mental health outcomes Black students experience as a result of participating in high-pressure academic environments and posit that conceptualizations of grit and perseverance do not include the impact of the racial microaggressions students of color experience (Carlone & Johnson, 2007; Hurtado et al., 2008). Moreover, hostile educational experiences and environments may affect students' academic motivation or behavior (Mc-Gee & Stovall, 2015; Solórzano et al., 2000; Yosso et al., 2009), which is not accounted for in the grit scales or theory.

Research has found that students of color in STEM uniquely benefit from other types of behavior and orientations, in addition to, or perhaps instead of, grit. Stereotype management, described as "students' developing understandings of racism and their developing senses of, negotiations of, and assertions of what it means to *be Black*," may be a key part of what can help students of color be successful (McGee & Martin, 2011, p. 1349). In particular, McGee and Martin (2011) studied high-achieving Black students in STEM and found that stereotype management helped students merge their identities as African Americans and as achievers in math and science, to forge new identities as successful Black engineers, mathematicians, or scientists. As students aged from K-12 to college, they developed more complex responses to microaggressions and also began to increasingly conceive of Black identity as collective. Specifically, the students were more likely to see their achievement as related to community goals rather than just their own. In this way, McGee and Martin (2011) believe that stereotype management is a more helpful way (than grit) to capture the achievement processes by which Black students navigate their experiences in STEM environments (e.g., classrooms, labs) in their pursuit of a degree. Researchers should continue to explore different ways of conceptualizing achievement processes that particularly incorporate the role that educational environments play in affecting student achievement.

Promising Institutional Interventions for Student Achievement in STEM

In previous sections of this chapter, we have discussed the limitations of the concept of grit in terms of theory, methodology, and its applicability for racially marginalized groups in higher education. We acknowledge the importance, broadly, of student motivation, behaviors, and perseverance. But institutional and structural barriers are essential for researchers and practitioners to address in order to improve the persistent rates of underachievement by certain groups (Chang et al., 2011). This section of the chapter highlights institutional practices and interventions that show promise for supporting and cultivating achievement among students of color in STEM fields. We explore this topic by highlighting the Meyerhoff Scholars Program (MSP) at the University of Maryland, Baltimore County (UMBC) which is nationally recognized for producing a significant number of graduates who go on to pursue doctoral degrees in STEM (Maton et al., 2012).

Participants of the MSP have reported that several program components played a role in their academic success, including the tuition assistance, academic advising, faculty-student interactions, and involvement of family members and community and cultural activities (Maton et al., 2012). Key reasons why MSP may have been so successful at graduating students (and encouraging them to pursue graduate studies) is because the program was structured to meet multiple needs that students who are the first in their families to pursue higher education have when they enter college. Programs that target multiple needs of students of color (e.g., financial, peer/social support, mentoring, and academic skills support) as structured interventions seem to be effective at reducing disparities and producing more STEM graduates (Hathaway et al., 2002; Maton et al., 2012).

Research suggests that targeted programs that include support for multiple areas of students' lives can increase students' sense of belonging to their campus and major (Hathaway et al., 2002; National Academies of Sciences, Engineering, and Medicine [NASEM], 2017). This is achieved through positive interactions with faculty members, mentors, and peers in "race positive" environments, defined as "involving interactions with same-race peers in settings where concern about the possibility of race-based rejection was absent" (Mendoza-Denton et al., 2002, p. 914). Improving the educational environments of students and making sure they have the information and resources they need are important alternatives to a narrow focus of conceptualizing achievement as individual efforts or based in genetics.

Another important feature about MSP as implemented at the UMBC campus is that the campus leaders who implemented the program changed the culture and mindset of the campus as well. Hrabowski (2014), founder of the program and president emeritus, argues that the reason the program has been so successful is because of how the institution and faculty in the STEM disciplines shifted to meet the needs of the students better. Initially upon arrival at the campus, Hrabowski observed that most of the faculty and staff believed that the students of color could not earn better than a "C" in most courses. University personnel did not believe the students were capable of being high-achieving. Literature suggests that when educators have low opinions of students they do not perform well (Musto, 2019). Hrabowski (2014) felt that it was important to develop "a setting, or climate that empowers students and sets the stage for them to excel academically" (p. 13). As president, he believed that there needed to be an institutional *and* disciplinary shift in terms of what campus staff and administrators and STEM faculty needed to do and believe to best support students.

Over the course of years, Hrabowski led the faculty at UMBC toward discussing student capabilities from a strengths-based approach (e.g., what do students contribute to our learning environment) instead of a deficit approach (e.g., what are students lacking). And through this transformation, students began to earn better grades and go to graduate schools in greater numbers. Institutional transformation seems to be an important part of the future of higher education and its continued ability to broaden access and support student achievement.

Discussion and Conclusions

Developed by Duckworth and colleagues, grit has been defined as "perseverance and passion for long term goals." Grit was conceptualized as an individual-level personality characteristic (Duckworth et al., 2007), influenced by genetics, but some research suggests it is also affected by educational and classroom environments (Farrington et al., 2012). Authors have published about and promoted grit through numerous articles and books and a well-known TED talk (Duckworth, 2013); as such, grit has captured the interest and imagination of parents, policymakers, researchers, and educators.

In the constant striving for the most effective strategies for improving student achievement, grit is one of the most recent to capture imaginations. Educators who embrace the grit concept administer assessments measuring it, which they then interpret and structure interventions for students to become more "gritty." In this chapter, we have summarized the concept of grit, presented some of its major critiques, and discussed possible future directions of research and practice in the study of achievement.

Duckworth has attributed the origins of the concept of grit to scholars such as Francis Galton who has espoused eugenicist ideals in the nineteenth century (see Maxwell, 2008; Valencia, 1997; Zuberi & Bonilla-Silva, 2008). These scholars emphasized innate individual attributes as being important to understand human behaviors and functioning. In addition, the eugenicist scholars also supported the "frontier thesis" of the qualities individuals needed to have to be successful for social mobility and achievement. This thesis is the belief that rugged individualism is a desired state and an aspirational goal for people to do well in U.S. society, and in effect be American (Kirchgasler, 2018). Given that this thesis was not developed with people of color in mind, the ideological foundations of grit seem ill-suited to its recommended application to diverse groups.

Grit has been assumed to be a "neutral" concept that can be applied universally to understand why some students are successful and others are not, but the origins of the concept belie this assumption. Researchers question the validity of grit altogether for students who experience race-related stress and discrimination, and there has been little empirical evidence to determine if the concept works as well for students of color as it seems to for white students (see Bowman et al., 2015; McGee & Stovall, 2015; Strayhorn, 2014).

Besides the conceptual concerns researchers have with grit, and whether grit is a useful concept for students of color and other marginalized groups, there are also several methodological critiques with grit. One is a validity concern: the grit scales may actually be measuring conscientiousness or perseverance (Credé et al., 2017). Others critique the measurement of grit and the structure of the grit scales (Credé et al., 2017). There are a number of reasons, conceptual, theoretical, and methodological, for educational researchers and practitioners to look in other directions to increase our understanding of what affects and supports student achievement. Credé (2018) thinks educational institutions may want to "focus their often limited financial and instructional resources on variables that have stronger relationships with success and performance and that can be more easily changed via interventions" (p. 5).

Researchers have suggestions for alternatives to pursuing grit: Farrington et al. (2012) suggest that focusing attention on the "academic mindset," which is described as the "psycho-social attitudes or beliefs one has about oneself in relation to academic work," may be an alternative framework to grit (p. 8). In the future, researchers may want to disentangle how grit (or perseverance) works and how well it may function (if at all) for different groups of students. We also suggest that a more fruitful direction for research is to better understand the ways in which marginalized students learn to navigate hostile school environments while also researching how we can make educational environments more welcoming.

Perhaps, too, we as educational researchers need to abandon the search for universal interventions and concepts designed to explain achievement strategies for the myriad of students our institutions will educate. It may be better to apply targeted theories and interventions for students or think more broadly in terms of classroom and school environments.

References

Akos, P., & Kretchmar, J. (2017). Investigating grit at a non-cognitive predictor of college success. *The Review of Higher Education*, *40*(2), 163–186. https://doi.org/10.1353/rhe.2017.0000

Almeida, D. J. (2016). Understanding grit in the context of higher education. In M. B. Paulsen (Ed.), *Higher education: Handbook of theory and research* (pp. 559–609). Springer.

Anderson, C., Turner, A. C., Heath, R. D., & Payne, C. M. (2016). On the meaning of grit… and hope… and fate control… and alienation… and locus of control… and… self-efficacy… and… effort optimism… and…. *The Urban Review*, *48*(2), 198–219. https://doi.org/10.1007/s11256-016-0351-3

Anderson, L. (2014, March 21). Lauren Anderson: Grit, Galton, and eugenics. *Living in dialogue: An Education Week blog*. http://blogs.edweek.org/teachers/living-in-dialogue/2014/03/lauren_anderson_grit.html

Bazelais, P., Lemay, D. J., & Doleck. T. (2016). How does grit impact college students' academic achievement in science? *European Journal of Science and Mathematics Education*, *4*(1), 33–43. https://doi.org/10.30935/scimath/9451

Bazzi, S., Fiszbein, M., & Gebresilasse, M. (2020). Frontier culture: The roots and persistence of "rugged individualism" in the United States. *Econometrica, 88*(6), 2329–2368. https://doi.org/10.3982/ECTA16484

Bejerano, A. R., & Bartosh, T. M. (2015). Learning masculinity: Unmasking the hidden curriculum in science, technology, engineering, and mathematics courses. *Journal of Women and Minorities in Science and Engineering, 21*(2), 107–124. https://doi.org/10.1615/JWomenMinorScienEng.2015011359

Bourdieu, P., & Passeron, J.-C. (1977). *Reproduction in education, society and culture.* Sage.

Bowman, N. A., Hill, P. L., Denson, N., & Bronkema, R. (2015). Keep on truckin' or stay the course? Exploring grit dimensions as differential predictors of educational achievement, satisfaction, and intentions. *Social Psychological and Personality Science, 6*(6), 639–645. https://doi.org/10.1177/1948550615574300

Carlone, H. B., & Johnson, A. (2007). Understanding the science experiences of successful women of color: Science identity as an analytic lens. *Journal of Research in Science Teaching, 44*(8), 1187–1218. https://doi.org/10.1002/tea.20237

Carter, D. F., Razo Dueñas, J., & Mendoza, R. (2019). Critical examination of the role of STEM in propagating and maintaining race and gender disparities in STEM. In M. B. Paulsen & L. W. Perna (Eds.), *Higher education: Handbook of theory and research.* Springer Nature Switzerland.

Chang, M. J., Eagan, M. K., Lin, M. H., & Hurtado, S. (2011). Considering the impact of racial stigmas and science identity: Persistence among biomedical and behavioral science aspirants. *The Journal of Higher Education, 82*(5), 564–596. https://doi.org/10.1353/jhe.2011.0030

Chen, X. (2013). *STEM attrition: College students' paths into and out of STEM fields* (NCES 2014-001). National Center for Education Statistics, Institute of Education Sciences.

Conant, J. B. (1959). *The American high school today: A first report to interested citizens.* McGraw-Hill Book Company, Inc.

Credé, M. (2018). What shall we do about grit? A critical review of what we know and what we don't know. *Educational Researcher, 47*(9), 606–611. https://doi.org/10.3102s0013189X18801322

Credé, M., Tynan, M. C., & Harms, P. D. (2017). Much ado about grit: A meta-analytic synthesis of the grit literature. *Journal of Personality and Social Psychology, 113*(3), 492–511. https://doi.org/10.1037/pspp0000102

Cross, T. M. (2014). The Gritty: Grit and non-traditional doctoral student success. *Journal of Educators Online, 11*(3), n3. https://doi.org/10.9743/JEO.2014.3.4

Duckworth, A., & Gross, J. J. (2014). Self-control and grit: Related but separable determinants of success. *Current Directions in Psychological Science, 23*(5), 319–325. https://doi.org/10.1177/0963721414541462

Duckworth, A. L. (2013, May 9). Grit: the power of passion and perseverance [Video]. YouTube. https://youtu.be/H14bBuluwB8.

Duckworth, A. L., & Eskreis-Winkler, L. (2013). True grit. *APS Observer, 26*(4). http://www.psychologicalscience.org/observer/true-grit

Duckworth, A. L., Peterson, C., Matthews, M. D., & Kelly, D. R. (2007). Grit: Perseverance and passion for long-term goals. *Journal of Personality and Social Psychology, 92*(6), 1087–1101. https://doi.org/10.1037/0022-3514.92.6.1087

Duckworth, A. L., & Quinn, P. D. (2009). Development and validation of the short grit scale (Grit-S). *Journal of Personality Assessment*, 91(2), 166–174. https://doi.org/10.1080/00223890802634290

Fancher, R. E. (2004). The concept of race in the life and thought of Francis Galton. In A. S. Winston (Ed.), *Defining difference: Race and racism in the history of psychology*. (pp. 49–75). American Psychological Association. https://doi.org/10.1037/10625-003

Farrington, C. A., Roderick, M., Allensworth, E., Nagaoka, J., Keyes, T. S., Johnson, D. W., & Beechum, N. O. (2012). *Teaching adolescents to become learners. The role of noncognitive factors in shaping school performance: A critical literature review*. University of Chicago Consortium on Chicago School Research.

Fosnacht, K., Copridge, K., & Sarraf, S. A. (2018). How valid is grit in the postsecondary context? A construct and concurrent validity analysis. *Research in Higher Education*, 60, 803–822.

Hathaway, R. S., Nagda, B. A., & Gregerman, S. R. (2002). The relationship of undergraduate research participation to graduate and professional education pursuit: An empirical study. *Journal of College Student Development*, 43(5), 614–631.

Hrabowski, F. A. III. (2014). Institutional change in higher education: Innovation and collaboration. *Peabody Journal of Education*, 89(3), 291–304. https://www.jstor.org/stable/43909773

Hurtado, S., Alvarez, C. L., Guillermo-Wann, C., Cuellar, M., & Arellano, L. (2012). A model for diverse learning environments. In J. C. Smart & M. B. Paulsen (Eds.), *Higher education: Handbook of theory and research* (pp. 41–122). Springer.

Hurtado, S., Eagan, M. K., Cabrera, N. L., Lin, M. H., Park, J., & Lopez, M. (2008). Training future scientists: Predicting first-year minority student participation in health science research. *Research in Higher Education*, 49(2), 126–152. https://doi.org/10.1007/s11162-007-9068-1

Hurtado, S., Newman, C. B., Tran, M. C., & Chang, M. J. (2010). Improving the rate of success for underrepresented racial minorities in STEM fields: Insights from a national project. *New Directions for Institutional Research*, 2010(148), 5–15. https://doi.org/10.1002/ir.357

John, O. P., & Srivastava, S. (1999). The Big-Five trait taxonomy: History, measurement, and theoretical perspectives. In L. Pervin & O. P. John (Eds.), *Handbook of personality: Theory and research* (2nd ed.). Guilford.

Kirchgasler, C. (2018). True grit? Making a scientific object and pedagogical tool. *American Educational Research Journal*, 55(4). https://doi.org/10.3102/0002831217752244

Kwon, H. W. (2017). The sociology of grit: Exploring grit as a sociological variable and its potential role in social stratification. *Sociology Compass*, 11(12). https://doi.org/10.1111/soc4.12544

Lee, Y.-G., & Ferrare, J. J. (2019). Finding one's place or losing the race? The consequences of STEM departure for college dropout and degree completion. *The Review of Higher Education*, 43(1), 221–261. https://doi.org/10.1353/rhe.2019.0095

Malone, K. R., & Barabino, G. (2009). Narrations of race in STEM research settings: Identity formation and its discontents. *Science Education*, 93(3), 485–510. https://doi.org/10.1002/sce.20307

Maton, K. I., Pollard, S. A., McDougall Weise, T. V., & Hrabowski, F. A. (2012). Meyerhoff Scholars Program: A strengths-based, institution-wide approach to increasing diversity in Science, Technology, Engineering and Mathematics. *Mount Sinai Journal of Medicine*, *79*(5), 610–623. https://doi.org/10.1002/msj.21341

Maxwell, E. (2008). *Picture imperfect: Photography and eugenics 1870–1940*. Sussex Academic Press.

McGee, E., & Stovall, D. (2015). Reimagining critical race theory in education: Mental health, healing, and the pathway to liberatory praxis. *Educational Theory*, *65*(5), 491–511. https://doi.org/10.1111/edth.12129

McGee, E. O., Botchway, P. K., Naphan-Kingery, D. E., Brockman, A. J., Houston, S., & White, D. T. (2022). Racism camouflaged as impostorism and the impact on black STEM doctoral students. *Race Ethnicity and Education*, *25*(4), 487–507. https://doi.org/10.1080/13613324.2021.1924137

McGee, E. O., & Martin, D. B. (2011). "You would not believe what I have to go through to prove my intellectual value!" Stereotype management among academically successful Black mathematics and engineering students. *American Educational Research Journal*, *48*(6), 1347–1389. https://doi.org/10.3102/0002831211423972

Mendoza-Denton, R., Downey, G., Purdie, V. J., Davis, A., & Pietrzak, J. (2002). Sensitivity to status-based rejection: Implications for African American students' college experience. *Journal of Personality and Social Psychology*, *83*(4), 896–918. https://doi.org/10.1037/0022-3514.83.4.896

Miriti, M. N. (2020, March). The elephant in the room: Race and STEM diversity. *BioScience*, *70*(3), 237–242. https://doi.org/10.1093/biosci/biz167

Morell, M., Yang, J. S., Gladstone, J. R., Turci Faust, L., Ponnock, A. R., Lim, H. J., & Wigfield, A. (2021). Grit: The long and short of it. *Journal of Educational Psychology*, *113*(5), 1038–1058. https://doi.org/10.1037/edu0000594

Muenks, K., Wigfield, A., Yang, J. S., & O'Neal, C. R. (2017). How true is grit? Assessing its relations to high school and college students' personality characteristics, self-regulation, engagement, and achievement. *Journal of Educational Psychology*, *109*(5), 599–620. https://doi.org/10.1037/edu0000153

Musto, M. (2019). Brilliant or bad: The gendered social construction of exceptionalism in early adolescence. *American Sociological Review*, *84*(3), 369–393. https://doi.org/10.1177/0003122419837567

National Academies of Sciences, Engineering, and Medicine [NASEM]. (2017). *Undergraduate research experiences for STEM students: Successes, challenges, and opportunities*. The National Academies Press. https://doi.org/10.17226/24622

National Science Board. (2018). *Science and Engineering Indicators 2018*. National Science Foundation (NSB-2018-1). https://www.nsf.gov/statistics/2018/nsb20181/report/sections/higher-education-in-science-and-engineering/highlights

Núñez, A. M., Rivera, J., & Hallmark, T. (2020). Applying an intersectionality lens to expand equity in the geosciences. *Journal of Geoscience Education*, *68*(2), 97–114. https://doi.org/10.1080/10899995.2019.1675131

Omi, M., & Winant, H. (2015). *Racial formation in the United States* (3rd ed.). Routledge/Taylor & Francis Group.

Park, D., Tsukayama, E., Yu, A., & Duckworth, A. L. (2020). The development of grit and growth mindset during adolescence. *Journal of Experimental Child Psychology*, *198*, 104889. https://doi.org/10.1016/j.jecp.2020.104889

Ris, E. W. (2015). Grit: A short history of a useful concept. *Journal of Educational Controversy, 10*(1), article 3.

Scelfo, J. (2016, April 8). Angela Duckworth on passion, grit and success. *The New York Times.* https://www.nytimes.com/2016/04/10/education/edlife/passion-grit-success.html

Smedley, A. (2013). Science and the idea of race: A brief history. In J. M. Fish (Ed.), *Race and intelligence: Separating science from myth* (pp. 145–176). Routledge ebook.

Solórzano, D., Ceja, M., & Yosso, T. (2000). Critical race theory, racial microaggressions, and campus racial climate: The experiences of African American college students. *Journal of Negro Education, 69*(1/2 Winter/Spring), 60–73. https://www.jstor.org/stable/2696265

SRI International. (2018). *Promoting grit, tenacity, and perseverance: Critical factors for success in the 21st century.* SRI International.

Strayhorn, T. L. (2014). What role does grit play in the academic success of black male collegians at predominantly White institutions? *Journal of African American Studies, 18*(1), 1–10. https://doi.org/10.1007/s12111-012-9243-0

Thomas, L. L., Kuncel, N. R., & Credé, M. (2007). Noncognitive variables in college admissions: The case of the non-cognitive questionnaire. *Educational and Psychological Measurement, 67*(4), 635–657. https://doi.org/10.1177/0013164406292074

Traweek, S. (1988). *Beamtimes and lifetimes: The world of high energy physicists.* Harvard University Press.

Valencia, R. (1997). *The evolution of deficit thinking: Educational thought and practice.* Falmer Press.

Vazsonyi, A. T., Ksinan, A. J., Ksinan Jiskrova, G., Mikuška, J., Javakhishvili, M., & Cui, G. (2019). To grit or not to grit, that is the question! *Journal of Research in Personality, 78*, 215–226. https://doi.org/10.1016/j.jrp.2018.12.006

Wolters, C. A., & Hussain, M. (2015). Investigating grit and its relations with college students' self-regulated learning and academic achievement. *Metacognition and Learning, 10*(3), 293–311. https://doi.org/10.1007/s11409-014-9128-9

Yosso, T. J., Smith, W. A., Ceja, M., & Solórzano, D. (2009). Critical race theory, racial microaggressions, and campus racial climate for Latina/o undergraduates. *Harvard Educational Review, 79*(4), 659–786. https://doi.org/10.17763/haer.79.4.m6867014157m7071

Zuberi, T., & Bonilla-Silva, E. (Eds.). (2008). *White logic, white methods: Racism and methodology.* Rowman & Littlefield Publishers.

3

CHALLENGING EVERYDAY STRUCTURAL RACISM

A Critical Race Analysis of Grit in STEM

Daniel G. Solórzano

I settled in my seat at the plenary session of the 2016 Annual Ford Fellows meeting at the National Academy of Sciences building in Washington, D.C. Our speaker was Dr. Keivan Stassun—a Professor of Physics & Astronomy at Vanderbilt University. His talk was centered on a program he co-directed with colleagues at Fisk University—a Historically Black College in Nashville, Tennessee (see Stassun et al., 2010). The program was titled *The Fisk-Vanderbilt Master's-to-PhD Bridge Program*. In his talk, Professor Stassun talked about how the program challenged the efficacy of the Graduate Record Exam (GRE) in graduate admissions (see Miller & Stassun, 2014). Professor Stassun also shared his story of how the Fisk–Vanderbilt Bridge Program used Angela Duckworth's work and her concept of grit as part of their holistic admissions program in the fields of astronomy, biology, chemistry, physics, and materials science (see Duckworth, 2016; Duckworth & Quinn, 2009; Powell, 2013). The program defined grit as perseverance combined with a passion for a long-term goal. Stassun and his team borrowed Duckworth's Grit Scale to develop an interview protocol for prospective students using the grit characteristics (see Duckworth & Quinn, 2009). They asked each candidate to (a) describe a challenging experience or obstacle, (b) their fears related to the obstacle, (c) how they pulled through, and (d) the resources or relationships on which they relied to overcome the obstacles. Stassun described how students admitted with the grit interview protocol not only persisted through the Ph.D. program but also excelled in these Science, Technology, Engineering, and Mathematics (STEM) fields. He also spoke of how the Fisk–Vanderbilt program faculty focused on the importance of mentoring for students' success. Keivan ended the presentation with

DOI: 10.4324/9781003332497-4

stories of some exemplary African American PhDs who graduated from the program and their contributions to STEM fields.

The talk was well-received by the Ford Fellows audience. I walked out of the auditorium with three strong feelings. First, I was really impressed with the African American students, the Fisk–Vanderbilt Bridge Program, and the commitments of the Fisk and Vanderbilt faculty and staff (see Stassun et al., 2010). Second, I knew of many other stories of African American post-baccalaureate success filled with examples of perseverance combined with a passion for a long-term goal (i.e., grit). Third, any examination of African American post-baccalaureate journeys must consider the impact of everyday structural racism (i.e., interpersonal, institutional, and internalized) on their completion or push out of the academy.

In this chapter, I begin by telling my story of coming to name and recognize everyday structural racism in the fields of Race and Ethnic Studies, Freirean Critical Pedagogy, and Critical Race Theory (CRT). Second, I put CRT in conversation with grit to show the importance of naming and recognizing everyday structural racism in the journeys of Students of Color. Next, I use Race and Ethnic Studies, Freirean Critical Pedagogy, and CRT to analyze the concept of grit. Finally, I look to some promising directions of CRT in STEM fields.

My Introduction to Race, Ethnic, and Gender Studies

I was first introduced to Race, Ethnic, and Gender Studies in 1968 in a first-year Collegiate Seminar at St. Mary's College. The professor assigned *The Autobiography of Malcolm X* (X & Haley, 1965). This was the first time I read a book centering on the experiences of People of Color generally and the African American community specifically.[1] This book started me on my journey to Race and Ethnic Studies. In my second year of college, I transferred to Loyola University of Los Angeles and eventually majored in Sociology with an emphasis in Mexican American Studies—as the field was then called. Now known as Chicana/o Studies, this interdisciplinary field examines the lives, histories, and cultures of Mexican-origin people coming to and living in the United States. Mexican American Studies at Loyola was structured so we had to take Black Studies classes to complete the program's pre-requisite, core, and elective courses. These courses enriched my experience by searching for answers to questions about everyday structural racism in both Mexican American and African American communities.

The narrative about the Chicana/o and African American experience focused on challenging the "cultural deficit" frame. This frame attributed Chicana/o and African American lack of social mobility to the "cultural deficiencies" of Black and Brown students, their families, and their communities (see Solórzano

& Solórzano, 1995; Valencia & Solórzano, 1997). In those years, many of us were reading foundational works in Chicana/o, African American, Native American, Asian American, and Gender Studies (see Solórzano, 2013). Some of the early core texts in these fields, along with my interdisciplinary training, led me to cultural nationalist frameworks (Asante, 1987, 1991), internal colonial paradigms (Acuña, 1972; Barrera, 1979; Barrera et al., 1972; Blauner, 1969, 1972, 2001; Bonilla & Girling 1973), Marxist and neo-Marxist texts (Barrera, 1979; Bowles & Gintis, 1976), and Women of Color Feminisms (Anzaldúa, 1987, 1990; Collins, 1986, 1990; hooks, 1990; Hurtado, 1996).

Like other Race and Ethnic Studies programs, Chicana/o Studies emerged in the context of the civil and human rights movements of the 1960s. I considered these Race and Ethnic Studies disciplines as areas of critical social inquiry that were embedded in interdisciplinary and historical analysis and were transformational for my journey to critical consciousness. These and other critical fields formed my intellectual foundation as I began to name and recognize systemic and everyday racism.

Recognizing Relational History to Name and Recognize Systemic and Everyday Racism

When studying everyday structural racism, we need to recognize how these forms of racism have played out in U.S. history (see Hannah-Jones, 2019, 2021). To tell the story, I share a short history of everyday structural racism confronting African Americans in the United States (see Figure 3.1) (see Solórzano & Pérez Huber, 2020). As one historical starting point, we start in 1619, when the first enslaved Africans were brought to the shores of Indigenous Powhatan land in what is now the United States at Jamestown—156 years before U.S. independence.[2]

From 1619 to 1865, African Americans were "legally" enslaved and served as chattel or property for the enslavers. That period represents 246 years of "legal" enslavement in what is now the United States—about 61% of U.S. history. From 1865 to 1965, African Americans lived in an era of Jim Crow. This 100-year period represented the "legal" separation and subsequent inequity of African Americans in all walks of social life—representing 25% of U.S. history. Under Jim Crow, by law or custom, African Americans could not live in the same neighborhoods as whites, attend the same schools as whites, work in the same jobs and factories as whites, accumulate the same economic wealth as whites, attend the same churches as whites, dine at the same restaurants as whites, have access to the same health care as whites, participate in the everyday political, civic, or social life as whites, or even be buried in the same cemeteries as whites. Enslavement and Jim Crow represent 86% of U.S. history. The years from 1965 to 2023 (present) embody the "modern" era of civil rights in the United States—these 57 years are sometimes referred to as the New Jim Crow and comprise about 14% of U.S. history (see Alexander, 2010). In this period, we had "civil rights" laws where African Americans and other People of Color could not be "legally segregated" in schools, workplaces, or other parts of social and political life. However, because of housing segregation and discriminatory *de facto* and *de jure* social policies and practices, African Americans and other People of Color continue to attend schools that have fewer resources, are kept out of the highest-paid and most secure occupations, have less access to quality health and wellness opportunities and have less accumulated wealth (Jones, 2000; Williams & Purdie-Vaughns, 2016; Williams et al., 2016).

U.S. racial history matters. While education and economic indicators for African Americans and other People of Color are improving, the opportunity and outcome gaps with whites remain very wide (Flores et al., 2019; Perez Huber et al., 2018). When discussing racism, we must acknowledge this 400-year (plus) history of everyday structural racism. We need to show that 86% of that history was spent in "legal" enslavement[3] or "legal" separation for African Americans. We need to show how the accumulation of that history still impacts the everyday lives of African Americans and other People of Color—especially their social mobility. Those who study social inequity and social mobility (like grit) in the current era must recognize this 400-year (plus) history of everyday structural racism. U.S. racial history matters; it mattered in 1619, and it matters in 2023.

To maintain these conditions over these four centuries, you need an ideology that justifies this arrangement—first as enslaved, then as *de jure*, and now as *de facto* second-class citizens. That ideology is white supremacy. I define white supremacy as the assigning of values to real or imagined differences to justify the perceived inherent superiority of whites over African Americans and other People of Color that warrants the right and power of whites to dominate others (see Solórzano & Pérez Huber, 2020). This short history is the evidence that many (including academics) are unaware of, ignore, or erase in their majoritarian stories of everyday structural racism. Studies of the perseverance and resilience of African Americans and other People of Color, combined with a passion for a long-term goal such as grit, must consider this history and the material conditions attached. Studies or programs using the grit framework must consider the community, familial, and individual tools and strengths these students utilize to navigate the worlds of academia—Community Cultural Wealth (see Solórzano & Villalpando, 1998; Yosso, 2005; Yosso & Solórzano, 2005). This racial history was critical as I started my teaching journey in 1972.

My Introduction to Paulo Freire

In 1972, after graduating from Loyola University, I began my formal teaching career as a high school social studies teacher at the Los Angeles County Central Juvenile Hall, a youth correctional and holding facility. I was part of a teacher training program called the *National Teacher Corps*. This was one of the first federally funded training programs to prepare teachers to work in underserved Communities of Color—urban and rural. The year I participated in *Teacher Corps*, the program focused on "urban corrections." As a first-year teacher, out of necessity and survival, I was introduced to the work of Paulo Freire—the Brazilian educator, activist, and critical social theorist.

Freirean Critical Pedagogy taught me that all education is political, and thus schools at any level are never neutral institutions (Freire 1970a, 1970b, 1973). Freire asserts that schools function either to maintain and reproduce the existing social order or, alternatively, to empower people to transform themselves and/or society. Freire argues that when schools domesticate, they socialize students into accepting the ideology, values, and structures of society's dominant class as legitimate. Conversely, when schools liberate, they engage students as subjects willing and able to act on their world. To create a liberating education, Freire developed the "problem-posing method," based on two-way dialogues of cooperation, reflection, and action between student and teacher (Freire 1970a, 1970b, 1973). I have continued my postsecondary teaching career using Freirean pedagogy at two California Community Colleges, two California State Universities, and one University of California campus in Chicana/o Studies, Sociology, and Education from 1975 to the present. Freire was and continues to be a critical foundation and bridge along my intellectual and pedagogical career path. Thus, Race and Ethnic Studies and Freirean Critical Pedagogy were pivotal and foundational as I made my way to CRT in the early 1990s.

My Journey to Critical Race Theory

In 1990, I arrived at UCLA as an assistant professor in Social Science and Comparative Education. In the summer of 1993, I read an article in the *Chronicle of Higher Education* by Peter Monaghan (1993) titled "'Critical Race Theory' Questions the Role of Legal Doctrine in Racial Inequality." The article introduced me to a new and emerging field in the law that challenged the orthodoxy of race and racism in the post-civil rights era (Bell, 1987, 1992). At that time, CRT in the law helped me explain the lack of racial progress from the 1960s to the 1990s. It also provided analytical tools to center race and racism in my academic research and teaching. In the months and years that followed, I immersed myself in the CRT artifacts in law libraries, conferences, and symposia. I worked to put CRT in the law in conversation with my research and teaching in Race, Ethnic, and Gender Studies, Freirean Critical Theory, and Education.

With the power of historical hindsight and the strength of multiple intellectual and community activist traditions, I worked with others (primarily graduate students at the University of California, Los Angeles) to use CRT as an analytical tool to help shape our methodologies as researchers and our practices as educators. I found that CRT informed our praxis (where theory and practice intersect) in multiple ways (Jain & Solórzano, 2014).

With this background, I defined critical race theory as an analytical framework that accounts for the role of race and racism in education and works toward identifying and challenging racism as part of a larger goal of identifying and challenging all forms of subordination. Along with this definition and my training in Race and Ethnic Studies and Freirean Critical Pedagogy, I initially developed and applied five tenets of CRT in education. The tenets are (a) the intercentricity of race and racism with other forms of subordination, (b) the challenge to dominant ideology, (c) the centrality of experiential knowledge, (d) the commitment to racial justice, and (e) the transdisciplinary perspective (see Figure 3.1) (Solórzano, 1997, 1998). These five intersecting elements of CRT were not new in and of themselves, but they collectively represented a challenge to some traditional modes of race scholarship. In the Freirean (1970b) problem-posing tradition, I found that CRT (a) names the racist injuries (i.e., educational inequity), (b)

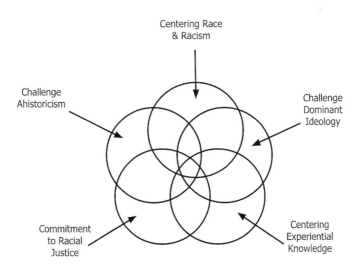

FIGURE 3.1   The intersecting tenets of critical race theory.

identifies their origins (i.e., systemic racism and white supremacy), and (c) seeks remedies for the injury (i.e., racial justice actions).

In CRT in education, we are often told to return to CRT's legal foundations and tenets. Although CRT in the law has been critical and foundational to CRT in education, I've also tried to show how CRT has deep roots in Race, Ethnic, and Gender Studies and Freirean Critical Pedagogy (Solórzano, 2013). Borrowing from Freirean Critical Pedagogy, I felt our responsibility was to "reinvent" or "reimagine" CRT for the various fields and contexts in which we work (see Freire & Macedo, 1987). This reinvention is what CRT scholars in education continue to practice. They engage with CRT in the context of the structures, processes, and discourses of educational research and praxis. In a Freirean sense, CRT continues to reinvent or reimagine itself to positively impact the communities we serve. Over the years, my colleagues and I have worked to reinvent or reimagine CRT in Education by developing "critical race tools."[4] These tools help us understand how People and Communities of Color experience racism, how they respond to racism, and how they use the cultural wealth and assets they possess to survive racism and other forms of oppression (see Solórzano & Villalpando, 1998; Yosso, 2005; Yosso & Solórzano, 2005).[5]

My intellectual histories in Race and Ethnic Studies and Freirean Critical Pedagogy prepared me when I read the 1993 Monaghan article and found CRT in the law. Reflecting on these academic and activist experiences and preparation, I was able to "see" the importance of CRT and that it represented a paradigm shift in the study of everyday structural racism (see Kuhn, 1970). Also, as I reflect on my introduction to the concept of grit at the Ford meeting and Professor Stassun's lecture, I again bring my intellectual and activist history and use the tools of CRT—specifically the five tenets—to better understand and critique grit.

My CRT>grit>STEM Analysis

Using my definition of Critical Race Theory, I take each of the five intersecting tenets in Figure 3.1 and put them in conversation with grit. Once again, I use my intellectual and activist history laid out earlier to engage in a preliminary *CRT>grit>STEM Analysis*.[6]

The Intercentricity of Race and Racism with Other Forms of Subordination

Critical Race Theory starts from the premise that race and racism are endemic, permanent, and in the words of Margaret Russell (1992), "a central rather than marginal factor in defining and explaining individual experiences of the law" (pp. 762–763). Although race and racism are at the center of a Critical Race Analysis, I also view them as intersecting with other forms of subordination, such as gender and class discrimination (Crenshaw, 1991). As Robin Barnes (1990) stated, "Critical race scholars have refused to ignore the differences between class and race as a basis for oppression. … Critical race scholars know that class oppression alone cannot account for racial oppression" (p. 1868). Critical Race Theory also acknowledges the inter-centricity of racialized oppression—the layers of subordination based on race, gender, class, immigration status, surname, phenotype, accent, and sexuality. Here, in the intersections of racial oppression, we can use Critical Race Theory to search for some answers to the theoretical, conceptual, methodological, and pedagogical questions related to the racialized experiences of People of Color.

CRT>grit>STEM Analysis

Grit focuses on the individual and their perseverance combined with a passion for a long-term goal. Grit rarely identifies or mentions the impact of race, racism (everyday or structural), or white supremacy as the Person of Color makes her way through achieving her long-term goal in STEM. Grit doesn't look at the intersecting forms of oppression—especially racism, sexism, and classism in STEM. A grit analysis rarely focuses on Students of Color, but on students in general. A CRT analysis centers on the lives and experiences of Students/Persons of Color by showing how everyday structural racism has a long history in STEM through various policies and practices along the educational pipeline. One example is the dearth of Faculty of Color in the natural, physical, and engineering sciences. For instance, at the University of California, Los Angeles, the Hispanic Serving Institution [HSI] Task Force published a final report and found that in 2019 the ratio of undergraduate STEM students to faculty by race was 130 to 1 for Latina/o students, 81 to 1 for Black students, 64 to 1 for Asian students, 10 to 1 for white students, and no Native American faculty (UCLA HSI Taskforce, 2022). Faculty of Color in STEM matters, and we should prioritize their hiring and retention.

The Challenge to Dominant Ideology

Critical Race Theory challenges the traditional claims that educational institutions make toward objectivity, meritocracy, colorblindness, race neutrality, and equal opportunity. Critical Race Scholars argue that these traditional claims act as a camouflage for the dominant groups' self-interest, power, and privilege in U.S. society (Calmore, 1992; Solórzano, 1997). Critical Race Theory challenges white privilege, rejects notions of "neutral" research or "objective" researchers, and exposes deficit-informed research that silences and distorts epistemologies of People of Color (Delgado Bernal, 1998).

CRT>grit>STEM Analysis

Grit rarely challenges objectivity, meritocracy, colorblindness, race neutrality, and equal opportunity. These are bedrock principles in STEM, and CRT challenges these principles in STEM and other academic fields across the educational pipeline. CRT also calls on STEM and other fields to challenge these principles and provide a culturally relevant and sustaining curriculum and pedagogy (see Dietz et al., 2022; Holly, 2021; Mejia et al., 2018; Mejia et al., 2022; Tsai et al., 2021). Once again, grit focuses on the individual and her perseverance combined with a passion for a long-term goal. Grit doesn't acknowledge that Students of Color have persevered, have resilience, have resisted, and have a passion for a long-term goal, yet are still disproportionally pushed out of STEM. The assumption is that if you fail in STEM, you don't have perseverance, resilience, or a passion for a long-term goal (i.e., grit). Thus, you are deficient and come from a culturally deficient family and community. Grit needs to challenge these deficit frameworks.

The Centrality of Experiential Knowledge

Critical Race Theory challenges traditional research paradigms, texts, and theories used to explain the histories and experiences of People of Color. Critical Race Theory recognizes that the experiential knowledge of People of Color is legitimate, appropriate, and critical to understanding, analyzing, and teaching about racial subordination. Critical Race Theorists view this knowledge as a strength and draw explicitly on the lived experiences of People of Color by including such methods as storytelling, family histories, biographies, scenarios, parables, *cuentos, testimonios*, chronicles, and narratives (Bell, 1987, 1992; Delgado, 1989, 1995; Olivas, 1990; Solórzano, 1997, 1998). CRT exposes deficit-informed research and methods that silence and distort the experiences of People of Color and instead focus on their racialized, gendered, and classed experiences as sources of strength (Solórzano & Solórzano, 1995; Valencia & Solórzano, 1997).

CRT>grit>STEM Analysis

Students of Color bring many strengths to the STEM fields. They bring their Community, Familial, and Individual Cultural Wealth to STEM. Grit doesn't recognize that cultural assets, strengths, and resilience are at the core of what Students of Color bring to the table while simultaneously acknowledging that STEM has racist structures embedded in their histories and current conditions.

The Commitment to Racial Justice

Critical Race Theory is committed to racial justice and offers a liberatory or transformative response to racial, gender, and class oppression (Matsuda, 1991). I envision a racial justice research agenda that leads toward the following:

- the elimination of racism, sexism, and poverty, and
- the empowering of minoritized groups

Critical Race researchers acknowledge that educational institutions operate in contradictory ways, with their potential to oppress and marginalize coexisting with their potential to emancipate and empower. Likewise, Critical Race Theory recognizes that multiple layers of oppression and discrimination are met with multiple forms of resistance. The histories of Communities of Color have shown that to be true.

CRT>grit>STEM Analysis

Because grit doesn't focus on a racial (CRT) analysis, it ignores or doesn't understand the importance of centering race and racism in STEM. It fails to recognize how STEM has its own racial and racist history and that it must be both acknowledged and challenged. There must be an explicit and unapologetic racial justice project in STEM to bring about initial change, leading toward long-term structural change in STEM fields.

The Transdisciplinary Perspective

Critical Race Theory challenges ahistoricism and the unidisciplinary focus of most analyses and insists on analyzing race and racism by placing them in historical and contemporary contexts (Delgado, 1984, 1992; Olivas, 1990). Critical Race Theory uses the transdisciplinary knowledge and methodological base of race and ethnic studies, women's studies, sociology, history, law, and other fields to guide research that better understands the effects of racism, sexism, and classism on People of Color.

CRT>grit>STEM Analysis

Grit doesn't recognize the history of racism and sexism in STEM. We must unearth, acknowledge, and tell that history to move STEM forward. A historical analysis of racism and white supremacy in STEM is an essential first step toward more structural change.

These five CRT tenets are not new in and of themselves, but collectively, they represent a challenge to the existing modes of scholarship. Indeed, Critical Race Theory names racist injuries and identifies their origins. In examining the origins, CRT finds that racism is often well-disguised in the rhetoric of shared "normative" values and "neutral" social scientific and educational principles and practices (Matsuda et al., 1993). However, when the ideology of racism is examined and racist injuries are named, the survivors of racism can find their voice. Furthermore, those injured by racism and other forms of oppression discover they are not alone in their marginality. They become empowered participants, hearing their own stories and the stories of others, listening to how the arguments against them are framed, and learning to make the arguments to defend themselves. The STEM fields would benefit from a CRT analysis and action plan to remedy the impact of everyday structural racism on both Students and Faculty of Color. The UCLA HSI Taskforce Report (2022) speaks to the importance of Student of Color spaces where these questions and issues around race, racism, and sexism could be acknowledged and engaged. The report and the student voices are clear that these spaces are rarely found in STEM fields, and there should be support for this type of student resource center.

Recent CRT Work in the Medical Sciences

In the Fall of 2021, I attended the *Critical Race Studies in Education Association* (CRSEA) annual conference.[7] I was on a panel on what the program calls "CriTalk" sessions. As part of the presentation, we discussed new and promising areas in CRT. At the very end of the panel, our colleague Margaret Montoya (one of the Founding Mothers of CRT in the Law) mentioned an article her daughter Diana had shared with her, titled "Seeing the Window, Finding the Spider: Applying Critical Race Theory to Medical Education to Make Up Where Biomedical Models and Social Determinants of Health Curricula Fall Short" (Tsai et al., 2021). Margaret called it MedCRT and mentioned the connections with the work at CRSEA. Tsai et al. (2021) assert that physicians should be taught critical theoretical frameworks to interrogate structural sources of racial inequities and achieve the goal of health equity. Their first significant contribution speaks to the importance of preparing medical school students and interns with a version of what we in Education call Critical Race Pedagogy (see Lynn, 1999; Lynn et al., 2013). MedCRT also uses some of the five tenets I shared earlier in this chapter to inform medical education—how they prepare trainees to work with Patients of Color.

In particular, they speak on how to combat health inequity in teaching medical school trainees by centering on racism and white supremacy in their curriculum and pedagogy. They also challenge the dominant frameworks in medical education, such as the biomedical and social determinants of health models. These models focus on the individual's failings—similar to cultural deficit theory—as opposed to examining the racist structural conditions in the community and in medicine that might better determine disparate health outcomes for People of Color. Tsai et al. (2021) argued that when they train medical personnel, they must focus on the "spider" and its relationship to the "web":

> A number of conditions—poverty, race, diet, sex—are labeled as "risk factors" entangled on a "web" of contributing elements that increase the likelihood of a given pathology. Importantly, however, the spider that weaves the web is absent in this metaphor. The material and historical conditions that create unequal distributions of power and resources—the conditions that spin the web of inequity such as racial supremacy, wealth concentration, neoliberal capitalism, and misogyny—are not included, considered, learned, or taught.
>
> *(p. 3)*

This article also challenges us and provides the tools for how we prepare teachers, school leaders, social workers, and others who serve the most underserved of committees—Communities of Color. It is exciting to see how CRT is moving into other important STEM areas like medicine, public health, and engineering.[8]

Conclusion

I don't want to downplay the importance of perseverance, resilience, and a passion for a long-term goal. These assets are critical to success for many of us. But People of Color already possess these grit characteristics. Both history and contemporary life stories are evidence of these characteristics. However, we can't ignore the impact of everyday structural racism that Students of Color experience in their collective and individual history in and out of STEM. Colleges and universities need to recognize and build on all of the strengths that Students of Color bring to STEM so they can not only survive but thrive.

From January to June 2020, Ahmaud Arbery, Breanna Taylor, and George Floyd (among others) were brutally murdered. The United States and the world responded with Black-led multiracial demonstrations and mobilizations. In the weeks, months, and years that followed, we have been going through "America's Racial Reckoning." This reckoning included anti-racist actions such as mobilizations, action plans, and statements for Racial Justice. Indeed, many discussions and actions utilized the essays in *The 1619 Project* (see Hannah-Jones 2019, 2021). Some might argue that the last time the United States saw such widespread racial justice mobilizations was the Civil Right Rebellions of the 1960s and 1970s (see Hannah-Jones, 2019, 2021). The 2020 attacks on Critical Race Theory began within the context of "America's Racial Reckoning" and the conservative pushback to the *1619 Project*.

On June 25, 2020, a month after the murder of George Floyd, the editorial team of the journal *Cell* responded to this "Racial Reckoning" by publishing an anti-racism statement. Many universities, professional societies, and academic journals responded similarly to the "Racial Reckoning." The *Cell* Editorial Team's (2020) response was titled "Science Has a Racism Problem." They conclude the Editorial with the following passage:

> We and our colleagues across Cell Press hope to serve as one small part of amplifying Black voices in STEM, and this is just the Editorial beginning. We are learning, and we will almost certainly make mistakes along the way. But silence is not, and never should have been, an option. *Science has a racism problem. Scientists are problem solvers.* Let's get to it.
>
> *(p. 1443, emphasis added)*

As the *Cell* Editorial Team states, "Scientists are problem solvers." To solve the racism problem, STEM would benefit from a CRT analysis and action plan to remedy the impact of everyday structural racism on Students, Staff, and Faculty of Color in the sciences. "Let's get to it."

Notes

1 The professor also introduced us to the speeches of Malcolm X on vinyl records. Later I found the 1972 documentary film titled *Malcolm X*. I also want to recognize Roberta Espinoza's (2011) concept of "pivotal moments." I've interpreted this to mean those interventions (involving people, places, written and visual material) that can point the way toward new ideas and new ways of interpreting the world. Reading *The Autobiography of Malcolm X* was a pivotal moment for me.
2 It should be noted that Indigenous peoples populated these lands for centuries before the first settler colonists came to what is now the *Americas* (North, Central, and South America). The settler colonists invaded, occupied, and committed genocide against the Native People throughout the *Americas*. The Indigenous peoples' story of structural racism begins when the first European settler colonists came to the *Americas*. It should also be noted that subsequent African American, Chicana/o, Asian American, other People of Color histories of systemic racism begin when settler colonists made contact with the Americas (see Acuña, 1972; Asante, 1987; Deloria, 1969; Takaki, 1989).

3 I recognize that there are differences between slavery and enslavement. Slavery is an identity and enslavement is a condition. For the same reason, I see the enslaver as those persons who dehumanized the enslaved person and thus reducing him/her to a commodity (see Hannah-Jones, 2019, 2021).

4 See, for example, research briefs on Latino Critical Theory, Tribal Critical Race Theory, Asian American Critical Race Theory, and BlackCrit and Critical Race methodologies at the *Center for Critical Race Studies in Education at UCLA* (For these and other CRT tools go to http://www.ccrse.gseis.ucla.edu/).

5 In 1995–1996, I started teaching a year-long Research Apprenticeship Course on Race, Racism, and Education. This course was foundational to developing CRT tools and applying CRT to education, to race, ethnic, and gender studies, and to Freirean Critical Pedagogy (see Solórzano, 2022).

6 While not comprehensive, there are three studies that explicitly use racism in their analysis of grit (McGee & Stovall, 2015; Sullivan, 2021; Tewell, 2020). Also, William Sedlacek (1999) has written about the salience of eight noncognitive variables in predicting Black student success on a number of outcome variables in higher education. One such variable is "understands and deals with racism." He states that this construct is based on a realistic and "personal experience of racism. Not submissive to existing wrongs, nor hostile to society, nor a 'cop-out.' Able to handle racist system. Asserts school role to fight racism" (p. 539). This predictive variable of Black students' education success is not used in grit analysis.

7 *Critical Race Studies in Education Association* is an interdisciplinary organization dedicated to the study of Critical Race Theory and the promotion of racial justice in education. It began in 2007 as an extension and critique of the annual *American Educational Research Association* meeting in Chicago.

8 There are other STEM fields using CRT that I need to mention. In the field of engineering colleagues are challenging the ways they train engineers, especially Engineers of Color (see Davis, 2022; Dietz et al., 2022; Holly, 2021; Martin & Garza, 2020; Mejia et al., 2018, 2022; Patrick et al., 2022).

References

Acuña, R. (1972). *Occupied America: The Chicano's struggle toward liberation.* Canfield Press.

Alexander, M. (2010). *The new Jim Crow: Mass incarceration in the age of colorblindness.* The New Press.

Anzaldúa, G. (1987). *Borderlands, la frontera: The new mestiza.* Aunt Lute Books.

Anzaldúa, G. (1990). Introduction. In G. Anzaldúa (Ed.), *Making face, making soul: Creative and critical perspectives by feminists of color* (xv–xxviii). Aunt Lute Books.

Asante, M. (1987). *The Afrocentric idea.* Temple University Press.

Asante, M. (1991). The Afrocentric idea in education. *Journal of Negro Education, 60*(2), 170–180. https://doi.org/10.2307/2295608

Barnes, R. (1990). Race consciousness: The thematic content of racial distinctiveness in critical race scholarship. *Harvard Law Review, 103,* 1864–1871.

Barrera, M. (1979). *Race and class in the Southwest: A theory of racial inequality.* University of Notre Dame Press.

Barrera, M., Muñoz, C., & Ornelas, C. (1972). The barrio as internal colony. *Urban Affairs Annual Reviews, 6,* 465–498.

Bell, D. (1987). *And we will not be saved: The elusive quest for racial justice.* Basic Books.

Bell, D. (1992). *Faces at the bottom of the well: The permanence of racism.* Basic Books.

Blauner, R. (1969). Internal colonialism and ghetto revolt. *Social Problems, 16,* 393–408.

Blauner, R. (1972). *Racial oppression in America.* Harper & Row.

Blauner, R. (2001). *Still big news: Racial oppression in America.* Temple University Press.

Bonilla, F., & Girling, R. (Eds.). (1973). *Structures of dependency.* Stanford Institute of Politics.

Bowles, S., & Gintis, H. (1976). *Schooling in capitalist America: Educational reform and the contradictions of economic life.* Basic Books.

Calmore, J. (1992). Critical race theory, Archie Shepp, and fire music: Securing an authentic intellectual life in a multicultural world. *Southern California Law Review, 65,* 2129–2231.

Cell Editorial Team. (2020). Science has a racism problem. *Cell, 181,* 1443–1444.

Collins, P. H. (1986). Learning from the outsider within: The sociological significance of Black feminist thought. *Social Problems, 33*(6), S14–S32. https://doi.org/10.2307/800672

Collins, P. H. (1990). *Black feminist thought: Knowledge, consciousness, and the politics of empowerment.* Routledge.

Crenshaw, K. (1991). Mapping the margins: Intersectionality, identity politics, and the violence against women of color. *Stanford Law Review, 43,* 1241–1299.

Davis, J. (2022). Disrupting research, theory, and pedagogy with critical race theory in mathematics education for Black populations. *Journal of Urban Mathematics Education, 15*(1), 9–30.

Delgado Bernal, D. (1998). Using a Chicana feminist epistemology in educational research. *Harvard Educational Review, 68*(4), 555–579.

Delgado, R. (1984). The imperial scholar: Reflections on a review of civil rights literature. *University of Pennsylvania Law Review, 132,* 561–578.

Delgado, R. (1989). Storytelling for oppositionists and others: A plea for narrative. *Michigan Law Review, 87,* 2411–2441.

Delgado, R. (1992). The imperial scholar revisited: How to marginalize outsider writing, ten years later. *University of Pennsylvania Law Review, 140,* 1349–1372.

Delgado, R. (1995). *The Rodrigo chronicles: Conversations about America and race.* NYU Press.

Deloria, V. (1969). *Custer died for your sins: An Indian manifesto.* McMillan.

Dietz, G., Douglas, E., McCray, E., Mejia, J., Pawley, A., & Revelo, R. (2022). Learning from anti-racist theories to reframe engineering education research on race. *Journal of Women and Minorities in Science and Engineering, 28,* 1–30. https://doi.org/10.1615/JWomenMinorScienEng.2022036609

Duckworth, A. L. (2016). *Grit: The power of passion and perseverance.* Scribner/Simon & Schuster.

Duckworth, A. L., & Quinn, P. D. (2009). Development and validation of the short grit scale (Grit-S). *Journal of Personality Assessment, 91*(2), 166–174. https://doi.org/10.1080/00223890802634290

Espinoza, R. (2011). *Pivotal moments: How educators can put all students on the path to college*. Harvard University Press.

Flores, A., Gaxiola Serrano, T., & Solórzano, D. (2019). Critical race theory, racial stratification in education, and public health. In C. Ford, D. Griffith, B. Marino, & K. Gilbert (Eds.), *Racism: Science and tools for the public health professional* (pp. 151–167). American Public Health Association.

Freire, P. (1970a). The adult literacy process as cultural action for freedom. *Harvard Educational Review, 40*(2), 205–225.

Freire, P. (1970b). *Pedagogy of the oppressed*. Continuum.

Freire, P. (1973). *Education for critical consciousness*. Seabury.

Freire, P., & Macedo, D. (1987). *Literacy: Reading the word and the world*. Bergin & Garvey.

Hannah-Jones, N. (2019, August). The 1619 project. *New York Times*. https://www.nytimes.com/interactive/2019/08/14/magazine/1619-america-slavery.html?searchResultPosition=2

Hannah-Jones, N. (2021). *The 1619 project: A new origin story*. One World.

Holly, J. (2021). Criticality is crucial: Fidelity in what we say and what we do. *Studies in Engineering Education, 2*(2), 46–53. https://doi.org/10.21061/see.78

hooks, b. (1990). *Yearning: Race, gender, and cultural politics*. South End Press.

Hurtado, A. (1996). *The color of privilege: Three blasphemes on race and feminism*. University of Michigan Press.

Jain, D., & Solórzano, D. (2014). A critical race journey of mentoring. In C. Turner & J. Gonzalez (Eds.), *Modeling mentoring across race/ethnicity and gender: Practices to cultivate the next Generation of diverse faculty* (pp. 125–142). Stylus Publishing.

Jones, C. (2000). Levels of racism: A theoretic framework and a gardener's tale. *American Journal of Public Health, 90*(8), 1212–1215. https://doi.org/10.2105/ajph.90.8.1212

Kuhn, T. (1970): *The structure of scientific revolutions* (2nd ed.). University of Chicago Press.

Lynn, M. (1999). Toward a critical race pedagogy: A research note. *Urban Education, 33*(5), 606–626. https://doi.org/10.1177/0042085999335004

Lynn, M., Jennings, M. E., & Hughes, S. (2013). Critical race pedagogy 2.0: Lessons from Derrick Bell. *Race Ethnicity and Education, 16*(4), 603–628. https://doi.org/10.1080/13613324.2013.817776

Martin, J., & Garza, C. (2020). Centering the marginalized student's voice through autoethnography: Implications for engineering education research. *Studies in Engineering Education, 1*(1), 1–19. https://doi.org/10.21061/see.1

Matsuda, M. (1991). Voices of America: Accent, antidiscrimination law, and a jurisprudence for the last reconstruction. *Yale Law Journal, 100*(5), 1329–1407. https://doi.org/10.2307/796694

Matsuda, M., Lawrence, C. III, Delgado, R., & Crenshaw, K. (1993). *Words that wound: Critical race theory, assaultive speech, and the first amendment*. Taylor & Francis.

McGee, E., & Stovall, D. (2015). Reimagining critical race theory in education: Mental health, healing, and the pathway to liberatory praxis. *Educational Theory, 65*(5), 491–511. https://doi.org/10.1111/edth.12129

Mejia, J., Revelo, R., Villanueva, I., & Mejia, J. (2018). Critical theoretical frameworks in engineering education: An anti-deficit and liberative approach. *Education Science, 8*(4), 158. https://doi.org/10.3390/educsci8040158

Mejia, J., Villanueva Alarcón, I., Mejia, J., & Revelo, R. (2022). Legitimized tongues: Breaking the traditions of silence in mainstream engineering education and research. *Journal of Women and Minorities in Science and Engineering, 28*(2), 53–77. https://doi.org/10.1615/JWomenMinorScienEng.2022036603

Miller, C., & Stassun, K. (2014). A test that fails. *Nature, 510,* 303–304. https://doi.org/10.1038/nj7504-303a

Monaghan, P. (1993, July 23). "Critical race theory" questions role of legal doctrine in racial inequality: Lani Guinier, ill-fated justice dept. Nominee is one of its traditional adherents. *Chronicle of Higher Education, 39*(42), A7–A9.

Olivas, M. (1990). The chronicles, my grandfather's stories, and immigration law: The slave traders chronicle as racial history. *Saint Louis University Law Journal, 34,* 425–441.

Patrick, A., Martin, J., & Borrego, M. (2022). Critical research methods in stem higher education: A state-of-the-art review. *Journal of Women and Minorities in Science and Engineering, 28*(3), 1–26. https://doi.org/10.1615/JWomenMinorScienEng.2022036570

Pérez Huber, L., Vélez, V. N., & Solórzano, D. (2018). More than "papelitos": A QuantCrit counterstory to critique Latina/o degree value and occupational prestige. *Race Ethnicity and Education, 21*(2), 208–230.

Powell, K. (2013). On the lookout for true grit. *Nature, 504,* 471–473.

Russell, M. (1992). Entering great America: Reflections on race and the convergence of progressive legal theory and practice. *Hastings Law Journal, 43,* 749–767.

Sedlacek, W. (1999). Black students on white campuses: 20 years of research. *Journal of College Student Development, 40*(5), 538–550.

Solórzano, D. (1997). Images and words that wound: Critical race theory, racial stereotyping, and teacher education. *Teacher Education Quarterly, 24*(3), 5–19. https://www.jstor.org/stable/23478088

Solórzano, D. (1998). Critical race theory, race and gender microaggressions, and the experiences of Chicana and Chicano scholars. *Qualitative Studies in Education, 11*(1), 121–136.

Solórzano, D. (2013). Critical race theory's intellectual roots: My email epistolary with Derrick Bell. In M. Lynn & A. Dixson (Eds.), *Critical race theory in education handbook* (pp. 48–68). Routledge.

Solórzano, D. (2022). My journey to this place called the RAC: Reflections on a movement in critical race thought and critical race hope in higher education. *International Journal of Qualitative Studies in Education, 36*(1), 87–98. https://doi.org/10.1080/09518398.2022.2042613

Solórzano, D., & Perez Huber, L. (2020). *Racial microaggressions: Using critical race theory to respond to everyday racism.* Teachers College Press.

Solórzano, D., & Solórzano, R. (1995). The Chicano educational experience: A proposed framework for effective schools in Chicano communities. *Educational Policy, 9*(3), 293–314. https://doi.org/10.1177/0895904895009003005

Solórzano, D., & Villalpando, O. (1998). Critical race theory, marginality, and the experience of minority students in higher education. In C. Torres & T. Mitchell

(Eds.), *Emerging issues in the sociology of education: Comparative perspectives* (pp. 211–224). SUNY Press.

Stassun, K., Burger, A., & Lange, S. (2010). The Fisk-Vanderbilt Masters-to-PhD Bridge Program: A model for broadening participation of underrepresented groups in the physical sciences through effective partnerships with minority-serving institutions. *Journal of Geoscience Education, 58*, 135–144. https://doi.org/10.5408/1.3559648

Sullivan, P. (2021). *Democracy, social justice, and the American community college: A student-centered perspective.* Palgrave Macmillan.

Takaki, R. (1989). *Strangers from a different shore: A history of Asian Americans.* Little, Brown & Company.

Tewell, E. (2020). The problem with grit: Dismantling deficit thinking in library instruction. *Libraries and the Academy, 20*, 137–159.

Tsai, J., Lindo, E., & Bridges, K. (2021). Seeing the window, finding the spider: Applying critical race theory to medical education to make up where biomedical models and social determinants of health curricula fall short. *Frontiers in Public Health, 9*, https://doi.org/10.3389/fpubh.2021.653643

UCLA HSI Taskforce. (2022). *Cultivating the seeds of change: Becoming a Hispanic Serving Institution. The final report of the Chancellor Appointed HSI Taskforce.* University of California, Los Angeles. https://ucla.app.box.com/v/HispanicServingInstitution.

Valencia, R., & Solórzano, D. (1997). Contemporary deficit thinking. In R. Valencia (Ed.), *The evolution of deficit thinking: Educational thought and practice* (pp. 160–210). Routledge Falmer.

Williams, D., Priest, N., & Anderson, N. (2016). Understanding associations between race, socioeconomic status and health: Patterns and prospects. *Health Psychology, 35*(4), 407–411. https://doi.org/10.1037/hea0000242

Williams, D., & Purdie-Vaughns, V. (2016). Needed interventions to reduce racial/ethnic disparities in health. *Journal of Health Politics, Policy and Law, 41*(4), 627–651. https://doi.org/10.1215/03616878-3620857

X, M., & Haley, A. (1965). *The autobiography of Malcolm X.* New York: Ballantine.

Yosso, T. (2005). Whose culture has capital? A critical race theory discussion of community cultural wealth. *Race Ethnicity and Education, 8*(1), 69–91. https://doi.org/10.1080/1361332052000341006

Yosso, T., & Solórzano, D. (2005). Conceptualizing a critical race theory in sociology. In M. Romero & E. Margolis (Eds.), *Blackwell companion to social inequalities* (pp. 117–146). Blackwell.

4

THE GRIT NARRATIVE

Shifting the Gaze and the Danger

Stephanie J. Waterman

Recently a friend tagged a Facebook photo of me receiving an award at a conference. Among posts of congratulations was one about being proud of me because I had overcome so much. I remember thinking, "Did I? I guess I did." But the post gnawed at me because I was clearly placed in a past, in a difficult *individual* past—at least through the perspective of the person who had initially posted that comment—and I had overcome that past by placing the award on my individual hard work and perseverance. I was perceived as an exception. Yes, there were issues in my educational path (financial barriers, lack of mentoring in my field, few scholars of color to work with), but I also had my home community, my family, and knowledge systems that supported me through structural hoops I had to navigate.

Indigenous students are often perceived as overcoming and of being resilient in persistence and retention narratives. Dr. Lindley and I used "perseverance" in our strength-based analysis of the educational experiences of Northern Arapaho women and Haudenosaunee women college completers (Waterman & Lindley, 2013). We explored our separate findings to identify similarities or differences in their educational experiences. Despite coming from very different communities, the women reported similar supports from their communities, and similar problems they encountered to persevere to degree completion. The assumptions that have informed, and still remain in the forefront of many people and higher education professionals, are that of overcoming, of having some inner drive to push back and remain resilient over an extended period of time against the many settler colonial environments we are educated in. In other words, the grit narrative.

DOI: 10.4324/9781003332497-5

In this chapter, I use my location as an Indigenous faculty member in the Western, settler colonial academy to interrogate terms such as "grit," and the closely related terms "resilience" and "perseverance." Two frameworks inform my discussion: critical inquiry (Gonzales, 2016; Pasque et al., 2011) and Indigenous feminist theories (Ross, 2009; Waterman, 2018). I argue that the grit narrative accepts as normative the structural roles of settler colonialism by putting the gaze on exceptional individuals while masking what matters, what students are being so resilient about—the focus of their perseverance and grit, cultural integrity and continuance as a people. I argue that the assumptions behind the term are dangerous. Concepts that support my argument are cultural integrity, community, a discussion of colonial constructs of time, (in)visibility, and an intriguing historical examination of the term by Ris (2015), as well as Tachine's (2022) use of monsters.

In the following section, I explore some of the literature regarding grit. I then share some examples of how a grit narrative masks structural roles of settler colonialism that continue to feed majoritarian stories (Stein, 2018) that deflect the responsibility higher education systems have toward marginalized students, particularly in relation to Indigenous populations.

Framework

> All things—stone, earth, flora, fauna (of which people are a small part)—are alive with their own spirit and reason for being. This premise puts us all on the same level.
>
> *(Maracle, 1996, p. 101)*

Objectivity, detachment, and individualism have long been characteristics and values of the academy. Yet, in the language of objectivity assumptions abound with often damaging consequences to marginalized peoples and the planet (Deloria & Wildcat, 2001). Imagine a student from a city, a suburb, a reservation, the bush, or a neighbor. An image immediately comes to mind depending upon an individual's physical location and socialization. Django Paris (2019) wrote, "A few years ago, after reading some tweets about education that employed common deficit-based terms for students of color, I tweeted this reply: "And by 'minority,' 'at-risk,' 'underserved,' 'achievement gapped,' 'struggling,' 'free & reduced,' you mean us? (Paris, 2015)" (p. 219). Similarly, when the term grit is used, we tend to imagine an "exceptional" person—one who is often male—and if this term describes a marginalized person, that person possesses exceptional abilities to overcome. What has been overcome—structural inequities, racism, etc.—is normalized, invisibilized. Critical theories help us turn the gaze to those structures to question assumptions that inform and maintain the status quo.

Critical Inquiry

> At the heart of grit research, then, is the desire to "fix" marginalized people so that they can participate in and replicate the system that they might have just narrowly survived.
>
> *(Gonzales, 2016, p. 116)*

My hope as a scholar and faculty member is to foster understanding and critical consciousness in the field so that Indigenous students, and other marginalized students, thrive in higher education instead of surviving it. My use of the word survive is not an exaggeration; Indigenous postsecondary (PSE) graduates have used the term "survive" when describing their educational experiences to me. Pasque et al. (2011) state that we "*must theorize explicitly* power, agency, and resistance" (p. 12, emphasis in original). Where is the power located in an uncritical grit narrative? How might an individualistic agency narrative play in enhancing the power of those who support the grit narrative? Marginalized people who complete PSE degrees are examples of agency, community, resistance, and other complex factors that a grit narrative can mask.

Critical inquiry embraces multiple truths. Educational success, for example, has many definitions. Dr. Cheryl Crazy Bull said that success *is* when a student completes one semester of coursework and then gets a job (2015 ASHE Keynote address). Kirkness and Barnhardt (1991) asked, "Why do universities continue to perpetuate policies and practices that historically have produced abysmal results for First Nations students … ?" (p. 2). More than 30 years have passed since Kirkness and Barnhardt asked these questions; if institutions would examine their policies and practices regarding Indigenous students, enrollment and graduation rates would be much higher. Yet, in what is called the United States, for example, "The 2016 total college enrollment rate for American Indian/Alaska Native youth adults (19 percent) was not measurably different from their 2000 rate" (NCES, 2017, p. 116). While these data are problematic—particularly after 2010 (see Burnette, 2022; Burnette et al., 2021) when the U. S. Department of Education counted students who identified as Native American *and* Hispanic as Hispanic only or if they identified with another category were counted as "two or more races"—these statistics function to inform institutional programming and fund programs. Critical theories turn the gaze on institutions that continue to marginalize.

Indigenous Feminist Theories

Feminist theories and Indigenous feminist theories disrupt tools of settler colonialism by re-storying majoritarian narratives (Ross, 2009; Waterman, 2018). My scholarly journey began when I worked on the NCES/IPEDS reports for the private NCAA Division I institution where I was once employed. Because of federal reporting guidelines, I witnessed the erasure of Indigenous students in the sample, and at the time, in the mid-to-late 1990s, most of the literature about Indigenous students ascribed to a deficit frame. Master narratives favor one story from which other stories are judged against or presented as exceptions. The federal reporting guidelines were based on a normalized cohort of first-time, full-time students, who entered in the fall semester, but Indigenous students tend to be part-time (39% reported in NCES, 2012, p. 182) and are thus not usually included in the cohort. Research about how marginalized students complete PSE degrees and Paris's tweet above are challenges to majoritarian terms that dehumanize. Tuck (2009) asked scholars "to consider the long-term repercussions of *thinking of ourselves as broken*" (p. 409, emphasis in original); we can easily extend that to *thinking of others as broken*. When researched as othered, a-people-to-fix, we can feel "overresearched, yet, ironically, made invisible" (p. 411). Terminology- and deficit-focused studies frame us in ways that assume we struggle and underlying that assumption is that it is *our* struggle, not the institution's.

Endarkened feminist theories include our voices and emotions (Delgado Bernal, 1998, see also Espino, 2012). Being heard in our own voice is re-storying (see Goeman, 2013; Waterman, 2018). The master narrative is incomplete and told through a settler colonial lens. In hooks' (1994) classrooms, she wrote, "I have students write short paragraphs that they read aloud so that we all have a chance to hear unique perspectives and we are all given an opportunity to pause and listen to one another" (p. 186). In this chapter, I share a perspective that a grit narrative can hide, and through these theories, we flip the gaze beyond the number of years an individual took to complete a university degree. In the following section, I discuss some of the literature related to grit and about Indigenous students.

Grit and Resilience Assumed

> Being asked to do more with less is inhumane.
>
> *(Cooper, 2018, p. 266)*

First, I acknowledge the assistance of Michael Denis O'Shea who assisted with the literature review when I could not read after my head injury.

As discussed more thoroughly in the introduction to this text, Duckworth et al. (2007) identified grit as an individual characteristic to persist to achieve one's goals, while facing obstacles, over a period of time. Applied to education, most research focuses on the K-12 environment and are quantitative studies that utilize a version of the Grit Scale (Duckworth et al., 2007). In the higher education setting, some examples are Duckworth and Quinn's (2009) study that applied the Short Grit Scale to determine if grit "predicted completion of the" U.S. Military Academy's "rigorous summer training program better than the Whole Candidate Score" which is used for admission" (p. 171). Another example is Strayhorn's (2014) quantitative study focused on "the role that grit plays in examining the academic success of Black male collegians' at 4-year PWIs [predominantly white institutions]" (p. 3). Strayhorn found that higher levels of grit were related to GPA. He suggested that educators engage in ways to nurture grit in Black male students instead of relying on "any myths that assume 'natural talent' or 'sheer genius' over sustained effort" (p. 8). Although Strayhorn may have named the problem of assumptions of natural talent and sheer genius of those who earn university degrees, by emphasizing on nurturing grit, he implies an individual focus rather than on institutional structures. While Nicolazzo (2017) does not use the term grit in her work about Trans* college students, she writes about the resilience of participants in her study and to think of resilience as a verb. Engaging in critical theories, Nicolazzo and Carter (2019) "use our experiences as trans* people across racialized and disability identities to discuss resilience as *a community-based practice* when looked at through crip theory (McRuer, 2006), queer theory (Cohen, 1997; Johnson 2001) and critical trans politics (Spade, 2015)" (p. 78, emphasis in original).

Akos and Kretchmar (2017) conducted a quantitative study regarding "self-reported grit scores" and whether they predicted "first-year GPA," if "informant-reported grit scores" (in this case, mostly parents or guardians) predicted first-year GPA, and "the relationship between self and informant grit scores" (p. 167). The authors found a relationship, writing that "we found evidence that the sub scores of grit predict GPA differently—in a model containing both subscores, perseverance of effort was a significant predictor of GPA, while consistency of interest was not" (p. 180). The authors go on to discuss the nuances of consistency and perseverance and discuss the possible role of social desirability response bias and negative stereotypes such as being lazy or having "low intelligence" (p. 181). They asserted:

A person might be gritty in musical endeavors, for example, and less gritty in their academic pursuits. While hesitant to label grit domain-specific, Duckworth and Gross (2014) nevertheless describe the gritty individuals as someone who is able to "actively suppress rival superordinate goals or

… lack(s) competing superordinate goals altogether" (p. 322). In other words, gritty people pursue one goal to the exclusion of all other goals.

(p. 184)

This is an important point—gritty individuals may have the privilege to focus on a singular goal.

Furthermore, the authors also raised this thought: "adolescent or young adult[s] *shouldn't* yet exhibit grit, particularly with respect to consistency of interest, except in the most rare instances" (p. 184, emphasis in original). According to an NCES 2017 Data Point report, 30% of students will change their major, and "About 1 in 10 students changed their majors more than once" (NCES 2017, p. 1) with the percentage varying by discipline. What are the circumstances of a gritty person? What was their schooling like, their community, their high school guidance, their early GPA? Particularly, what were their institutions like, student supports, staff demographics, location, leave policies, etc., of institutions with students who do not score high on the grit scales? Akos and Kretchmar (2017) suggested further areas of quantitative research to complicate grit. I acknowledge that the grit scales are not designed to measure the challenges individuals may encounter. Grit scales could identify institutions that require particularly gritty students and populations of students who exhibit grittiness to identify barriers and systems of oppression woven into the institutional system. Then we could examine those institutions.

Indigenous Students and Grit

Higher education articles that focus on grit often name Native students in their study sample, albeit small, as in Akos and Kretchmar's (2017) study of "grit as a non-cognitive predictor of success" (p. 163) or as in a description of the institutional demographics and sample, such as Broghammer's (2017) dissertation of grit as a predictor of first-year academic success, or what can be commonly found in quantitative studies, in a description of the racial category of "other" like in Moreno-Hernandez and Mondisa's (2021) study of first-year engineering students.

The term grit is used in Native American higher education literature most often as a descriptor along with terms such as persistence and resilience. In Petsko's (2021) dissertation study of Native American women graduates, factors that contributed to resilience included spirituality and their connection to community. Referring to Waterman and Lindley's (2013) study in which women college graduates completed their degrees within a 5–35 year period, Petsko wrote, "Indigenous women demonstrate exceptional grit and resilience in achieving their educational goals" (p. 3).

Uink et al. (2021) focused their study of Aboriginal women in university in Australia. They use the term grit once in their discussion of the perseverance expressed by participants, as "all women [in their study] referenced an ability to overcome challenges as a necessity for remaining at university" (p. 187). A participant in Poolaw's (2018) study of Indigenous men in higher education mentioned witnessing the grit of his parents as contributing to their success "at this point in life" (p. 158). When asked for "helpful tips to young Native men who are going into graduate programs" (p. 175) this same participant also mentioned grit: "I think resilience is key ... it's like resilience and grit!" (p. 176).

A large body of literature exists concerning Indigenous students' retention and persistence. Family and community support, their spirituality, adequate financial aid, the presence of elders, Indigenous studies, and Native student affairs offices are factors that support persistence and resilience (see, for example, Falk & Aitken, 1984; Guillory & Wolverton, 2008; Larimore & McClellan, 2005; Mosholder & Goslin, 2013). We did not find a body of literature that employs grit scales specifically with Indigenous students. In the following section, I share my thoughts regarding the grit narrative beginning with settler colonialism and related concepts such as time.

Assumptions of Grit

In their discussion of settler colonialism, Tuck and Wang (2012) asserted that "settlers come with the intention of making a new home on the land, a homemaking that insists on settler sovereignty over all things in the new domain" (p. 5). Their claimed domain becomes defined by settlers including relationships with land, people, and other forms of violence such as the boarding school. All the systems we encounter and work in today—education, the economy, etc.—are built upon settler colonialism.

As noted, grit is defined as a focus on a goal over an extended period of time, often despite encountering difficulties. Settler colonialism interrupted Indigenous ways of being by violently imposing Western ontologies, axiologies, and epistemologies. The Western concept of time interrupted Indigenous ways of thinking about our bodies, the seasons, ceremonies, and harvest, for example.

"The concept of time that undergirds the Western academy derives from a Judaeo-Christian notion of time as linear, constant, and irreversible" (Lee & Liebeanu, 2000, in Shahjahan, 2014, p. 490). In Western-based institutions, we are all expected to be on the same calendar and to value time in identical ways. In higher education, we have due dates for assignments, limited time span to degree completion, and deadlines to pay the bursar. Applications for admission, scholarships, fellowships, and grant proposals have firm, unforgiving due dates that can sometimes feel cruel. Degrees are expected to be completed within a certain time frame or one might have to start over, repeat courses, or possibly lose financial aid. "As hyper extensions of colonial time, neoliberal logics operate to measure, splice, and commodify time in ways that is affectively experienced by individuals navigating the academy" (Shahjahan, 2014, p. 491).

Consider this orientation to time. In an article titled "Cultural Conflicts, Important Factors in the Academic Failures of American Indian Students," Sanders (1987) provides a list of cultural differences between "American Indian" and "Anglo-Americans." Although a broad essentialization, I agree with many of them, for example, Indigenous students often consider group needs before their own and "interject less"; in other words, Indigenous students are more collective and are less likely to interrupt a speaker (p. 82). On this list is: "Present goals considered important—future accepted as it comes" (p. 83). This can easily be misinterpreted as having no goals at all or being unmotivated. Referencing Sando (1973), Sanders further explains:

> A present-time orientation and lack of importance placed on future goals is reflected in the concept of sharing, in which American Indians keep for themselves only enough to satisfy present needs. This is the opposite of Anglo-Americans, who rigidly adhere to fixed time schedules and place value on a future-time orientation in which long-range goals, acquisitiveness of material comforts, and saving for the future are all a major focus (Kluckholn & Strodtbeck, 1991).
>
> *(p. 84)*

Leaving school to care for family, participate in ceremony, or to work has been interpreted as being unable to value long-term goals (Waterman & Bazemore-James, 2019). Sharing and not taking more than you need respects Creation while ensuring the well-being of everyone in the present community and in the future. Taking care of the present is more than being present-oriented as it cares for a future beyond majoritarian imaginations.

Through a critical and Indigenous feminist lens, how might a "present time" orientation be interpreted? Given the attempt to eliminate Indigenous peoples to acquire our lands through violence, physical warfare, biological warfare, education/assimilation policies, removal, and starvation tactics, continuation as a people is fundamental (Waterman & Lindley, 2013). As Haudenosaunee, we are to make decisions based on how that decision impacts "the welfare of its generations yet unborn" (Mohawk, 1992, p. 28). This is what many people mean by the phrase considering the seventh generation. "This philosophy is perhaps best reflected in the Iroquois [Haudenosaunee] Confederacy—that we must consider the impact of a decision made today on the impact on the seventh generation from now" (LaDuke, 2002, p. 276). I have argued (Springer et al., 2010) that many Indigenous peoples are considering so far into the future that Western cultures do not recognize our future-thinking. Taking care of, and taking time for, family, ceremony, Indigenous language, and Mother Earth are actions that ensure there will literally be a future. Taking care of family now, taking care of ceremony now, taking care of Mother Earth now, ensures a future. For everyone and all of Creation.

An elder told a group of us at an education conference in Arizona many years ago that when we want something, to respectfully ask Creation. He said to ask only once and to not go chasing after it. It will happen when it's meant to be, and when the time is right, it will come to you. The late Onondaga Chief Leon Shenandoah, Tadodaho, said, "I never call on the Creator for anything. I don't have to. Nobody else does either" (Wall, 2001, p. 16). Creation provides everything. Knowledge is relational and experiential, it "choos[es] who it reveals itself to and under what circumstances" (Adams et al., 2015, p. 30).

What might this orientation to time look like in a higher educational setting? As settler colonialism has been intent on our removal and assimilation, "[i]ntegral to continuation as a people is the maintenance of relationships that establish young people in the community" (Waterman, 2018, p. 65). For example, an Onondaga university graduate "always knew she wanted to be a teacher, … took 11 years after her two-year degree before she completed her bachelor's degree. The participant established herself in the community, married, started a family, and then completed her degree" (p. 65) becoming an elementary school teacher. Continuation of one's community is not reflected in years to degree completion or the focus of one's grittiness. As reflected in education literature, grit does not reflect such complexity. For many minoritized students who exhibit grit, the focus of their grittiness is their cultural integrity and self-preservation.

When Donna (Mohawk) was a new student, she did not participate in her institution's summer bridge program "because her aunt had passed and there were cultural commitments she and her family had to attend to" (Waterman, 2021, p. 9). She later transferred from her state's flagship institution to a smaller local college to help her family, prolonging her years as a student because she switched to part-time enrollment. And Melanie (Mohawk), who shared that her auntie warned her that she would "have to work twice as hard as White people," exhibited grittiness to balance tradition with university (Waterman, 2007, p. 31). When Melanie was in graduate school, she realized the advice was literally about working hard. She reflected:

It was the connection to the community that um, "Oh here I am" you know, we're going, running back to ceremonies, and oh, I'm going to miss two weeks of classes because I have to go to Mid-winter [ceremony], and on the side we're trying to learn language.

(p. 31)

Traditional Indigenous ceremonies do not follow the Christian calendar and are rarely recognized by non-Native Colleges and Universities (NNCU) (Shotton et al., 2013), making Melanie's ability to practice her spirituality harder. Indigenous traditions are invisibilized when not included in official university calendars and when faculty and staff are not educated about our ceremonies requiring a dedication and resiliency, or grit, to continue spiritual traditions.

Role of Invisibilization in Grit Narratives

As Tachine (2022) writes, "most people we encounter" in what is known as the United States "do not know about us" and many think we no longer exist (p. 139). When we do appear, "out of place" such as the university, we can invoke fear. This may seem out of the ordinary, but I recall non-Indigenous women pulling their children away from me at the Wegmans supermarket in an upper-class neighborhood in the city in which I was living at the time. More than once. My visibility as a person of color, out of place, frightened the women.

Our erasure is intentional. Paris (2019) writes about the many terms used "to name students of color" and their use to "avoid the prominence of race, racialization, and racism. This erasure—and it is an erasure—is no coincidence" (p. 218). Tachine (2022) centers her book upon the Diné Twin Warriors story about monsters that attempt to disrupt Diné life. Using this frame she writes about the "systemic monsters of white supremacy, settler colonialism, racism, erasure, heteropatriarchy, and capitalism" (p. 9) that the students who shared their stories with her encountered as they pursued a higher education degree and the "*Indigenous weapons*" (p. 11, emphasis in original) the strengths "that are rooted in Navajo ways of knowing of k'é (kinship; relational-based) that build survivance and reawaken the power and sovereignty of Indigenous presence and belonging" (p. 11) that students engaged in to defeat the monsters.

Like Melanie, the students in Tachine's (2022) study worked hard to be Indigenous while being a student. Tachine makes visible the settler colonial structures (the monsters) that requires us to be resilient. Tachine names the structures that grit narratives hide. Monsters are scary and perceived as dangerous. In the following section, I focus on danger.

Dangerous Thinking and Privilege

> One time, in a meeting on my campus, in a discussion about the hardships children of color face, a white woman remarked dismissively, "Oh, but children are resilient!" Celebrating the resilience of poor folks is a perverse way of acknowledging the unreasonable demands placed upon people who already are struggling to make it.
>
> *(Cooper, 2018, p. 266)*

The quoted remark above is the danger I see in an uncritical use of the grit narrative. Struggle on the part of certain populations is normalized. We are expected to overcome hardships such as poverty. We are expected to be from poverty and as Tachine (2022) points out, structures are in place to ensure economic gains are not made. When an individual does overcome, it's a celebration for the individual.

Ris (2015) complicates grit through a historical lens that is helpful in understanding the term's connection to class and privilege and that supports settler colonial concepts of individualism. Academic and popular literature and media outlets have used the term to blame the victim, as "victims of circumstance" and "underperformers" (p. 2). Ris traced how the term was defined by the white middle and upper class and then applied to disadvantaged populations as a way to rationalize poverty and failure (2015). He takes us through nineteenth-century literature that feature (male) characters who overcome poverty, in particular, "rags to riches" books like Twain's *Huckleberry Finn* and books by Horatio Alger Jr. "'Grit,' 'pluck,' and 'resolve' are terms used interchangeably in Alger's work, always reflecting a dogged refusal to succumb to obstacles on the path to occupational success" (Ris, 2015, p. 4). These books were not meant for the masses as they were expensive for their time; their intended audience was "the children of the middle and upper classes" (p. 4). Interestingly, Ris argues that grit was something that the offspring of the elite were lacking; they "coddle" their children or what today might be referred to as "affluenza: the disadvantages caused by a childhood advantage" (De Graff et al., 2001, as cited in Ris, 2015, p. 3). Ris argued that young people needed hardship to "build character" and traces discourse of grit as it was used through time: the 1910s and 1920s when "publishers often slapped an athletic scene on the cover" (p. 6); how it became associated with football, Little League, and paper routes; when Alger's books were reissued after World War II including the establishment of the Horatio Alger Awards in 1947 "celebrating individuals who had risen from poverty to national prominence" (Ris, 2015, p. 6). He then connects the grit narrative to economic periods.

After 1972 there was a decline in Boy and Girl Scouts participation, "organizations primed to provide grit to middle-class children" (Ris, 2015,

p. 7). During the 1960s and 1970s, "income inequality was historically low" (p. 7); Ris (2015) offered this interpretation:

> The relative lack of grit discourse in these decades could be theoretically linked to two conclusions: that the rising tide of prosperity lessened anxiety about downward mobility in privileged classes, or, more cynically, that the ebbing of extreme poverty meant that the grit narrative was no longer needed as a rationalization for systemic hardship. If either of these is the case, then grit's reemergence in the national discourse in recent years, simultaneous with widening economic inequality, is not a coincidence.
>
> *(p. 7)*

The focus on grit today is not on building character in middle- and upper-class youth; the focus today is developing grit in disadvantaged youth so they can climb out of poverty. Different programs and schools have been developed to close achievement gaps. I am simplifying his argument for sake of space.

Ris (2015) argues there are two sides: the grit narrative is today's version of the "culture of poverty" (p. 10) rhetoric of the 1960s and that the middle and upper class uses grit, or the lack of grit, as an excuse for their own children's failures, "without claiming a lack of ability" (p. 9). The focus is on developing grit—think of character education programs in school, work policies for social programs—hence, settler colonial systems that maintain hardships are ignored:

> This conversation, of course, takes on a dangerous character. If grit provides the pathway to success, and grit comes from persevering through hardship, then the way to help poor people is to make sure their lives remain difficult. Climbing over obstacles will make them stronger and more mobile.
>
> *(Ris, 2015, p. 11)*

Education for Indigenous people was not intended to educate. This cruel policy of assimilation and attempted cultural destruction was based on hardship. Adams (1995) writes about the emphasis these schools had on hard labor; "[students] spent approximately half the school day either learning industrial skills or performing manual labor" (p. 149). School and student success was often measured in production, such as the number of shirts or harnesses produced. The Superintendent at Fort Stevenson, Dakota "boasted that 'a vast amount of hard labor' was required to extract" the coal for the school (p. 151). The emphasis on work, very little on actual instruction for reading, writing, or say accounting, left the students with few marketable skills to earn an income. Irene Stewart, a boarding school survivor, wrote, "We were too tired to study" (p. 153). It wasn't just hard labor, students nearly starved and were not provided adequate healthcare (Adams, 1995). It was literally dangerous to attend these schools.

Grit was necessary to *survive* at these schools. My grandparents attended residential schools. When I hear "grit," this is what I think of, the sheer effort to survive the hard labor imposed at school, the expectation that students work and forego any other interests to the detriment of their own identity; the sheer grit necessary to withstand the attack on one's personhood.

> But you know, you can't subject to someone's stupid idea and ignorance. You just have to get over the fact that there's always going to be the people that aren't pleased with people going to college and stuff like that.
> *(Cecelia, in Tachine, 2022, p. 163)*

Grit masks the dangerous monsters (Tachine, 2022) of settler colonialism. The master narrative of settler colonialism defines how, when, and what is learned in higher education, it defines who succeeds and who is expected not to. These definitions are normalized, unquestioned; they become assumptions. Ris (2015) made the argument of popular fiction's dangerous role in fueling the necessity of hardship for some that he connected to the economy, as he argued, to rationalize poverty. Boarding schools were tied to the economy. They were efforts to strip us of our culture to gain land and resources, but also to replace a collective mindset with an individualistic one (Adams, 1995). While settler colonialism tries hard to erase Indigenous knowledge and our history, we continue. Grit narratives also mask the Indigenous weapons (Tachine, 2022) and cultural integrity (Waterman, 2007), the strengths of our communities we use to continue as a people.

Time and Again

In summary, the assumptions that support the grit narrative are based in settler colonialism. Institutional calendars are structures that rarely include or accommodate Indigenous ceremonial calendars. Melanie had to work hard at university, an Ivy League, to maintain a GPA to get into medical school while learning her language and practicing her traditions. She had to exhibit grit to maintain and strengthen her Indigeneity.

Racism invisibilizes the normalcy of an Indigenous student engaging in higher education. If anyone doubts the role of invisibility, consider the experiences of two Mohawk students, Thomas Kanewakeron Gray and Lloyd Skanahwati Gray, who were removed from a campus tour at Colorado State University when "a parent in the group [tour] reportedly called 911 and alleged that the two were 'definitely not part of the tour.'" The caller said "'they stand out,' 'their behavior is odd,'" that "'they were 'creepy kids,' and 'made me feel sick'" (Keene & Tachine, 2018); Indigenous people out of place, being hypervisible in higher education.

Duckworth and Quinn's (2009) study data included exceptional people. It is not common for someone to desire to participate in spelling bee competitions that lead to the National Spelling Bee competition or to desire to attend the United States Military Academy at West Point. The authors acknowledged this. The path to West Point is not just academic, there are physical qualifications as well. The grit behavior of exceptional individuals was then applied to populations who are simply seeking a higher education. The exceptionality of grit feeds the myth of extraordinary people as college material. In Strayhorn's (2014) study, he warned that we should not rely on assumptions of "natural talent or sheer genius" (p. 8) for students to succeed. If those who are "underserved" and who "overcome" are considered an exception (what does that say for the rest of us) when there is achievement, there can only be a few who earn degrees, or very few identified as high achievers. The assumption that we all can't overcome reinforces erasure and invisibility, scarcity of resources, celebrates the few, with no incentives to change the system. Tuck (2009) writes that Indigenous people are both hypervisible (see the above campus tour) while invisible. The rest of us, like Thomas Kanewakeron Gray and Lloyd Skanahwati Gray, must be made invisible because damage-centered thinking requires keeping us in a certain place in a certain image. Tachine (2022) would describe this as an example of the racism monster.

Pasque et al. (2011) ask us to examine power, agency, and resistance. The power of settler colonialism is to maintain systems that make it hard for us. The terms Paris (2019) identified (like "at-risk") "are always filtered through the White gaze and that they are explicitly and implicitly set against whiteness as the norm" (p. 218). That power maintains rules and assumptions that are dangerous. Goward (2020) writes about their experience as a first-generation Black scholar in the academy. There are multiple stressors on marginalized first-generation students and the grit and resilience she had to engage in made her sick, literally, sick. Goward, like Tachine (2022) point to harmful systemic structures (monsters).

> The conversation about who is marked as "at risk," or needing to be more resilient, are often the ones who have background characteristics have been demonstrated to predict lower grades and test scores not because the students are not capable, but because their families have been historically denied opportunities that would have given them access to quality schools. … And yet higher education is asking these same students to be more resilient and to exhibit more grit.
>
> *(Goward, 2020, p. 175)*

Agency is calling out the harm of these structures and exposing strengths of marginalized communities. Higher education's relationship with students is reciprocal. Higher education has responsibilities, too (Kirkness & Barnhardt, 1991). Goward (2020) states, "Any good therapist is going to ask the people in a relationship how they contributed to the breakdown between them" (p. 176). Turning the gaze then, let's consider which community is broken (Tuck, 2009). Can we critically question the systems that harm communities, are dangerous, and make us sick?

Through critical theories and an Indigenous feminist lens in this chapter I shared some of my experience and that of others in reference to the grit and resiliency literature. These experiences, these "desires" (Tuck, 2009), were examples of maintaining and strengthening cultural integrity. A grit narrative in higher education invisibilizes that part of us in the academy. Despite the formal efforts to literally remove us, schooling to assimilate us and destroy our communities, the dehumanization, the Murdered and Missing Women and Girls (Bychutsky, 2017), we seek Western educations to give back (Lopez & Tachine, 2021) and strengthen our communities. We are learning our languages and practicing our spirituality even if the university doesn't recognize academic credit for language learning or excused absences for our spiritual ceremonial days. A grit narrative deflects the institution's responsibility to support our efforts to strengthen our traditional ways, and yet, NNCUs were so instrumental in attempts to remove our ways of being to make us invisible. Critical theories are tools to question policies and to seek alternatives to high-stakes competition, hurried notions of time, and community and family as barriers.

Paris's (2019) discussion of terms and naming that erase people and places, such as naming buildings after enslavers and the term minority for non-whites, states that "these less-than namings, and framings operate on explicit and implicit logics of White superiority" (p. 219). Naming is foundational to settler colonialism, and grit narratives play directly into that logic. Paris asks for a flip, a move to "desire-based naming" refusing "deficit-based naming" (p. 220). I don't want to be resilient all the time and I should not need to exhibit grit to be a faculty member. I don't want higher education to be something we merely survive; we should be able to thrive in this environment.

As my dear friend, Dr. Ruth Harper, commented about having to be resilient: "One thing I've said sometimes is 'I'm sorry you've had to be so strong.'" That's an acknowledgement that there's something wrong and it's not me or the person who exhibits resiliency. As an Indigenous cis-woman tenured faculty member defined by some as a "'minority,' 'at-risk,' 'underserved,' 'achievement gapped,' 'struggling,' ..." (Paris, 2015, p. 219) exception, I ask that you be critical, to turn your gaze away from "what is 'wrong'" with students" and ask "why the academy reverts to putting the onus of student departure solely on the student" (Goward, 2020, p. 176) and the role of grit.

References

Adams, D. H., Wilson, S., Heavy Head, R., & Gordon, E. W. (2015). *Ceremony at a boundary fire: A story of Indigenist knowledge*. Sydney eScholarship Repository.

Adams, D. W. (1995). *Education for extinction: American Indians and the boarding school experience: 1875–1928*. University Press of Kansas.

Akos, P., & Kretchmar, J. (2017). Investigating grit at a non-cognitive predictor of college success. *The Review of Higher Education*, *40*(2), 163–186. https://doi.org/10.1353/rhe.2017.0000

Broghammer, S. M. (2017). *Grit as a predictor of academic success for first-time undergraduate students* [Unpublished doctoral dissertation]. University of North Carolina, Chapel Hill. https://digscholarship.unco.edu/dissertations/463

Burnette, J. D. (2022). Why is the total enrollment of American Indian and Alaska Native precollegiates such a difficult number to find? *Journal of American Indian Education*, *60*(1&2), 162–186. muse.jhu.edu/article/840607

Burnette, J. D., Younker, J. T., & Wick, D. P. (2021). Statistical termination or fewer self-identified students: What is causing the decline in American Indian and Alaska Native College enrollments? *Journal of Economics, Race, and Policy*, *4*(4), 237–256. https://doi.org/10.1007/s41996-020-00057-y

Bychutsky, R. (2017). *Social denial: An analysis of missing and murdered Indigenous women and girls in Canada* [Unpublished master's thesis]. University of Ottawa.

Cohen, C. (1997). Punks, bulldaggers, and welfare queens: The radical potential of queer politics? *GLQ: A Journal of Lesbian and Gay Studies*, *3*, 437–465.

Cooper, B. (2018). *Eloquent rage: A black feminist discovers her superpower*. Picador.

Crazy Bull, C. (2015). ASHE keynote address. https://www.youtube.com/watch?v=S_6nFmua-_s

De Graaf, J., Wann, D., & Naylor, T. H. (2001). *Affluenza: The all-consuming epidemic*. Berrett-Koehler Publishers.

Delgado Bernal, D. (1998). Using a Chicana feminist epistemology in educational research. *Harvard Educational Review*, *68*(4), 555–582. https://doi.org/10.17763/haer.68.4.5wv1034973g22q48

Deloria, V. Jr., & Wildcat, D. R. (2001). *Power and place: Indian education in America*. Fulcrum.

Duckworth, A. L., Peterson, C., Matthews, M. D., & Kelly, D. R. (2007). Grit: Perseverance and passion for long term goals. *Journal of Personality and Social Psychology*, *92*(6), 1087–1101. https://doi.org/10.1037/0022-3514.92.6.1087

Duckworth, A. L., & Quinn, P. D. (2009). Development and validation of the short grit scale (Grit-S). *Journal of Personality Assessment*, *91*(2), 166–174. https://doi.org/10.1080/00223890802634290

Duckworth, A., & Gross, J. J. (2014). Self-control and grit: Related but separable determinants of success. *Current Directions in Psychological Science*, *23*(5), 319–325. https://doi.org/10.1177/0963721414541462

Espino, M. M. (2012). Seeking the "truth" in the stories we tell: The role of critical race epistemology in higher education research. *The Review of Higher Education, 36*(1), 31–67. https://doi.org/10.1353/rhe.2012.0048

Falk, D. R., & Aitken, L. P. (1984). Promoting retention among American Indian college students. *Journal of American Indian Education, 23*(2), 24–31.

Goeman, M. (2013). *Mark my words: Native women mapping our nations.* University of Minnesota Press.

Gonzales, L. D. (2016). Revising the grounds for the study of grit: Critical qualitative inquiry in post-secondary education organizational research. In P. A. Pasque & V. M. Lechuga (Eds.), *Qualitative inquiry in higher education organization and policy research* (pp. 113–128). Routledge.

Goward, S. L. (2020). Resilience and grit are for rich people: How "making it" through higher education has made me sick. In J. A. Van Galen & J. Sablan (Eds.), *Amplified voices, intersecting identities: Volume 2: First-gen PhDs navigating institutional power in early academic careers* (pp. 170–176). Brill Sense.

Guillory, R. M., & Wolverton, M. (2008). It's all about family: Native American student persistence in higher education. *The Journal of Higher Education, 79*(1), 58–87. https://www.jstor.org/stable/25144650

hooks, b. (1994). *Teaching to transgress: Education as the practice of freedom.* Routledge.

Johnson, E. P. (2001). "Quare" studies, or (almost) everything I know about queer studies I learned from my grandmother. *Text and Performance Quarterly, 21*(1), 1–25.

Keene, A., & Tachine, A. (2018, May 7). State university tour incident is nothing new for Native students. *TeenVOGUE.* https://www.teenvogue.com/story/csu-incident-native-students-nothing-new

Kirkness, V. J., & Barnhardt, R. (1991). First Nations and higher education: The four Rs—respect, relevance, reciprocity, responsibility. *Journal of American Indian Education, 30,* 1–15. https://www.jstor.org/stable/24397980

Kluckhohn, F. R., & Strodtbeck, F. L. (1960). *Varieties in the basic values of family systems. A Modern Introduction to the Family.* Row Peterson and Co.

LaDuke, W. (2002). *The Winona LaDuke reader.* Voyageur Press.

Larimore, J. A. , & McClellan, G. S. (2005). Native American student retention in U.S. postsecondary education. In M. J. Tippeconnic Fox, S. C. Lowe, & G. S. McClellan (Eds.), *New directions for student services: Serving Native American students* (pp. 17–32). Jossey-Bass.

Lee, H., & Liebeanu, J. (2000). Time and the internet at the turn of the millennium. *Time & Society, 9*(1): 43–56. https://doi.org/10.1177/0961463X00009001003

Lopez, J. D., & Tachine, A. R. (2021). Giving back: Deconstructing persistence for indigenous students. *Journal of College Student Development, 62*(5), 613–618.

Maracle, L. (1996). *I am woman: A Native perspective on sociology and feminism.* Press Gang Publishers.

McRuer, R. (2006). *Crip theory: Cultural signs of queerness and disability.* NYU Press.

Mohawk, J. (1992). The Indian way is a thinking tradition. In J. Barreiro (Ed.), *Indian roots of democracy* (pp. 20–29). Akwe:kon Press.

Moreno-Hernandez, A. D., & Mondisa, J. L. (2021). Differences in the self-perceptions of resilience, grit, and persistence among first-year engineering undergraduates. *International Journal of Engineering Education*, *37*(3), 701–711. https://www.ijee.ie/1atestissues/Vol37-3/12_ijee4061.pdf

Mosholder, R., & Goslin, C. (2013). Native American college student persistence. *Journal of College Student Retention: Research, Theory & Practice*, *15*(3), 305–327. https://doi.org/10.2190/CS.15.3.a

National Center for Education Statistics (NCES). (2012). Higher education: Gaps in access and persistence study. NCES 2012-046. Institute of Education Sciences, U.S. Department of Education.

National Center for Education Statistics (NCES). (2017). *Data Point, NCES 2018-434. Percentage of 2011-12 First Time Postsecondary students who had ever declared a major in an associate's or bachelor's degree program within 3 years of enrollment, by type of degree program and control of first institution: 2014.* Institute of Education Sciences, U.S. Department of Education.

Nicolazzo, Z. (2017). *Trans* in college: Transgender students' strategies for navigating campus life and the institutional politics of inclusion.* Stylus.

Nicolazzo, Z., & Carter, R. (2019). Resilience. In E. S. Abes, S. R. Jones, & D.-L. Stewart (Eds.), *Rethinking college student development theory using critical frameworks.* Stylus.

Paris, D. (@django_paris) (2015). "And by 'minority,''diverse,''at-risk,''underserved,' 'achievement gapped,' 'struggling,''free & reduced,' you mean us?" Tweet.

Paris, D. (2019). Naming beyond the white settler colonial gaze in educational research. *International Journal of Qualitative Studies in Education*, *32*(3), 217–224. https://doi.org/10.1080/09518398.2019.1576943

Pasque, P. A., Carducci, R., Gildersleeve, R. E., & Kuntz, A. M. (2011). Disrupting the ethical imperatives of "junior" critical qualitative scholars in the era of conservative modernization. *Qualitative Inquiry*, *17*(7), 571–588. https://doi.org/10.1177/1077800411409878

Petsko, M. T. (2021). *Stories of resilience: Collecting narratives on the determination of Indigenous women seeking graduate degrees* [Unpublished doctoral dissertation]. Villanova University.

Poolaw, J. (2018). *Modern warriors: An exploration of Indigenous male graduates* [Unpublished doctoral dissertation]. University of Oklahoma.

Ris, E. W. (2015). Grit: A short history of a useful concept. *Journal of Educational Controversy*, *10*(1), article 3.

Ross, L. (2009). From the "F" word to Feminisms/Indigenisms. *Wicazo Sa Review*, *24*(2), 39–52.

Sanders, D. (1987). Cultural conflicts: An important factor in the academic failures of American Indian students. *Journal of Multicultural Counseling and Development*, *15*(2), 81–90. https://doi.org/10.1002/j.2161-1912.1987.tb00381.x

Sando, J. (1973). Educating the Native American: Conflict in values. In L. A. Bransford, L. Baca, & K. Lane (Eds.), *Cultural university and the exceptional child* (pp. 58–65). Council for Exceptional Children.

Shahjahan, R. A. (2014). Being "lazy" and slowing down: Toward decolonizing time, our body, and pedagogy. *Educational Philosophy and Theory*, *47*(5), 488–501. https://doi.org/10.1080/00131857.2014.880645

Shotton, H., Lowe, S., & Waterman, S. (2013). *Beyond the asterisk: Understanding Native American college students.* Stylus Publishing.

Spade, D. (2015). *Normal life: Administrative violence, critical trans politics, and the limits of law.* Duke University Press.

Springer, M., Ecklund, T., Thunder, A., & Waterman, S. J. (2010, March). *NASPA IPKC and ACPA NAN: Student affairs partnerships and collaborations to promote Native American student success.* Presentation at the *American College Personnel Association national conference,* Boston, MA.

Stein, S. (2018). Confronting the racial-colonial foundations of US higher education. *Journal for the Study of Postsecondary and Tertiary Education, 3,* 77–98. https://doi.org/10.28945/4105

Strayhorn, T. L. (2014). What role does grit play in the academic success of Black male collegians at predominantly white institutions? *Journal of African American Studies, 18*(1), 1–10. https://doi.org/10.1007/s12111-012-9243-0

Tachine, A. R. (2022). *Native presence and sovereignty in college: Sustaining Indigenous weapons to defeat systemic monsters.* Teachers College Press.

Tuck, E. (2009). Suspending damage: A letter to communities. *Harvard Educational Review, 79*(3), 409–427. https://doi.org/10.17763/haer.79.3.n0016675661t3n15

Tuck, E., & Wang, K. W. (2012). Decolonization is not a metaphor. *Decolonization: Indigeneity, Education & Society, 1,* 1–40.

U. S. Department of Education. (December 2017). *Data Point: Beginning college students who change their majors within 3 years of enrollment, NCES 2018-434.* https://nces.ed.gov/pubs2018/2018434.pdf

Uink, B., Bennett, R., & van den Berg, C. (2021). Factors that enable Australian Aboriginal women's persistence at university: A strengths-based approach. *Higher Education Research & Development, 40*(1), 178–193. https://doi.org/10.1080/07294360.2020.1852185

Wall, S. (2001). *To become a human being: The message of Tadodaho Chief Leon Shenandoah.* Hampton Books.

Waterman, S. J. (2007). A complex path to Haudenosaunee degree completion. *Journal of American Indian Education, 46*(1), 20–40. https://www.jstor.org/stable/24398461

Waterman, S. J. (2018). Indigeneity in the methods: Indigenous feminist theory in content analysis. In R. Minthorn & H. S. Shotton (Eds.) *Reclaiming Indigenous research in higher education* (pp. 178–190). Routledge.

Waterman, S. J. (2021). "They won't do it the way I can": Relationality and goodness in theorizing the work of Haudenosaunee higher education personnel. *Journal of Diversity in Higher Education.* https://doi.org/10.1037/dhe0000352

Waterman, S. J., & Bazemore-James, C. (2019). It's more than us: Knowledge and knowing. In E. Abes, S. R. Jones, & D-L. Stewart (Eds.), *Rethinking college student development theory using critical frameworks* (pp. 158–170). Stylus.

Waterman, S. J., & Lindley, L. (2013). Cultural strengths to persevere: American Indian women in higher education. *NASPA Journal About Women in Higher Education, 6*(2), 139–165. https://doi.org/10.1515/njawhe-2013-0011

Waterman, S. J., & Sands, T. L. (2016). A pathway to college success: Reverse transfer as a means to move forward among the Haudenosaunee (Iroquois). *Journal of American Indian Education, 55*(2), 51–74. https://doi.org/10.5749/jamerindieduc.55.2.0051

5

SOMETIMES YOU'RE GRITTY, AND SOMETIMES YOU'RE NOT

The Racialization of Grit for Asian Americans

Jacqueline Mac, Rikka J. Venturanza, Megan Trinh, and Varaxy Yi

An Axe to Grind with Grit

We have an axe to grind with grit. Grit is a false narrative that preys on the desire and hope of achieving the American Dream by centering the merito-cratic belief that you can overcome adversity by developing gritty character-istics. As we discuss in the following sections, grit has become an increasingly popular concept in education. The attraction to an idea such as grit is that some individuals believe grit is something that can be influenced and devel-oped in others as a solution for educational disparities. Because of this mal-leability, however, it is easy to weaponize grit as a label to determine who is gritty, deserving, or not. Grit is another form of racial labeling that assigns the value of educational success to students of color based on their academic performance (see Reed & Jeremiah, 2017). Scholars, educators, and com-munity activists have critiqued this popularity as yet another way to rein-force inequitable educational conditions by locating the responsibility of academic success on whether individual students have or have not devel-oped grit. Toward this end, how grit has been wielded both neutralizes and strengthens racialized processes and contributes to systemic inequity.

Nevertheless, in the grit discourse, the race-based analyses of the concept and its inequitable impact on Asian American students and our communities are noticeably missing and have yet to be empirically examined. Presently, there is a strong possibility that many institutional leaders have or will employ grit as a measure within admissions criteria and other programs to support students given the Supreme Court's 2023 ruling against affirmative action. Even more troubling is that the 2023 cases decided upon by the Supreme

DOI: 10.4324/9781003332497-6

Court frame Asian American students as victims of race-conscious admissions and use Asian Americans as a political wedge to dismantle affirmative action (Lee, 2021); discussing grit concerning Asian Americans is ever more important.

According to one study, Asian American community college students reported less grit than other student populations (Zentner et al., 2016). So, we wonder, how does grit—the discourse about it, the way grit is used—impact Asian Americans, a community for whom the model minority myth has become the central narrative to characterize their universal success? In our discussion, several questions surface: How does the racialization of Asian Americans as experiencing success in education, vis-à-vis the model minority myth, play a role? Does this mean they have "less grit"? Or perhaps they have so much grit, their success is taken for granted, rendering their struggles invisible? What about Asian American students who are characterized as a deviant minority, such as Southeast Asian American students who are deemed so academically inferior that they drop out, join gangs, become "welfare" sponges, and resist assimilation into American life (Museus, 2013; Yi Borromeo, 2018)? Further, what implications does grit have for a population that is also simultaneously racialized as perpetual foreigners? Might Asian American students feel compelled to overachieve to prove that they fit into American society—to achieve the American Dream? Indeed, some scholars have found that Asian Americans use the model minority myth as a strategy to cope with the discrimination and racism they face (Lee et al., 2017).

The overlap between the concept and discourse of grit with the model minority myth is glaring. We provide a more in-depth discussion of both topics but briefly define the model minority myth. We use Yi et al.'s (2020) critical race definition of the model minority myth:

> A white supremacist racial project that strategically frames Asian Americans as a universally successful racial group to maintain systems that enact differential forms of violence on all communities of color. The myth perpetuates such violence through mechanisms that include, but are not limited to, the racial exclusion of Asian Americans (and sometimes Pacific Islanders) from many aspects of society and the perpetuation of deficit ideologies that deny the existence of inequitable structures of access and opportunity while blaming other People of Color for not working hard enough or having the right cultural values.
>
> *(p. 551)*

The concepts of grit and the model minority myth are presented and sometimes perceived as neutral, even well-intended in some settings. Both concepts are universalized to depict accessible outcomes to all and promote an individualized process concerning educational attainment. Both concepts (and the material consequences resulting from deploying these concepts) work to maintain white supremacy in education by promoting meritocracy and glorifying individual efforts toward the American success story. Such promotion and glorification are how grit and the myth are weaponized, rendering invisible structural barriers and minimizing Asian Americans in conversations about and efforts to advance educational equity.

In this chapter, we propose that rather than help dismantle educational inequities, how grit is wielded services the existing inequitable educational system. We examine the possibility that grit operates at the confluence of the model and deviant minority myths. Together, these dual myths perpetuate existing inequitable systems that drive wedges between groups of color and reify the conditional status of Asian Americans as people of color in service of white supremacy. The dual myths are important to understand as Asian Americans are conditionally racialized, which often results in the entire population being misrepresented, mischaracterized, and overlooked. Such conditional racialization impacts how Asian Americans form their individual and collective identities. Further, like the model minority myth (Yi et al., 2020), grit implicates everyone, but grit harms Asian Americans in specific ways.

In the following sections, we make these arguments in the context of the historical and contemporary racialization of Asian Americans in American society in general and higher education in particular. As Asian American scholars and activists, we are concerned that the critical lessons from how the model minority myth has negatively impacted our community have not been learned, so we end this chapter with some cautions. Before we do so, we provide our readers with a note about our positionality and journey in writing this piece.

A Note about Asian American Things to Our Readers

Collectively, we are a group of Asian American women from refugee, immigrant, low-income, and first-generation backgrounds. We are doctoral students and faculty members who believe in the power of our collective wisdom, stories, and intuition. We naturally gravitated toward and centered critical race and women of color feminist epistemologies in our day-to-day work, especially in our approach to this piece you are reading. As we practice a more human and embodied approach to our work, we recognize that we ideated and wrote this piece during complex and powerful realities: a university-system-wide strike for labor equity, an enduring global pandemic, journeying into pregnancy and motherhood, and navigating the wisdom our research and dissertation participants imparted. Although these realities are not the focus of this piece, living in these moments has indeed informed our thinking and writing.

In our discussion of the possibilities of this chapter, a recurring theme is "how much word count should we devote to explaining Asian American things?" This question arose from lived experiences when journal reviewers would ask us to justify why Asian Americans mattered. When we have read education policy reports from the last 30 years that continually omit Asian Americans from their analysis. When statistics would provide an asterisk next to "Asians" or institutions lump "Asian" students together with white students. When professors, colleagues in the field, and others looked curiously at us when we shared our research interests. As scholars with an explicit interest in Asian American things, we work and live inside the tension that our society has very low literacy regarding Asian American things because of how Asian Americans are racialized. Yet, we can still be frustrated by devoting treasured word count to explain things that have been explained elsewhere, and no amount of word count can convince someone Asian American things matter if they are unwilling to seek out the plethora of resources that exist already.

We have a few more notes about "Asian American things" that we want our readers to recognize. First, we grappled with great difficulty in having this conversation about grit because some people in our community greatly agree with this concept. After all, it resonates deeply with their lived experiences. There are also people in our community who have been greatly harmed. Adding to this difficulty is that when our community is being used as a pawn to dismantle racial equity efforts, there are few opportunities to come together to unpack how we are being used and racialized.

This brings us to the second Asian American thing, which required persistence, audacity, deep emotional wells, and the work of generations of organizers and scholars to articulate. Asian Americans are racialized in many ways to be a population of convenience—a population included, excluded, or omitted to support whatever picture of race and equity an author or institution sees fit. We are referenced when denying imperative and equitable support for marginalized populations, including support that would benefit Asian Americans. We are scapegoated for taking up unnecessary resources, inducing unnecessary competition, or causing disease. Sometimes we are included in "diversity," and sometimes, we are not. We are sometimes simply omitted, and to figure out why we must engage in contorted mental gymnastics. Sometimes, we actively participate in one of these examples without fully understanding the consequences. In one of our conversations, we described this as an experience of "constantly being used while never given or having space even to understand what is happening to us or with us." In short, how we are used as a wedge is "never about our own stories." We hope that through centering our agency, desires, and complexity in this piece, we can expose the inequities facing our communities while interrupting the conditional and damaging ways our stories have been used (Tuck, 2009).

For the readers looking for a period to punctuate a complete and watertight argument in this chapter, you may be disappointed to know we did not do this for some of the reasons we listed above. To honor the racial realities of this conversation and the realities we are navigating, we consider this piece our best attempt in this moment with what we currently know, recognizing that the conversation must go further. For readers willing to go on this journey with us, we invite your thoughts and wisdom to advance this exploration and conversation.

The Conceptualization of Grit in Higher Education

As a construct, *grit* has been universalized in the workplace and education to explain how individuals persevere and maintain success. Grit was introduced in 2007 and is defined as "perseverance and passion for long-term goals" (Duckworth et al., 2007, p. 1087) and has quickly become part of the general lexicon within educational discourse. Popularized through a Ted Talk, Duckworth's (2013) concept of grit has gained widespread recognition as a key to achievement and success (Credé, 2018). Duckworth et al. (2007) differentiate grit from talent and intelligence, suggesting grit is a trait one can develop. The belief that one can develop grit is intriguing and has been adopted without reservation within schools, workplaces, and even the U.S. Department of Education to evaluate students (Credé, 2018; Gonzales, 2016). The idea that an individual can develop to be "more gritty" reinforces the concept that individuals bear the responsibility for their educational achievement. Furthermore, the belief that grit can be fostered among all racial groups is intriguing.

This infatuation with grit as an indicator of success is reflected in the broader research and teaching of grit in educational spaces (Credé, 2018; Gonzales, 2016). Grit is appealing because it allows educators and parents to explain, manage, and control student success narratives. For those students experiencing educational challenges, grit is proffered as a "solution," whereby focusing on hard work and dedication to one's studies should yield positive outcomes. Simultaneously, scholars raised questions about the validity of grit as both a standalone construct and its lack of empirical validity (Credé, 2018; Fosnacht et al., 2019). Additionally, Almeida (2016) noted that most studies on grit utilize quantitative methodologies, whereas qualitative exploration of grit is limited. Few of these studies currently include Asian American students as a focal group. Zentner et al. (2016) conducted the only study involving Asian American and Pacific Islander (AAPI) students, comparing their grit scores to the general population. They found that non-AAPI students have a statistically significant overall higher grit score than AAPI students. However, this study offers just one data point for consideration. Without continued focus and inclusion of Asian American populations in future studies and discussions of grit, we miss out on opportunities to better understand grit and its implications.

Grit has also begun making its way into postsecondary spaces, becoming a lens to frame and support student success in college (Almeida, 2016; Gonzales, 2016). Initially, Duckworth and Quinn (2009) validated their scale in a postsecondary setting and showed how grit predicted retention. Later, Strayhorn (2014) extended the grit scale and framework further into higher education research by exploring grit's role in Black male collegians' academic success, suggesting that grit may be an "effective lever to raising Black male academic success" (p. 7). Strayhorn also suggested that grit is a malleable trait. These and similar studies reinforce grit as a useful concept in explaining success among college students. As a result, many college campus programs and resources may consciously and unconsciously leverage this idea of grit to guide their approach to student success. For example, the University of Utah's First Ascent and Opportunity First Scholars programs prioritize recruiting students with grit (Jaschik, 2022).

However, scholars have mentioned how these stories of individual success through grit are stories of exception—not the rule (Gonzales, 2016; Love, 2019). These scholars assert that the glitziness of grit as an explanatory factor in student success both masks and detracts from the role that systemic oppression plays in society (Almeida, 2016; Gonzales, 2016; Love, 2019; Schreiner, 2017). Schreiner (2017) critiqued the idea of grit as an individual personality trait, noting that variation in grit levels is based on the environments in which we live and were raised, illuminating the inherent privilege embedded within the concept. According to Schreiner, four dangers result due to this emphasis on a student's grit that (a) focuses on the individual, (b) is founded on deficit ideology, (c) is framed as able to be cultivated, and (d) places the inordinate focus and use of grit to determine admission status. Similarly, Gonzales (2016) further problematized the conceptualization of grit, highlighting the "desire to 'fix' marginalized people" while "idealizing and idolizing individuals who persevere in the face of historical inequities and marginalization" (p. 116). Gonzales noted that this default understanding of student success leaves structures in place. Thus, the idea that students can "grit" their way out of inequities is concerning.

A vital critique of grit is its story about success, social mobility, and the American Dream. Grit reinforces the concept of working hard despite enduring prolonged challenges; this will result in an individual's success against all odds. However, this narrative pathologizes students who experience significant barriers that are at once institutionalized and systemic. Ultimately, students are the focal point while the structures and systems that have created barriers and upheld educational disparities are masked. The danger of a grit-based ideology leads students, parents, and educators to be socialized into deficit-oriented beliefs that those who do not achieve are at fault and lack grit (Gorski, 2016). Moreover, this leads to the reproduction of a deficit narrative for student populations that experience educational disparities—most of whom are low-income and racially minoritized students. Grit becomes another method of labeling which students are deserving or not—ultimately, grit shapes the value our students bring to our education system.

The time to reckon with grit as a dangerous tool and ideology is now before it continues to proliferate into higher education spaces and exacerbate harm for all our students. To do so, we center Asian Americans in this conversation involving grit, not only to dismantle the specious arguments upholding grit as a concept but also to highlight how Asian Americans have always been implicated in these conversations albeit without acknowledgment of our agency and influence.

The Meritocratic Asian American

To reinforce the narrative of meritocracy, white supremacy, and systems of inequity in the United States, Asian Americans are given racial scripts (Molina, 2014) to perform disparate roles as model citizens, deviant and dangerous citizens, or people who may never be American enough (Paek & Shah, 2003; Takaki, 1998). To maintain these scripts, Asian Americans are often racialized based on their achievement and ability to assimilate, thus manifesting the characterizations of grit. Asian Americans are simultaneously racialized as forever foreigners and model minorities (Lee et al., 2009)—two narratives that may complement or contradict one another but always depend upon how American, or un-American, one is. On one end, Asian Americans are perceived as an enemy or foreign threat, taking over schools and employment opportunities. Conversely, the model minority myth characterizes Asian Americans as naturally successful and, therefore not in need of support. A critical contradiction of these racialized narratives facing Asian Americans has shown how they have had or can perform attributes of being American. In striving to explore and understand the connection of grit to how Asian Americans experience race and racism, this section explores how Asian Americans have been historically racialized and, in turn, how this history shapes the contemporary realities conveniently connected to grit.

In reviewing educational scholarship on Asian American racialization, scholars argue that historically, Asian Americans embraced the model minority myth as a strategy to resist and cope with discrimination and racism (Lee et al., 2017). By pursuing a good education, getting a well-paying job, and obtaining social capital, Asian Americans can achieve the American Dream—a symbol of assimilation and Americanness. For example, during the Jim Crow era, early Chinese American students living in the Mississippi

Delta faced policies that excluded them from being able to attend white schools. School segregation and exclusion policies were based on a white and Black binary, resulting in Chinese American students and their parents having to position themselves closer to whites to gain access to these schools. In other words, to minimize the racism they faced in school, Chinese parents and students believed that by working hard and being "grittier," their children would be safer from discrimination and racism (Lee et al., 2017). The historical ways that Chinese American parents and students resisted their racialization by performing a model minority identity helps challenge the idea that Asian Americans are inherently "successful" model minorities with a natural, hard work ethic. Instead, it reveals that Asian Americans are *not* model minorities but *had* to embrace this racialized narrative of the model minority to survive a system rooted in white supremacy.

A consequence of these strategies for survival and protection against racism has led to the reproduction of the harmful model minority myth within our communities and with the perception of our communities. This reproduction of the model minority myth has continued to marginalize and obscure the needs of communities such as Southeast Asian Americans. Southeast Asian Americans who seldom fit neatly into the model minority narrative are racialized as deviant minorities and perceived through a deficit lens (Museus & Park, 2015; Yi Borromeo, 2018). Thus, the model minority myth is both a strategy of resistance and a tool of oppression (Lee et al., 2017).

Although the model minority and perpetual foreigner stereotypes are the dominant racialized narratives shaping the lives of Asian Americans, Southeast Asian Americans (e.g., Cambodian, Hmong, Lao, and Vietnamese) face another pervasive racialized narrative—the deviant minority myth. The deviant minority myth associates Southeast Asian Americans with welfare dependence, gang affiliation, and cultural deficiency, which have been used to explain their lower educational attainment compared to other Asian American groups (Yi Borromeo, 2018). Yi Borromeo (2018) found that Cambodian/Khmer student participants had a more salient racialization with the deviant minority myth. However, other subgroups, such as Vietnamese American students, experience more polarized racialization where they are perceived on extreme ends as either model or deviant minorities, depending on the context (Ngo & Lee, 2007). Thus, Southeast Asian Americans experience complex and polarized racialization.

This polarized racialization is further seen in how Southeast Asian American cultures have been discussed as a source of their success or a reason for their lack of success (Museus & Park, 2015; Ngo & Lee, 2007; Yi Borromeo, 2018). Many Southeast Asian Americans are refugees or descendants of refugees who have faced war, displacement, genocide, and institutional and systemic barriers. To focus on cultural, religious, and family values to explain the achievement rates of Southeast Asian Americans is to deflect from the systemic inequities and racism facing this community. Like how grit centers the success of students based on their ability to develop "grittiness," grit is manifested through both the model and deviant minority myths where Southeast Asian American students are either used to support the American Dream and meritocracy ideology or to explain the achievement gap within the Asian American community and other communities of color. Ultimately, labeling our communities as successful or unsuccessful, or as "gritty" or "not gritty," illustrates that our value is defined by our achievements, further promoting meritocracy and individual journey toward the American Dream. Such labeling directly shapes the sociopolitical and cultural dimensions of our communities' educational experiences.

Despite trying to work their way to Americanness, access, and safety, history reveals to us that Asian Americans have never been safe from racism—or specifically anti-Asian racism, which brutally intensified during the height of the pandemic—no matter how much success and grit they possess. During the COVID-19 pandemic, Asian Americans are experiencing increased anti-Asian racism, hate crimes, and xenophobia. In schools, Asian American students are bullied and harassed for their racial and ethnic identities (Gutierrez et al., 2021). Clearly, anti-Asian racism is not new. Asian Americans continue to be uplifted as an example of our nation as a land of equal opportunity, but also used as a scapegoat for our nation's economic downfall and disease because, by extension, Asian Americans are deemed a threat to white people's privilege and well-being (Li & Nicholson, 2021). How Asian Americans have been praised or despised based on their success and proximity to whiteness gives us a sense of how grit can be conflated with the racialization of Asian Americans.

Considering the power and influence of race and racism, Asian Americans have been at odds with American society since they first migrated to the United States. The distinct racialization of Asian Americans continues to be unyielding as more concepts like grit further reinforce racial mischaracterizations of immigrant-origin communities tasked to continuously prove they are not the other, the enemy, that they are, in fact, American, at the very least assimilable to be part of American society. As such, the potential force grit may generate in alignment with this history is deeply concerning as our community contends with the internalization of racism that directly impacts their mental health and overall well-being (Chopra, 2021; Hwang, 2021). The concept of grit and the way it is used reproduce harmful racial scripts in which Asian Americans who prove themselves through accomplishments are racialized as model citizens and those who "fail" to are racialized as inherently deficient and dangerous. Omi and Winant (2014) argued that racial formation is "the sociohistorical process by which racial identities are created, lived out, transformed, and destroyed" (p. 109). While we aspire to eradicate concepts that further fuel racist ideology toward our communities, we hope to strengthen the case against the movement toward grit by telling the Asian American journey. This journey remains a historically compounded experience of being othered, with the added dimensions of being deemed perpetual foreigners, model, and/or deviant minorities.

Racialized Grit and the Model and Deviant Minority

As the trajectory of grit takes hold in mainstream American society and maintains a steady momentum, the forces generated by the model minority myth discourse may likely intensify, given the similarity between the two concepts. This is especially concerning given the high stakes of national race-based legal cases surrounding affirmative action likely to point blame at Asian Americans for the possible repeal of such legislation. Considering this high degree of alignment, Asian Americans' Americanness will likely be endorsed or challenged through their grittiness—or left out of the conversation altogether. As such, the amalgamation of grit and model minority characteristics will likely reinforce or strengthen how Asian Americans are essentialized, valorized, or omitted, further fortifying the mistreatment and harm our communities have historically endured and presently experience—especially within educational contexts. As such, we must consider this inquiry: what if the confluence of the model minority and deviant minority myths is how Asian Americans are racialized regarding how grit is used and applied in education? If grit is conceptualized as a universal color-evasive tool wielded to maintain inequities in education, then for Asian Americans, how grit is used is similarly conditional as the model minority myth. Specifically, grit, then, is a conditional, racialized construct that underscores two racialized narrative binaries. The logic would operate something like this: first, some Asian Americans are universally successful (model minority myth), and therefore, grit is not an applicable measure or necessary for individual Asian Americans to develop. Second, other Asian American subgroups (e.g., Southeast Asian Americans; deviant minority myth) are so lacking in grit that they are undeserving of support. To explore this inquiry, we locate the parallels between grit and the model and deviant minority myths, discuss the possibilities of what learning is advanced with this understanding, and share the limitations of this framing.

There indeed are some glaring parallels between the discussion of grit and the model and deviant minority myths. Conceptually, grit and the model minority myth are perceived as well-intentioned and neutral in quality. However, both concepts also generate extreme harm when wielded to support the bygone assumption that American society is a meritocratic society. In doing so, both concepts serve white supremacy by maintaining that all students and learners can be successful if they work hard enough. At the same time, by not even naming those individuals or groups deemed "unsuccessful" in education, the concepts of grit and the model minority myth only work when those individuals can be individually blamed for their lack of success and are therefore undeserving of additional support. For example, Southeast Asian American (SEAA) students are highlighted as the undeserving foil to the model minority myth as they experience significant educational disparities that are often attributed to a perception of cultural deficiency, overreliance on social welfare systems, and involvement in deviant behaviors (Cowart & Cowart, 1993; Truong, 2007). Instead of educators and educational leaders creating the necessary resources for these students to succeed, such positioning has resulted in the internalized belief that SEAA students are "less than" and further creates significant academic and psychological challenges throughout their educational experiences (Yi Borromeo, 2018; Yi et al., 2020).

Several important implications arise with the framing of grit for Asian Americans that exist at the intersection of the model and deviant minority myths. First, our exploration of racialized grit for Asian Americans reveals another mechanism of how insidiously the model minority myth works. In general, the myth is understood as part of a racial project that harms all groups of color (Yi et al., 2020). Often, the people not labeled the "model" are other communities of color. Yet, in our exploration here, we agree with other scholars and educators that the "other" also includes Asian American subgroups (Yi et al., 2020). We extend this position by offering the confluence of the model minority myth with the deviant minority myth as necessary to more fully understand how the former works to shape the lives of Asian Americans, especially those often omitted or ignored (Yi Borromeo, 2018).

Second, by understanding the way grit is racialized for Asian Americans, we can continue to lift the veil of color-neutral approaches to educational equity efforts. Specifically, by identifying how grit is used as another racial label and how the concept of grit is conditionally wielded in the case of Asian Americans, we can directly point out how these concepts continue to service white supremacy.

Finally, our exploration in this chapter is an example of trying to understand how racism shows up in our lives, especially elements that are not easily seen or identified as racism but are, in fact, racist. Our work as activists, educators, and scholars includes unveiling such mechanisms. In this case, we tried to take apart the increasingly popular and alluring concept of grit and reveal how it is wielded in our community. Yet, as we described earlier, figuring this out is hard. The journey is made only slightly easier by approaching this exploration with a feminist and critical race lens (Espiritu

& Duong, 2018; Fujiwara & Roshan-Ravan, 2018; hooks, 1984; Ladson-Billings & Tate, 1995; Tintiangco-Cubales & Sacramento, 2009), through the embracing of subjectivity (Mac et al., 2021), and recognizing the importance of our endeavor as Asian Americans (Matsuda, 1996). If we can try to start figuring this out, it can help Asian Americans and all communities combat white supremacy and reduce racial inequities and harm in higher education.

We recognize that there are limitations to understanding racialized grit for Asian Americans as operating at the confluence of the model and deviant minority myths. While the model minority myth is a behemoth narrative shaping the lives of Asian Americans, we recognize that not every subgroup within the Asian American community is impacted the same way by how the myth is wielded. As such, we may be limited in understanding how racialized grit shapes the educational experiences of those groups. Further exploration with other subgroups is needed, such as South Asian and Desi communities and recent Burmese and Bhutanese refugee communities.

Another limitation is that we did not fully examine the implications of individual versus social group racialization that grit and the deviant and model minority myths produce. We recognize that these concepts and how they are used are experienced and lived at both individual- and group-based levels. For example, Yi Borromeo (2018) found that Southeast Asian American students experienced conflicting messages that while Asian Americans are viewed as successful, their communities are seen as deficient, significantly impacting how they viewed themselves individually as learners. Some students in Yi Borromeo's study chose to reject the model minority archetype and intentionally failed in school. We maintained most of our focus at the social group level, yet more exploration is needed to understand how a narrative of an individual characteristic such as grit implicates individual Asian Americans, who are often viewed as having unique cultural and group-based values perceived to drive their universal success. How does this narrative of "individual-" versus "group-" based rationale for educational success implicate Asian Americans? Are individual Asian Americans less gritty because their successes are tied to their group membership?

A Cautionary Tale for Higher Education

Our exploration in this chapter further shows that grit—the concept and how it is used—cannot be separated from our current system of educational inequities. Consequently, we cannot untangle the solution to these inequities. Treating grit as an individualized concept deflects our collective focus from meaningfully addressing systemic racial inequities in our education system. Rather, we must recognize that grit is a racialized construct that maintains and advances the current system of inequities. We centered on

Asian American lived experiences and racialization that contradicts the supposed universality of grit as a blanket explanation for educational success. Through doing so, we also furthered our collective understanding of how broad narratives about the "successes" and "failures" of Asian Americans are interwoven.

In addition to some of the limitations to our exploration, we offer additional inquiries from this chapter that are worthy of further examination.

- What are the experiences of Asian American students related to the use of grit as a concept in schools and colleges? What meaning do they make of these experiences? What messages do they want to share with policymakers and leaders of their educational institutions?
- How do other communities respond to (or not) the conditional grittiness of Asian American students? What implications do these responses (or lack thereof) have on Asian American students?
- In what ways does the confluence of the model and deviant minority myths shape policy aimed to advance educational equity? And how might this influence further shape conversations about grit?
- What dimensions of internal and external racialization processes do Asian Americans experience related to grit? How are those dimensions related to each other?

As individuals who have experienced being a racialized group of convenience, we offer a cautionary tale for higher education—especially those administrators and leaders seeking to adopt grit as a concept. The allure of grit—a concept to recognize dedication through adversity and as a label used to name who is and is not deserving—is powerful. Using grit in such a way can do to other communities of color what the model minority myth did and continues to do to Asian Americans. Some of these harms include positioning some individuals of color as more deserving than others, assessing individual worth and value based on their educational achievements, attributing individuals' efforts in education to their culture, and reducing members of a group who are labeled as "undeserving" to the margins. In short, the plethora of educational experiences of an entire group of people is minimized, invisibilized, and largely omitted from educational equity efforts and society. We urge leaders, policymakers, and educators to heed our call to avoid haphazardly applying and using grit without fully considering the possible irreparable harm they may cause. We urge you to do the hard work required to address educational equity.

Postsecondary leadership can combat the perils of racializing Asian Americans in these harmful ways and attempt to address the harms that have been caused meaningfully. We are not the first to try to identify meaningful actions, but we do highlight the following as the most relevant to our chapter:

- Resist the urge to reinforce and uphold hegemonic narratives about Asian Americans. Recognize your opportunity to learn by committing to understanding the depths and complexities of this heterogeneous group.
- Evaluate your institutional priorities and root out how those priorities obscure, thwart, and omit efforts to understand and serve Asian Americans on your campus and in your community. Invest material resources in understanding and supporting your Asian American student body, faculty, and staff.
- Stop using Asian American stories to advance other agendas. Period. Instead, center Asian American stories and experiences to better serve them. Asian American communities are worthy of being centered.

We conclude our exploration with this query we found ourselves returning to: Given our exploration, is there a silver lining to grit? Is there a way that grit can be used for good? Can grit be used to advance the progress of racial equity? We are not optimistic and leave you, our readers, with this poetic reflection.

> *I'm holding a mirror up to myself to understand my reflection*
> *but I find it hard even to see myself.*
> *Parts of me are still obscured*
> *because of these outside narratives about who I'm supposed to be*
> *and what I'm supposed to represent.*
> *The clothes I'm wearing are not my own*
> *like the tools given to me to use were made by others*
> *who have yet to understand who, where, what I come from.*
> *While I don't have the tools to dress myself,*
> *see myself,*
> *I no longer want to be fitted as*
> *the side-kick,*
> *the wedge,*
> *the symbol to serve*
> *your story.*
> *I want to be*
> *the main character*
> *of my own story.*

References

Almeida, D. J. (2016). Understanding grit in the context of higher education. In M. B. Paulsen (Ed.), *Higher education: Handbook of theory and research* (pp. 559–609). Springer.

Chopra, S. B. (2021). Healing from internalized racism for Asian Americans. *Professional Psychology: Research and Practice, 52*(5), 503–512. https://doi.org/10.1037/pro0000407

Cowart, M. T., & Cowart, R. E. (1993). Southeast Asian refugee youth and the cycle of violence. *NASSP Bulletin, 77*(557), 41–45. https://doi.org/10.1177/019263659307755709

Credé, M. (2018). What shall we do about grit? A critical review of what we know and what we don't know. *Educational Researcher, 47*(9), 606–611. https://doi.org/10.3102s0013189X18801322

Duckworth, A. L. (2013). Grit: *The power of passion and perseverance* [Video]. TED Conferences. https://www.ted.com/talks/angela_lee_duckworth_grit_the_power_of_passion_and_perseverance?language=en

Duckworth, A. L., Peterson, C., Matthews, M. D., & Kelly, D. R. (2007). Grit: Perseverance and passion for long term goals. *Journal of Personality and Social Psychology, 92*(6), 1087–1101. https://doi.org/10.1037/0022-3514.92.6.1087

Duckworth, A. L., & Quinn, P. D. (2009). Development and validation of the short grit scale (Grit-S). *Journal of Personality Assessment, 91*(2), 166–174. https://doi.org/10.1080/00223890802634290

Espiritu, Y. L., & Duong, L. (2018). Feminist refugee epistemology: Reading displacement in Vietnamese and Syrian refugee art. *Signs: Journal of Women in Culture and Society, 43*(3), 587–615. https://doi.org/10.1086/695300

Fosnacht, K., Copridge, K., & Sarraf, S. A. (2019). How valid is grit in the postsecondary context? A construct and concurrent validity analysis. *Research in Higher Education, 60*(6), 803–822.

Fujiwara, L., & Roshan-Ravan, S. (2018). Introduction. In L. Fujiwara & S. Roshan-Ravan (Eds.), *Asian American feminisms and women of color politics* (pp. 3–24). University of Washington Press.

Gonzales, L. D. (2016). Revising the grounds for the study of grit: Critical qualitative inquiry in post-secondary education organizational research. In P. A. Pasque & V. M. Lechuga (Eds.), *Qualitative inquiry in higher education organization and policy research* (pp. 113–128). Routledge.

Gorski, P. C. (2016). Poverty and the ideological imperative: A call to unhook from deficit and grit ideology and to strive for structural ideology in teacher education. *Journal of Education for Teaching, 42*(4), 378–386. https://doi.org/10.1080/02607476.2016.1215546

Gutierrez, R. A. E., Le, A., & Teranishi, R. T. (2021). A racial reckoning: Anti-Asian racism and exclusion in higher education. *Education Trust—West.* https://west.edtrust.org/wp-content/uploads/2017/11/EducationTrust_2021_ANTI-ASIAN-RACISM-AND-EXCLUSION-IN-HIGHER-EDUCATION-_v5.pdf

hooks, b. (1984). *Feminist theory: From margin to center.* South End Press.

Hwang, W. C. (2021). Demystifying and addressing internalized racism and oppression among Asian Americans. *American Psychologist, 76*(4), 596–610. https://doi.org/10.1037/amp0000798

Jaschik, S. (2022, November 14). University of Utah seeks students with grit. *Inside Higher Ed.* https://www.insidehighered.com/admissions/article/2022/11/14/university-utah-seeksstudents-grit

Ladson-Billings, G., & Tate, W. IV. (1995). Toward a critical race theory of education. *Teachers College Record*, *97*(1), 47–68. https://doi.org/10.1080/10282580701850413

Lee, J. (2021). Asian Americans, affirmative action, & the rise in anti-Asian hate. *Daedalus*, *150*(2), 180–198. https://doi.org/10.1162/DAED_a_01854

Lee, S. J., Park, E., & Wong, J. H. S. (2017). Racialization, schooling, and becoming American: Asian American experiences. *Educational Studies*, *53*(5), 492–510. https://doi.org/10.1080/00131946.2016.1258360

Lee, S. J., Wong, N.-W. A., & Alvarez, A. N. (2009). The model minority and the perpetual foreigner: Stereotypes of Asian Americans. In N. Tewari & A. N. Alvarez (Eds.), *Asian American psychology: Current perspectives* (pp. 69–84). Routledge/Taylor & Francis Group.

Li, Y., & Nicholson, H. L. Jr. (2021). When "model minorities" become "yellow peril"—Othering and the racialization of Asian Americans in the COVID-19 pandemic. *Sociology Compass*, *15*(2). https://doi.org/10.1111/soc4.12849

Love, B. L. (2019, February 12). "Grit is in our DNA": Why teaching grit is inherently anti-Black. *Education Week*. https://www.edweek.org/leadership/opinion-grit-is-in-our-dna-why-teaching-grit-is-inherently-anti-black/2019/02

Mac, J., Yi, V., Na, V., Thaviseth, L., Phommasa, M., & Pheng, L. M. (2021). The SEAAster scholars collective: A story of homemaking in academia. *Journal of Southeast Asian American Education and Advancement*, *16*(1). https://doi.org/10.7771/2153-8999.1233

Matsuda, M. J. (1996). *Where is your body? And other essays on race gender and the law*. Beacon Press.

Molina, N. (2014). *How race is made in America: Immigration, citizenship, and the historical power of racial scripts*. University of California Press.

Museus, S. D. (2013). Unpacking the complex and multifaceted nature of parental influences on southeast Asian American college students' educational trajectories. *Journal of Higher Education*, *84*(5), 708–738. https://doi.org/10.1353/jhe.2013.0031

Museus, S. D., & Park, J. J. (2015). The continuing significance of racism in the lives of Asian American college students. *Journal of College Student Development*, *56*(6), 551–569. https://doi.org/10.1353/csd.2015.0059

Ngo, B., & Lee, S. J. (2007). Complicating the image of model minority success: A review of Southeast Asian American education. *Review of Educational Research*, *77*(4), 415–453. https://doi.org/10.3102/0034654307309918

Omi, M., & Winant, H. (2014). *Racial formation in the United States*. Routledge.

Paek, H. J., & Shah, H. (2003). Racial ideology, model minorities, and the "not-so-silent partner": Stereotyping of Asian Americans in U.S. magazine advertising. *Howard Journal of Communication*, *14*(4), 225–243. https://doi.org/10.1080/716100430

Reed, L., & Jeremiah, J. (2017). Student grit as an important ingredient for academic and personal success. *Developments in Business Simulation and Experiential Learning*, *44*, 252–256.

Schreiner, L. A. (2017). The privilege of grit. *About Campus*, *22*(5), 11–20. https://doi.org/10.1002/abc.21303

Strayhorn, T. L. (2014). What role does grit play in the academic success of Black male collegians at predominantly white institutions? *Journal of African American Studies, 18*(1), 1–10. https://doi.org/10.1007/s12111-012-9243-0

Takaki, R. T. (1998). *Strangers from a different shore: A history of Asian Americans* (Updated and Revised ed.). Little, Brown and Company.

Tintiangco-Cubales, A., & Sacramento, J. (2009). Practicing Pinayist pedagogy. *Amerasia Journal, 35*(1), 179–187. https://doi.org/10.17953/amer.35.1.98257024r4501756

Truong, M. H. (2007). Welfare reform and liberal governance: Disciplining Cambodian-American bodies. *International Journal of Social Welfare, 16*(3), 258–268. https://doi.org/10.1111/j.1468-2397.2006.00479.x

Tuck, E. (2009). Suspending damage: A letter to communities. *Harvard Educational Review, 79*(3),409–428.https://doi.org/10.17763/haer.79.3.n0016675661t3n15

Yi Borromeo, V. (2018). *A phenomenological inquiry in the racialized experiences of Southeast Asian American community college students* [Unpublished doctoral dissertation]. University of Denver.

Yi, V., Mac, J., Na, V. S., Venturanza, R. J., Museus, S. D., Buenavista, T. L., & Pendakur, S. L. (2020). Toward an anti-imperialistic critical race analysis of the model minority myth. *Review of Educational Research, 90*(4), 542–579. https://doi.org/10.3102/0034654320933532

Zentner, A., Gutierrez, R., Bell, E., & Pham, P. (2016). Exploring Asian-American/Pacific Islander student grit within the two-year college system. *Social Science Research Network Electronic Journal.* https://doi.org/10.2139/ssrn.2846623

PART II

College Structural Barriers and Research Studies

6

MORE THAN GRIT

Toward Critical Race College Retention and Persistence for Latina/o/x Students

Nancy Acevedo

Due to a gap between the percentage of white students and Latina/o/x students who (a) enroll in four-year colleges (Lopez & Fry, 2013), (b) persist in the second-year of college (National Student Clearinghouse, 2022), (c) attend selective institutions (Lopez & Hill, 2022), and (d) graduate from college (Excelencia in Education, 2020), it remains urgent that we improve the college transition experiences and increase persistence rates for Latina/o/x students (Lee et al., 2022). While parents are key actors in initiating the urgency of earning a college degree (Conchas & Acevedo, 2020), academic and college preparation experiences during high school represent a key influence on college access and transition (Michel & Durdella, 2019). Research finds that students who graduate from policed, under-resourced high schools believe that the lack of college preparation in high school will hinder their high school to college transition (Acevedo-Gil, 2022; Madrigal-Garcia & Acevedo-Gil, 2016). In high school, students are socialized through policies and practices that serve as measures to control their behaviors and limit them from engaging in self-advocacy and independence (Acevedo-Gil, 2022; Madrigal-Garcia & Acevedo-Gil, 2016).

These schools consist of New Juan Crow Education (NJCE) environments, which include measures of control that are socially and spatially situated, resulting in Latina/o/x students experiencing a criminalizing and policed schooling context at higher percentages than white and Asian American students (Kasprisin, 2013). Furthermore, Stovall (2016) contended:

DOI: 10.4324/9781003332497-8

the relationship between schools and jails represent a school to prison nexus, marking a space where both institutions operate as one in the same under the same set of rules ... school can serve as the reminder that *you are in jail.*

(p. 2, emphasis in original)

However, previous literature traditionally examined the experiences of students within such K-12 contexts and the experiences of Latina/o/x students while in higher education, separately. Therefore, the present study aimed to address a dearth in the literature by examining the transition to four-year colleges for Latina/o/x students who were previously socialized within a NJCE context. Some studies that examine the experiences of Latina/o/x students overcoming obstacles in K-12 and higher education engage in individual-centered decontextualized analysis of student grit (Hochanadel & Finamore, 2015). This chapter applies a structural lens by accounting for and challenging the role of inequitable and racist structures.

This qualitative case study connects the college preparation and socialization that one Latina student experienced in high school with her transition from high school to a four-year college in order to challenge the deficit, meritocratic notion that students need more levels of grit to succeed. Using testimonio (Booker, 2002), this chapter shares an example of a Latina student enacting community cultural wealth (CCW), alongside accessing institutional resources to develop, maintain, and meet college aspirations, which informed the development of a critical race college retention and persistence framework.

Theoretical Frameworks

This study used two frameworks to connect school contexts and student resources—NJCE and CCW. NJCE allowed the study to account for racialized institutional processes and experiences with intersectionality (Crenshaw, 1991). CCW builds on and challenges the traditional sociological concepts of social and cultural capital. Combined, these two frameworks account for the marginalizing schooling contexts and highlight the student-level assets used to challenge them. Examining both the institutional context and student cultural wealth helps contest the individualistic notion of grit.

New Juan Crow in Education

The New Juan Crow in Education framework (Madrigal-Garcia & Acevedo-Gil, 2016) is defined as an interconnected "web of power and relegation" that occurs at the intersection "inadequate school resources," "zero tolerance (practices), and a high-security environment" (Madrigal-Garcia & Acevedo-Gil, 2016, p. 7). NJCE builds on the concepts of New Jim Crow (Alexander, 2020) and Juan Crow (Lovato, 2008). New Jim Crow acknowledges the U.S. era of Jim Crow that allowed for legal segregation and unequal treatment for African Americans, solely on the basis of race. Alexander (2020) noted that under the New Jim Crow era, the prison industrial complex maintains a racial caste system, which serves the same purpose as pre–Civil War slavery and the post–Civil War Jim Crow laws. Alexander also explained that the education system serves a role in New Jim Crow through the "unequal educational opportunities these children are provided" (Sokolower, 2012, para. 2).

While Alexander (2020) first defined the New Jim Crow with the African American U.S. historical context and experience in mind, Lovato (2008) used the term Juan Crow to bring the concept into the Latino community. With waves of immigration throughout the United States, Lovato defined Juan Crow as "the matrix of laws, social customs, economic institutions and symbolic systems enabling the physical and psychic isolation needed to control and exploit undocumented immigrants" (para. 6). Lovato developed the concept after researching the experiences of undocumented Latina/o/x immigrants in Atlanta, Georgia and noted that they "now occupy a separate, unequal, and clandestine place that has made it increasingly difficult for them to work, rent homes, or attend school" (para. 8).

By considering both the relevance of the New Jim Crow to the education system and the implications for Latino communities of Juan Crow, Madrigal-Garcia and Acevedo-Gil (2016) examined schooling contexts for Latina/o/x students. They found that Latina/o/x students were "socially and spatially" marginalized and "experience a hostile, punitive, criminalizing, and militarized environment as a result of zero-tolerance and high-stakes testing policies that portray these students as disposable" (Madrigal-Garcia & Acevedo-Gil, 2016, p. 156). A NJCE framework contends that the secondary and postsecondary educational pathways of Latina/o/x students are hindered through racialized "policies, practices, and daily interactions" (Madrigal-Garcia & Acevedo-Gil, 2016, p. 7). For this study, the author used a NJCE framework to guide the examination of a Latina student as she experienced high security and surveillance along with high-stakes testing and anti-immigrant policies and practices within an NJCE context, which influenced her schooling experiences.

Community Cultural Wealth

Duckworth et al. (2007) defined grit as "perseverance and passion for long-term goals" (p. 1087). They further detailed grit as a process that:

entails working strenuously toward challenges, maintaining effort and interest over years despite failure, adversity, and plateaus in progress. … Whereas disappointment or boredom signals to others that it is time to change trajectory and cut losses, the gritty individual stays the course.

(p. 1088)

An individual engages in grit when they persist toward their goals, despite encountering obstacles. As noted by Duckworth and colleagues, persistence occurs throughout multiple years and contexts. However, this does not consider the unequal and inequitable contexts of K-12 schools and higher education systems. As Gonzales (2016) explained, "The conventional approach to studying grit aims to understand how students 'make it' through barriers, and there is not an attempt to revise the organizational, structural, and cultural causes of said barriers" (p. 121). Instead of addressing the "difficulties" as noted above, Duckworth and colleagues simply measure the student's effort; they focus on the student's ability to persist, regardless of racialized and structural inequities.

CCW (Yosso, 2005) uses critical race theory as a lens to detail six forms of capital that communities of color enact to navigate such inequitable and marginalizing K-12 schooling contexts for which grit does not account. CCW moves beyond the individual's ability to persist and acknowledges that students possess "accumulated assets and resources in the histories and lives of Communities of Color" (p. 77). The six interconnected forms of capital consist of familial, social, navigational, linguistic, resistant, and aspirational.

Familial capital refers to cultural knowledge that is nurtured among family that carries a sense of community history, memory, and cultural intuition. Social capital refers to the networks of individuals and resources in the community. Navigational capital refers to skills that are used to maneuver social institutions. Linguistic capital entails the ability to communicate in various forms, including language, music, art, and poetry. Resistant capital includes the skills that individuals gain through oppositional identities and behaviors that aim to challenge inequality.

Aspirational capital entails remaining committed to goals, even when facing obstacles and lacking the resources to overcome such barriers. A key difference between aspirational capital and grit (Duckworth et al., 2007) is that CCW is founded on critical race theory and begins with the acknowledgement of structural barriers of racism, capitalism, sexism, and other systems of oppression that intend to exclude Students of Color. Yosso (2005) elaborated that aspirational capital must be contextualized within the social and familial settings. Family and community members often foster aspirational capital; thus, it is not an individualistic and decontextualized variable.

Although previous studies examine the role of individual capitals, as opposed to the CCW model in its entirety, Yosso cautioned that the forms of capital are not "mutually exclusive or static," and "aspirational capital overlaps with each of the other forms of capital, social, familial, navigational, linguistic and resistant" (p. 77). Therefore, this study focused on examining the role, not only of aspirational capital, but how the participant enacted CCW to sustain aspirational capital.

Literature Review

The first section of the literature review integrates two strands from the NJCE context: high-security surveillance environments and a lack of institutional resources. The literature begins with an overview of surveillance and policing and continues with a discussion of inadequate resources and concludes with the anti-immigrant policies that affect the educational pathways of undocumented Latina/o/x students. To discuss the subjugating schooling conditions experienced by Latina/o/x students, the second section of the literature review evaluates previous studies that have examined how Latina/o/x students access and transition from high school to college successfully.

Surveillance and Policing in K-12

A NJCE context entails a process that is socially and spatially situated wherein Students of Color experience a punitive, criminalizing, and policed schooling context at higher percentages than other students (Advancement Project, 2010). Students of Color are disproportionately impacted at both the point of disciplinary referral and when administrators decide the type of punishment (Welch & Payne, 2012). The schooling contexts are informed by accountability measures, criminalizing measures of control, zero-tolerance policies, and high-stakes tests (Madrigal-Garcia & Acevedo-Gil, 2016).

Such policies and practices portray Students of Color as disposable and actively push them out of school on a path toward incarceration (Wald & Losen, 2007). Michelle Alexander conceptualized that the education system serves as a "cage" in New Jim Crow through the "unequal educational opportunities these children are provided at a very early age coupled with the constant police surveillance they're likely to encounter" (Sokolower, 2012, para. 13). Thus, the aforementioned policies and practices situate students on the educational margins and perpetuate the criminalizing processes for Students of Color by socializing them in highly structured and policed contexts. Such marginalization results in school contexts that reproduce inequality and stratification though disparate treatment for Students of Color.

High-Stakes Testing

Wald and Losen (2007) argued that high-stakes standardized tests aim to make students invisible and push them out of the educational pipeline. Some scholars assert that one implication of high-stakes tests is to push out students in earlier grades because if academically low-achieving students are not in schools, they cannot decrease overall exam scores (Wald & Losen, 2007). Figlio (2006) concluded that, when compared to higher-achieving students, Florida educators used disciplinary practices to keep lower-performing students at home on test days. Other studies revealed that school districts and states will manipulate student data and exam scores to increase overall performance numbers and meet standards (Contreras & Rodriguez, 2021; Winerip, 2003). High school exit exams required for students to earn a diploma are also examples of high-stakes tests that are correlated with lowered college aspirations for Latina/o/x students (Rodriguez & Arellano, 2016).

Inadequate Academic Resources

The final strand to contextualize the NJCE context experienced by Latina/o/x students is the role of inadequate academic resources in schools (Madrigal-Garcia & Acevedo-Gil, 2016). Various studies have established and reaffirmed that Latina/o/x students attend schools with less structural resources than schools in wealthy communities that enroll primarily white students (Lee et al., 2022). In particular, Latina/o/x students experience academic under-resourced schooling through spatial and social measures (Lee et al., 2022). This contributes to racial segregation in schools greater than before *Brown v. Board of Education* eliminated de jure segregation (Orfield & Lee, 2007).

As such, Latina/o/x students are more likely than white students to attend schools that are under-resourced. Kucsera et al. (2015) found a "systemic trend of severe school segregation, strongly related to inequality in both opportunities and outcomes, and further compounded by a climate of high stakes standards and accountability" (p. 564). An example of unequal and inequitable access to opportunities includes student access to Advanced Placement (AP) courses. Despite court cases aiming to improve access to AP, studies continuously find inequitable enrollment patterns in AP courses (Naff et al., 2021; Palencia & Shakeshaft, 2022) and disparate exam scores (Judson & Hobson, 2015) for Latina/o/x students, when compared with white and Asian American groups.

To counter deficit schooling contexts, scholars have developed the notion of a school-wide college culture. Guided by the elements present in the college-going opportunities available to white wealthy students who attend private schools, a college culture is defined as a school environment where all students are prepared to make informed postsecondary decisions by receiving structural, motivational, and experiential college preparatory opportunities (McClafferty Jarsky et al., 2009). Education scholars contend that a college culture can counter the educational limitations experienced by low-income, Students of Color, and potential first-generation college students. Nevertheless, the amount and type of resources available to a school influence the level of college-going opportunities available in K-12 schools (Tierney & Colyar, 2005). As such, students who attend schools in low-socioeconomic areas have access to a watered-down form of college-going culture, which has implications for students being less likely to attend college (Palardy, 2015).

Enacting Community Cultural Wealth to Access and Transition to College

Students of Color enact CCW both as they access and transition to college (Huber, 2009; Liou et al., 2009). Researchers have found that Latina/o/x students enact social capital as a form of CCW by reaching out to local organizations for support (Liou et al., 2009) and such community connections allowed participants to enact navigational capital. The concept of "marginalization as motivation" has been connected to the resistant capital that emerged when Latina/o/x students work toward accessing college-going information (Liou et al., 2009, p. 546). Pérez (2014) examined how enacting linguistic, resistant, and navigational capital eased the academic and social transitions to college. In a study conducted by Martín (2014), however, findings revealed that Latina/o/x students may not always be aware of their cultural wealth that they could enact to navigate their educational journeys. Additionally, Martín highlighted that institutions seldom recognize and elevate the CCW that students bring with them to college. While students may not always leverage capitals strategically within their CCW to navigate college, it may be activated by serving as a protective factor when they experience microaggressions along their college journey (Acevedo & Solórzano, 2021). Nevertheless, participation in a college preparation program allowed the participants to understand how they could enact CCW throughout their postsecondary journey (Martín, 2014). Overall, findings in the literature revealed that Latina/o/x students depend on more than grit or aspirations to achieve postsecondary goals.

Methods

This chapter uses testimonio methodology to conceptualize the relationship between grit and community cultural wealth as well as between a school-prison nexus and college pathways. Testimonio serves to document the experiences of oppressed groups and challenge injustices (Booker, 2002). Cruz (2006) explained that testimonio connects "with a reader or an audience, positioning a reader or an audience for self-reflection. A reader or an audience member becomes complicit as an observer and as witness" (p. 31). The role of the researcher is to compile and translate "the story into written form" (p. 34). While other qualitative methods, such as oral history, position the researcher as someone who collects data, testimonio methodology positions the research participant as "a witness who is moved to narrate by the urgency of the situation" (Yúdice, 1985, p. 4). In other words, the research participants understand they experienced injustices and want to voice their concerns.

Data were derived from descriptive statistics available through the California Department of Education, the school website, and one oral history interview with a Latina PhD student, conducted in 2017. The data were gathered to triangulate whether the high school from which the participant graduated aligned with a NJCE context—the participant came from a low-income background, had parents who did not earn a four-year college degree in the United States, and identified as Chicana/Latina. She graduated from a high school in Southern California and attended a campus of the University of California (UC). She participated in a testimonio interview that lasted 70 minutes, where a small number of interview questions resulted in her reflecting on and sharing her lived experiences. The interview was transcribed and then coded deductively and inductively (Saldaña, 2015). The interview was coded deductively to examine the experiences with NJCE in K-12. The initial coding was followed by then analyzing the high school website and previous statistics served to triangulate the interview data. Deductive coding revealed the importance of having access to institutional resources.

Findings

First, Diana's experience indicated that the high school context affected her as a Latina student and her perceptions of educational possibilities and enrollment in college. Diana reflected on her experiences of educational inequities, control and policing, and high-stakes tests, which align with a NJCE context. A lack of academic preparation in K-12 contributed to Diana struggling with her academic transition to higher education. Nevertheless, enacting CCW allowed Diana to navigate college access and transition successfully. Although aspirational capital supported this process, it was the intersection of familial, linguistic, social, navigational, and resistant capital that maintained aspirational capital. Next, I elaborate on this process.

Navigating a New Juan Crow Education

Diana's experiences resonated with the elements present in a New Juan Crow in Education. In particular, Diana's high school represented a context that was characterized by educational inequities, high-stakes testing, and policing. She explained:

> In the 90s, there was a lot of anti-immigrant sentiments in California. ... I began to learn what it meant to be Mexican (in the U.S.), it meant that we weren't going to have services, we weren't going to have support, that we were going to be segregated, that we were going to be put in these classes that were lower, that our expectations would be lower. ... My high school was the worst.

As she recalled how she learned to identify ethnically, Diana noted the anti-immigrant sentiments and policies in California during the late 1990s, such as Propositions 209 and 187. The injustices she witnessed and experienced developed her social justice lens and abilities to understand that in the United States, individuals from Mexican background were simultaneously denied access to institutional resources and marginalized through segregation. Her social justice lens allowed Diana to rationalize that marginalizing policies and practices continued in K-12 schools, which resulted in low expectations of academic potential. The low expectations were also present spatially in the school; Diana detailed her high school context by noting that the physical building was "always abandoned" and felt like a "warehouse."

She elaborated on her high school context, which aligned with a NJCE context, by explaining the following:

> There's no love. ... It was always about controlling students, rather than to provide support or services and activities for students. if anything, those things were always taken away. ... Students couldn't wear certain things, certain colors. ... I experienced it in a different way because my style was more rebellious, you couldn't wear bracelets with spikes. ... School hadn't even started, I went to get my schedule. And the security guard called me over: "You, come here! Give me your bracelet!"

Diana highlighted the dehumanizing notions of control and policing, present in a NJCE context. Such schooling hindered the educational resources and enrichment opportunities present for students. Instead, students had to control the way they dressed and their behaviors. Such mechanisms of control and policing intersected with a loss of resources, which had negative implications for her, as an academically high-achieving student. By being in a school where they could not express their identities through their outward appearance, students received the message that they had to conform to a certain aesthetic because their authentic selves did not belong in school. The mechanisms of control resulted in students receiving clear messages that they do not belong in school as they are, that they could not be trusted to behave, and that they had to conform even when school was not in session. In other words, Diana could not be herself *and* be academically high-achieving in her school because she fit the profile of a behavior problem.

Document analysis confirmed Diana's depiction of her high school as under-resourced and over-policed. During the years she attended the school, about 65% of teachers were fully credentialed, 20% were university interns, 6% were pre-interns, and 9% had an emergency credential. In other words, about 35% of teachers in the school did not have the credentials to teach students. Furthermore, a recent review of the school website continued to mirror the discipline policies and practices to which Diana referred. The website stated that students must follow various behavioral standards and could be disciplined for: "defying the authority of adults," "wearing hats or any kind of headgear at school," and "any behaviors deemed inappropriate by the administrative team."

The discipline policies translated to 15% of Latina/o/x students and 28% of African American students being suspended during a school year. Out of 214 suspensions for African American students, 139 were for defiance and out of 183 suspended Latina/o/x students, 135 were for defiance. Thus, the majority of students were being suspended for defying the constructed definition of authority influenced by social expectations established for People of Color. The inequities present in academic resources and discipline likely influenced the graduation rates, where only 47% of incoming twelfth-grade students graduated during Diana's graduation year. Furthermore, in 2018, only 15% of Latina/o/x students met the UC/CSU course admission requirements upon graduation—just 5 out of 34 Latinas. The graduation outcomes informed the school being classified as a "persistently low-achieving school" by the Assessment and Accountability Division in the California Department of Education.

The NJCE context was compounded with teacher turnover rates. Diana explained that teachers leaving mid-year had direct implications for her learning opportunities and educational outcomes. She noted:

> One of my AP teachers left in the beginning of the first quarter. … it sucks for us because the rest of the year we had this AP class with substitutes. … I had another AP English teacher; she just left the first quarter too. … I had another teacher who left in the first semester. She left because she also got another job within the district … I had an AP Spanish teacher who

left to another state because the houses are cheaper and bigger … When they left, I would get another teacher who was a replacement who didn't have the experience or the credentials to teach so they were really easy, easy "A," or a substitute—and substitutes, we knew them by name because teachers, they would just leave us.

Diana recalled various instances when her teachers left mid-year due to professional and personal ventures. Within seconds, she listed four teachers leaving, three of whom taught AP courses. Diana's lived experiences resonated with other students who have to cope with high turnover rates.

Teachers leaving had direct implications for the educational opportunities available to students in such schools. For students who were in AP courses, in particular, a teacher leaving meant they would not be able to prepare for the exam. She recalled:

> For AP, it meant that we were not prepared but we could take [the exam].
> … We knew we weren't going to pass them. I mean, like the English, I still studied for it but we knew we weren't going to pass it could barely do good on the standardized tests, or the CAHSEE. I was two points away from failing it and I was supposed to be one of the best students, one of the "smart" students.

When recalling her educational experiences in high school, Diana highlighted the implications of numerous teachers leaving in the middle of the academic year. In alignment with a NJCE context, teachers leaving the school hindered the lack of academic preparation that students had to pass the AP exam and receiving college credit. Although Diana was excelling academically, she "barely" passed the high school exit exam. Her school maintained below-average passing rates where 49% passed the English exam and 32% passed the math portion, compared with 75% and 74% statewide, respectively.

Beyond test scores, teachers leaving mid-year resulted in students interpreting it as abandonment due to not being valued. Diana noted:

> It made us feel like "They don't care about us" like, "We are not important," or "Our academic success is not important." Because they would try to prepare us or stay here; they wouldn't leave us. It just created more resentment; I had a lot of resentment. I had a lot of rage, all of that definitely fueled it.

Students interpreted the teachers leaving mid-way through the academic year as educators disregarding their value. Her explanations rooted in students feeling like teachers did not care about their personal nor academic well-being. However, Diana provided insights into how students processed the emotional toll of feeling like teachers did not care; it created resentment and rage. Students understood that they were continuously left behind for better economic opportunities.

Enacting Community Cultural Wealth within New Juan Crow Education

Nevertheless, students resisted within the NJCE context of being devalued and disregarded by educators and deficit policies. Diana's explanation connected back to her earlier recounting of being segregated in English learning classes because of her ethnicity:

> I always had to fight to be in honors English instead of Puente.[1] I was enrolled as a freshman, and I was like, "I want to be in honors English, not Puente." She was like "No, Puente will help you get to college," I was like, "I know my A-Gs." The teacher came to convince me. ... It triggered me like, all the Latino kids get segregated into one class. ... They said the only way to get in honors was if a student dropped. During lunch that day, I told my friends and one said "I'll switch with you, I don't want honors, that's too hard." So, we went to the counselor. That's what I always had to do. That's the reason I was able to go to college. I always had to fight my counselors about my classes.

Diana exemplified that she enacted navigational, linguistic, and resistant capital to access a college-going pathway. Her resistant capital was rooted in the previous experiences that she had with being segregated in English learning courses; despite the culturally relevant pedagogical and college-going practices, she refused to be segregated into the Puente Program. Instead, she enacted navigational capital to access a college-going pathway in the honors program by using linguistic capital.

Nevertheless, Diana's navigational and resistant capital was rooted in social capital, given that she learned about the A-G course requirements in middle school through a college preparation program. She explained:

> I was in other programs in middle school, that taught me what to do, in terms of what classes to take to be not just eligible but competitive. ... I was in MESA, I was in EAOP. ... These programs would reiterate the same information. Like, workshops on A-G (admission requirements), this is a university, these are the Cal States, this is a community college, and these are the differences, these are the Ivy Leagues. I was learning all these different things that I had never learned. I knew I wanted to go to

the university. ... More importantly, they said all of you are going to this high school, and they basically told us the A-G, what classes they offered. I already knew what classes I needed to take. That's why I was I was able to advocate for myself when I went to high school because I had those tools with me.

Through the middle school college access program, Diana was equipped with accurate information and understood the context of her high school, which informed her abilities to self-advocate as a teenager in ninth grade. Her experience with the program serves as evidence for the need to supplement community cultural wealth with institutional resources that provide concrete opportunities, particularly in schools where the cultural capital is not brokered to future first-generation college students. Diana emphasized the detailed and repetitive explanations of information to contextualize college knowledge. Thus, by high school, she had the proper cultural capital and the confidence to self-advocate and enact both resistant and navigational capital to access the limited college-going opportunities available in her school.

Maintaining College Aspirations

Although Diana benefited from access to college information through college-going programs, she noted the need for continual validation throughout the college choice process, which strengthened her aspirational capital. She recalled her experience with asking the college counselor for a letter of recommendation to the Bill and Melinda Gates Millennium Scholars Program:

> When you don't have the confidence, you need someone to guide you, in terms of "You *can* do it." I remember when I was applying to the Gates scholarship, and I broke down because I was really looking forward to applying and hopefully be the first one in my high school to get this. I went to get my letter of recommendation, I had already asked for a letter, it was only going to be a matter of changing a few things here and there. But she was like "No, it's too late, I told you to that you need to tell me two weeks in advance." I understand she was preparing us for the real world, which is good. But in this case, when so few of us ever get to do any of this, I would think there would be a little more flexibility. ... I remember leaving her office crying; thinking, "There goes my opportunity, how am I going to pay?"

In this example, it is evident that Diana's aspirational capital did waver, it was not constant but instead fluctuated based on her the access to institutional resources. In her reflection, Diana also highlighted that despite her access to college information, she maintained financial fears and believed she would be unable to afford a college education.

The activation of Diana's social capital allowed her aspirational capital to continue. She explained that after being turned away from the counselor, a teacher offered support:

> I remember going to MESA (Math, Engineering, and Science Achievement) after school, and the teacher was like, "What's wrong with you?" and I told her. She was like, "Well, I'll recommend you … I'll write you a really good letter." I had never thought about asking her. And she did. I ended up getting it, I was the first one in my high school to get it and it was a really big deal. I remember the college and career counselor trying to get credit because she's supposed to and I was like, "No, you wouldn't even recommend me for this."

Diana's ability to maintain aspirational capital and meet her established goal to have been the first in her high school to be a Millennium Scholar entailed her not just remaining committed to a goal and maintaining passion for the goal but also having to find an alternative route when the career counselor proved to be an institutional obstacle she had to overcome. Through the support from an asset-based teacher, who understood the implications of the scholarship and Diana's context, she was able to earn the prestigious award. To note, the Gates Millennium Scholars Program evaluates applications using criteria from Kalsbeek, Sandlin and Sedlacek's (2013) noncognitive variables about college readiness—aspirational capital such as Diana's is vital for a person's long-term success, research shows. Also evident in Diana's experience was her enactment of resistant capital because she was not complacent in allowing the counselor to receive credit for her award.

Transitioning to College

Upon transitioning to college, Diana shared the postsecondary implications of a NJCE K-12 context, which she managed to negotiate by enacting CCW. Before transitioning to a UC campus, she participated in a summer bridge program, offered through the Educational Opportunity Program (EOP). She explained, "That summer bridge program, it did what all those other programs did for me in high school. … You get to live on campus, take some classes to give you a refresher on what (college) would be like." In her explanation of the summer bridge program, Diana understood that in middle school and high school, she had benefitted from various institutional programs. Similarly, the EOP summer bridge program prepared her with access to navigational and social capital that would benefit her as an undergraduate student. As indicated by the EOP website, the program aimed to provide "support and information" with the intent to "validate" students and foster "a sense of participation, belonging and empowerment." With EOP, Diana could have access to academic preparation, mentorship, and advising.

Just as important was that the program provided Diana access to develop new social capital because it represented a form of structural support. She elaborated:

> I created a family. ... That really helped me because I basically knew all the Black and Brown people on campus, first-generation, low-income. When I got to campus, I already knew who I was going to roll with, who were the people that I could relate to.

Given her participation in the two-week summer orientation program, Diana knew that she would begin at the UC campus with a cohort of peers who would provide both academic and social support as she transitioned to the UC campus.

Diana went from having to enact resistant capital in her high school classrooms by pointing out the lack of ethnic and gender representation in textbooks to enrolling in Ethnic Studies courses. She explained:

> I took courses in Chicano Studies and Black Studies and, finally, people were articulating all the things that I felt. ... I began to have a language to articulate my suffering, my pain, to describe what we had gone through. It empowered me in a way ... I (was) doing a lot of organizing on campus but also off campus, with families, I felt like, "Wow, so this is why I'm going to the university. I want to create change; I want to help my community. But what does that look like?" I started to find that and be surrounded by other people who were doing that and I felt inspired.

Upon transitioning to the UC campus, Diana explained that she benefited from her ability to apply her critical lens in Ethnic Studies courses. In these courses, she was validated that she belonged in college because her perspective was welcomed. Diana also strengthened her linguistic capital by being able to understand and explain the oppressive systems of power. This was helpful both in reflecting on her individual experiences and to engage her linguistic capital with community organizing. She was then able to apply the linguistic capital to her work as an activist both on-campus and off-campus. Collectively, these experiences strengthened her aspirational capital. She was able to be her authentic self in both the academic and activist settings. Providing a support to communities that aligned with her own community fueled Diana's aspirational capital and motivation to earn a bachelor's degree.

However, Diana's academic preparation in a K-12 NJCE context, such as the teacher turnover and lack of qualified teaching staff, hindered her post-secondary academic experiences. Given her inequitable access to educational opportunities, Diana was not prepared academically for college:

> I didn't have academic skills. I didn't have writing skills. I didn't have reading skills. I didn't have the basic skills that most students go into the university having. ... I remember we were talking once my first year. "How long did it take you to write your essay?" "Oh, it took me like nine hours, here and there throughout the week." And I was like "What?! It took me two weeks; it took me two weeks, working on it every day, for hours." I saw that disparity that I was going to have to work three times as hard as a student if I'm going to make it through the university.

Thus, implications of the educational inequities resulted in Diana having to invest more time and energy in her academics, in attempts to pass her courses. In comparison to other students, Diana knew she would have to invest more time and energy to meet academic standards. Time was a limited commodity because although Diana was able to access financial funds as a Gates Scholar, she had to work a graveyard shift to ensure that she could support herself financially. In this process, Diana enacted her resistant capital, as she knew that she would have to work harder than most students to keep up academically. However, doing so also meant sacrificing sleep and well-being, a notion that the concept of grit does not take into account.

Persisting in College

Diana explained that although her high school did not prepare her academically, she possessed a skillset that the majority of her peers lacked: "Even though I did not have academic skills, I had something they didn't have, which was critical thinking skills because it was really hard for some people to think critically about some things." Diana's critical thinking skills aligned with resistant capital because she enacted her abilities to challenge inequality. Diana attributed her critical thinking skills to her socioeconomic and ethnic background and the marginalization she experienced and witnessed in her community. She knew that interpreting readings and assignments critically was a strength rooted in her background, which other students often lacked.

When it came to persisting and navigating higher education, Diana credited the social and navigational capital brokered by EOP. She explained:

You get to sit down with the EOP counselors. Who you could relate to. … They were EOP counselors and they helped to start EOP, as a movement. They brought in with them something different. It was not just a job. When I would struggle with an essay question that seemed basic for everyone else but for a hood-girl like me, straight out of (my city), I didn't understand what the question was and I was too ashamed to ask my peers, I didn't want to seem stupid. I would go and ask, "What are they asking me in this question? I don't understand it." They would be like, "Let's break it down." And I was like, "Oh that's what they are asking, why couldn't they just say that?" (Laughing) They [professors] make it so complicated.

As an academically underprepared student, Diana was fortunate to have access to counselors who reinforced the notion that she belonged in college through the institutional resource of EOP. Because she received support from college outreach and preparation programs in middle school and high school, she knew that it would be essential to reach out for help to EOP counselors. Moreover, she was able to reach out because the counselors were culturally relevant and proactively built rapport with Diana, who knew she could be vulnerable with them. The program employed counselors who had a history of supporting and advocating for students. Therefore, Diana was able to enact social and navigational capital in her transition to higher education from a NJCE setting, which fueled her abilities to persist.

Discussion and Implications

Duckworth et al. (2021) operationalized grit to entail both passion and perseverance, or "commitment and goal striving" (p. 574). A key study used to develop the concept of grit comes from a study conducted by Cox (1926), using IQ testing to understand individuals classified as geniuses. At that time, however, IQ testing was developed as an instrument to uphold white supremacy and justify racist explanations around higher intelligence and abilities of white individuals. Choosing to base a concept on a racist foundation continues to reinforce white supremacy in contemporary times and ignores the NJCE contexts that Latina/o/x students likely have to navigate when maintaining a commitment to their goal.

Aspirational capital entails "the ability to maintain hopes and dreams for the future," which may seem in alignment with the commitment portion of grit. However, unlike grit, aspirational capital acknowledges that students will likely face institutional barriers. If a Latina/o/x student has to navigate a NCJE context, she will have to move beyond the policing and control discipline policies that intertwine with suspensions and dehumanizing experiences. This challenge is rarely shared by white students, who experience lower suspension rates than Latina/o/x in schools with the same discipline policies (Gray, 2019). Latina/o/x students who experience a NCJE context will have to maintain their commitment to a goal even after experiencing a loss of resources, including high teacher turnover rates, and having to self-advocate when an institutional agent represents a roadblock, such as the counselor at Diana's high school. Finally, a Latina/o/x student will likely have to negotiate academic under-preparation and financial hardships once they transition to college. None of the NJCE elements affect white students in the same manner, and none of those elements are accounted for when studying grit using the traditional operationalization. Ultimately, grit exists in a vacuum that does not account for inequitable access to resources and marginalizing practices.

Duckworth et al. (2021) contended that "remaining steadfastly committed to a goal should incline one to strive diligently to achieve it, and diligent striving toward a goal could for a variety of reasons bolster one's devotion" (p. 574). I developed Figure 6.1 to illustrate the process of bolstering devotion, where passion informs perseverance, which in turn "bolsters" perseverance, resulting in grit.

I reflected on Diana's testimonio to propose a model for critical race college retention and persistence, depicted in Figure 6.2, which challenges the simplistic, decontextualized, and meritocratic notion of grit. The model for critical race college retention and persistence acknowledges the importance of having access to institutional resources, when aspiring to earn a college degree. The model begins with acknowledging that Latina/o/x students enact CCW to establish college aspirations. They navigate marginalizing schooling structures with NJCE contexts, which entails various obstacles. The CCW continues with the student and when they have access to institutional resources, students can identify and circumvent obstacles.

The Depiction of College Retention and Persistence model acknowledges that while CCW can serve as a protective barrier against racial

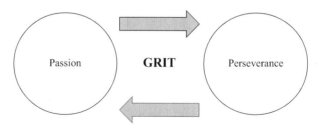

FIGURE 6.1 Illustration of grit process.

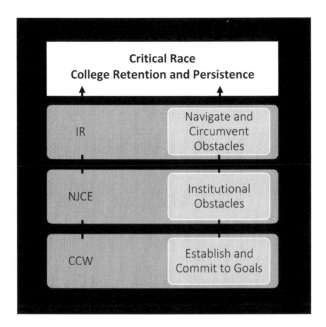

FIGURE 6.2   Depiction of College Retention and Persistence.

microaggressions (Acevedo & Solórzano, 2021), institutional resources—such as outreach programs, supportive counselors, summer bridge programs, and scholarships—are critical for students to navigate both NJCE and postsecondary contexts. In Figure 6.2, the black background represents the NJCE contexts that students likely navigate in high school (Acevedo-Gil, 2022; Madrigal-Garcia & Acevedo-Gil, 2016). Given the NJCE context, preparation and guidance in middle school become even more important for Latina/o/x students to maintain *and* meet aspirations. For instance, once in college, Diana was able to enroll in ethnic studies courses, which allowed her to channel her frustrations with inequities and injustices into scholar-activism. With the financial support of the Bill and Melinda Gates Millennium Scholarship, she did not have to endure harsh financial hardships like other Latina/o/x college students from low-income backgrounds (Muñoz & Rincon, 2015). Finally, by having access to culturally relevant EOP counselors, Diana was able to navigate the academic expectations that were incongruent with her previous schooling experiences. Diana's testimonio exemplifies the need to move beyond grit and instead understand a reciprocal connection between CCW, NJCE, and institutional resources for Latina/o/x student pathways to earn a college degree.

Conclusion

For some researchers, Diana's testimonio reflects a sample of n = 1 with no statistical significance. For others who engage in critically conscious approaches to research by acknowledging the implications of colonial and racist ideologies that U.S. schooling institutions were founded upon, Diana's testimonio exemplifies the insidious nature of white supremacy. Grit was developed in alignment with (Duckworth et al., 2007) and reframed (Duckworth et al., 2021) to be in alignment with IQ research (Cox, 1926) and depends on individualistic notions of meritocracy and commitment to success. Instead of focusing resources on developing individual student grit, educational leaders, educators, and researchers need to ensure Students of Color have access to equitable institutional resources to navigate and compensate for previous marginalizing policies and practices.

Note

1 The Puente Project aims to "increase the number of educationally underrepresented students who enroll in four-year colleges and universities, earn college degrees and return to the community as mentors and leaders to future generations." See: https://www.thepuenteproject.org/.

References

Acevedo, N., & Solórzano, D. G. (2021). An overview of community cultural wealth: Toward a protective factor against racism. *Urban Education*. https://doi.org/10.1177/00420859211016531

Acevedo-Gil, N. (2022). New Juan Crow education as a context for institutional microaggressions: Latina/o/x students maintaining college aspirations. *Urban Education, 57*(8), 1358–1386. https://doi.org/10.1177/0042085918805152

Advancement Project. (2010). Test, punish, and push out: How "zero tolerance" and high-stakes testing funnel youth into the school-to-prison pipeline. *Advancement Project.* http://www.advancementproject.org/resources/entry/test-punish-and-push-out-how-zero-tolerance-and-high-stakestesting-funnel

Alexander, M. (2020). *The new Jim Crow: Mass incarceration in the age of colorblindness.* The New Press.

Booker, M. (2002). Stories of violence: Use of testimony in a support group for Latin American battered women. In L. H. Collins, M. R. Dunlap, & J. C. Chrisler (Eds.), *Charting a new course for feminist psychology* (pp. 307–320). Praeger Publishers/Greenwood Publishing Group.

Conchas, G. Q., & Acevedo, N. (2020). *The Chicana/o/x dream: Hope, resistance, and educational success.* Harvard Education Press.

Contreras, F., & Rodriguez, J. (2021). Investing in educational equity for Latinos: How accountability, access, and systemic inequity shape opportunity. In E. G. Murillo Jr., S. A. Villenas, R. T. Galván, J. S. Muñoz, C. Martínez, & M. Machado-Casas (Eds.), *Handbook of Latinos and education* (pp. 103–113). Routledge.

Cox, C. M. (1926). *Genetic studies of genius: Volume II. The early mental traits of three hundred geniuses*. Stanford University Press.

Crenshaw, K. (1991). Mapping the margins: Identity politics, intersectionality, and violence against women. *Stanford Law Review, 43*(6), 1241–1299. https://doi.org/10.2307/1229039

Cruz, C. (2006). *Testimonial narratives of queer street youth: Towards an epistemology of a brown body* [Unpublished doctoral dissertation]. University of California, Los Angeles.

Duckworth, A. L., Peterson, C., Matthews, M. D., & Kelly, D. R. (2007). Grit: Perseverance and passion for long term goals. *Journal of Personality and Social Psychology, 92*(6), 1087–1101. https://doi.org/10.1037/0022-3514.92.6.1087

Duckworth, A. L., Quinn, P. D., & Tsukayama, E. (2021). Revisiting the factor structure of grit: A commentary on Duckworth and Quinn (2009). *Journal of Personality Assessment, 103*(5), 573–575. https://doi.org/10.1080/00223891.2021.1942022

Excelencia in Education. (2020). Latino college completion: United States. https://www.edexcelencia.org/research/latino-college-completion

Figlio, D. N. (2006). Testing, crime and punishment. *Journal of Public Economics, 90*(4–5), 837–851. https://doi.org/10.1016/j.jpubeco.2005.01.003

Gonzales, L. D. (2016). Revising the grounds for the study of grit: Critical qualitative inquiry in post-secondary education organizational research. In P. A. Pasque & V. M. Lechuga (Eds.), *Qualitative inquiry in higher education organization and policy research* (pp. 113–128). Routledge.

Gray, M. (2019). Blocking the bathroom: Latino students and the spatial arrangements of student discipline. *Critical Education, 10*(2). https://doi.org/10.14288/ce.v10i2.186371

Hochanadel, A., & Finamore, D. (2015). Fixed and growth mindset in education and how grit helps students persist in the face of adversity. *Journal of International Education Research (JIER), 11*(1), 47–50. https://doi.org/10.19030/jier.v11i1.9099

Huber, L. P. (2009). Challenging racist nativist framing: Acknowledging the community cultural wealth of undocumented Chicana college students to reframe the immigration debate. *Harvard Educational Review, 79*(4), 704–730. https://doi.org/10.17763/haer.79.4.r7j1xn011965w186

Judson, E., & Hobson, A. (2015). Growth and achievement trends of advanced placement (AP) exams in American high schools. *American Secondary Education, 43*(2), 59–76. https://www.jstor.org/stable/43694211

Kalsbeek, D., Sandlin, M., & Sedlacek, W. (2013). Employing noncognitive variables to improve admissions, and increase student diversity and retention. *Strategic Enrollment Management Quarterly, 1*(2), 132–150.

Kasprisin, L. (2013). The school-to-prison pipeline: A civil rights and a civil liberty issue. *Journal of Educational Controversy, 7*(1), article 1.

Kucsera, J. V., Siegel-Hawley, G., & Orfield, G. (2015). Are we segregated and satisfied? Segregation and inequality in Southern California schools. *Urban Education, 50*(5), 535–571. https://doi.org/10.1177/0042085914522499

Lee, H., Shores, K., & Williams, E. (2022). The distribution of school resources in the United States: A comparative analysis across levels of governance, student subgroups, and educational resources. *Peabody Journal of Education, 97*(4), 395–411. https://doi.org/10.1080/0161956X.2022.2107369

Liou, D. D., Antrop-González, R., & Cooper, R. (2009). Unveiling the promise of community cultural wealth to sustaining Latina/o students' college-going information networks. *Educational Studies*, *45*(6), 534–555. https://doi.org/10.1080/00131940903311347

Lopez, M. H., & Fry, R. (2013). *Among recent high school grads, Hispanic college enrollment rate surpasses that of whites*. Pew Research Center.

Lopez, S., & Hill, C. B. (2022). *Underrepresentation of Black and Latino undergraduates at America's most selective private colleges and universities*. Research Report. ITHAKA S+ R. https://sr.ithaka.org/wp-content/uploads/2022/03/SR-Report-Underrepresentation-of-Black-and-Latino-Students-at-Selective-Private-Colleges-and-Universities-20220330.pdf

Lovato, R. (2008, May). Juan Crow in Georgia: Immigrant Latinos live under a matrix of oppressive laws, customs and institutions. *The Nation*. https://www.thenation.com/article/archive/juan-crow-georgia/

Madrigal-Garcia, Y. I., & Acevedo-Gil, N. (2016). The new Juan Crow in education: Revealing panoptic measures and inequitable resources that hinder Latina/o postsecondary pathways. *Journal of Hispanic Higher Education*, *15*(2), 154–181. https://doi.org/10.1177/1538192716629192

Martín, L. (2014). *The hidden curriculum exposed: How one outreach program bridges cultural capital and cultural wealth for Latina/o community college transfer students* [Unpublished doctoral dissertation]. University of California, Los Angeles.

McClafferty Jarsky, K., McDonough, P. M., & Núñez, A. M. (2009). Establishing a college culture in secondary schools through P-20 collaboration: A case study. *Journal of Hispanic Higher Education*, *8*(4), 357–373. https://doi.org/10.1177/1538192709347846

Michel, R., & Durdella, N. (2019). Exploring Latino/a college students' transition experiences: An ethnography of social preparedness and familial support. *Journal of Latinos and Education*, *18*(1), 53–67. https://doi.org/10.1080/15348431.2017.1418356

Muñoz, J., & Rincon, B. (2015). Unpacking the layers: Financial aid and Latino high school students' postsecondary plans. In P. Perez & M. Ceja (Eds.), *Higher education access and choice for Latino students: Critical findings and theoretical perspectives* (pp. 38–54). Routledge.

Naff, D., Parry, M., Ferguson, T., Palencia, V., Lenhardt, J., Tedona, E., Stroter, A., Stripling, T., Lu, Z., & Baber, E. (2021). *Analyzing advanced placement (AP): Making the nation's most prominent college preparatory program more equitable*. Metropolitan Educational Research Consortium. https://scholarscompass.vcu.edu/merc_pubs/121/

National Student Clearinghouse. (2022). *Persistence and retention: Fall 2020 beginning postsecondary student cohort*. https://nscresearchcenter.org/wp-content/uploads/PersistenceRetention2022.pdf

Orfield, G., & Lee, C. (2007). Historic reversals, accelerating resegregation, and the need for new integration strategies. *The Civil Rights Project at UCLA*. https://civilrightsproject.ucla.edu/research/k-12-education/integration-and-diversity/historic-reversals-accelerating-resegregation-and-the-need-for-new-integration-strategies-1

Palardy, G. J. (2015). High school socioeconomic composition and college choice: Multilevel mediation via organizational habitus, school practices, peer and staff attitudes. *School Effectiveness and School Improvement, 26*(3), 329–353. https://doi.org/10.1080/09243453.2014.965182

Palencia, V., & Shakeshaft, C. (2022). All in?: Inequities in Hispanic access and enrollment in Advanced Placement. *Journal of Latinos and Education*, 1–13. https://doi.org/10.1080/15348431.2022.2057990

Pérez, D. (2014). Exploring the nexus between community cultural wealth and the academic and social experiences of Latino male achievers at two predominantly White research universities. *International Journal of Qualitative Studies in Education, 27*(6), 747–767. https://doi.org/10.1080/09518398.2014.901573

Rodriguez, J. M., & Arellano, L. (2016). The impact of high-stakes testing on Latina/o students' college aspirations. *Journal of Hispanic Higher Education, 15*(2), 113–135. https://doi.org/10.1177/1538192715627192

Saldaña, J. (2015). *The coding manual for qualitative researchers.* Sage.

Sokolower, J. (2012). Schools and the New Jim Crow: An interview with Michelle Alexander. *Rethinking Schools.* http://www.rethinkingschools.org//cmshandler.asp?archive/26_02/26_02_sokolower.shtml

Stovall, D. O. (2016). Schools suck, but they're supposed to: Schooling, incarceration and the future of education. *Journal of Curriculum and Pedagogy, 13*(1), 1–3.

Tierney, W. G., & Colyar, J. E. (2005). The role of peer groups in college preparation programs. In W. G. Tierney, Z. B. Corwin, & J. E. Colyar (Eds.), *Preparing for college: Nine elements of effective outreach* (pp. 49–68). SUNY Press.

Wald, J., & Losen, D. J. (2007). Out of sight: The journey through the school-to-prison pipeline. In S. Books (Ed.), *Invisible children in the society and its schools* (pp. 23–38). Routledge.

Welch, K., & Payne, A. A. (2012). Exclusionary school punishment: The effect of racial threat on expulsion and suspension. *Youth Violence and Juvenile Justice, 10*(2), 155–171. https://doi.org/10.1177/1541204011423766

Winerip, M. (2003, August 13). The "zero dropout" miracle: Alas! Alack! A Texas tall tale. *New York Times.* https://www.nytimes.com/2003/08/13/nyregion/on-education-the-zero-dropout-miracle-alas-alack-a-texas-tall-tale.html

Yosso, T. (2005). Whose culture has capital? A critical race theory discussion of community cultural wealth. *Race Ethnicity and Education, 8*(1), 69–91. https://doi.org/10.1080/1361332052000341006

Yúdice, G. (1985). Letras de emrgencia: Claribel Alegría. *Revista Iberoamericana, 51*(132), 953–964.

7

GRITTY ENOUGH?

African American Science, Technology, Engineering, and Mathematics (STEM) Student Success Factors

Melissa M. Mahoney

Why African American STEM Achievement Matters

The U.S. Bureau of Labor Statistics (2022) has projected 165.4 million STEM workers will be needed by 2030 to replace retirees and to meet the demands of the growing STEM (science, technology, engineering, and mathematics) industry. Not only do STEM fields offer significant employment prospects, but these jobs also pay more than other fields. Accordingly, as the demand for qualified STEM personnel continues to grow, STEM bachelor's degree attainment remains imperative (U.S. Department of Education, Civil Rights Data Collection, 2009). African Americans make up 5.8% of the STEM workforce (Cheeseman Day & Martinez, 2021), though they make up more than 13% of the U.S. population (U.S. Census Bureau, 2021b). This disproportionately low representation means fewer opportunities to take advantage of the STEM field's benefits and persistently lower representation in this important and highly publicized industry.

While higher education enrollment has decreased to 15.8 million students, National Center for Education Statistics (NCES, 2022a) predicts undergraduate enrollment at postsecondary institutions will increase to near pre-pandemic numbers—17.5 million in 2009 compared to 17.1 million in 2030. Moreover, enrollment among certain students of color has increased drastically between 2009 and 2020: Hispanic enrollment increased by 86%, Asian/Pacific Islander enrollment increased by 26%, and Black enrollment increased by 14% (NCES, 2022a). As a result, federally-funded initiatives have been implemented nation-wide to address the need for STEM bachelor's degree attainment among historically underrepresented and low-income

DOI: 10.4324/9781003332497-9

populations. Some program features include personalized academic counseling, financial support, early course registration, test preparation and graduate application review, and mentoring from STEM faculty, all while engaging with a group of like-minded peers. Despite programs being established, bachelor STEM degree attainment among African American and Latino students does not equal or surpass rates of their white and Asian counterparts (Hill & Green, 2007; NCES, 2022b).

Population Growth and the Diversity of the STEM Pipeline

With the Hispanic/Latino population being the fastest growing group in the United States (Gonzalez & Kuenzi, 2014; U.S. Census Bureau, 2021a), multiple initiatives focusing on the retention and STEM degree attainment for this population have been developed. According to the Bureau of Labor Statistics (2022), STEM occupations are projected to grow to near 11 million by 2031. Upon examining the diversification of the STEM pipeline, retaining all students of color in the STEM field is a necessity since it is a cost-effective way to increase the number of prepared STEM professionals in the field (Olson & Riordan, 2012). The programs also have the opportunity to increase the number of historically underrepresented populations in STEM professions.

STEM degree attainment boasts upward social mobility and job security while the STEM retention programs supporting students serve a dual purpose of expanding science ownership and diversifying the science-related questions we seek to answer. Vakil and Ayers (2019) described science as "both culturally-mediated and socially constructed," serving as humanity's collective intergenerational inquiry, rooted in our desires to explore the complex world around us, to push boundaries and make life-improving advancements. Despite such collectivist roots of STEM, scientific knowledge is presented absolutely rather than ever-evolving. This in turn has resulted in erasure of science's impacts on historically underrepresented, non-dominant populations, leaving accomplishments by diverse persons, largely ignored. When people of color participate in STEM, lines of inquiry and the impacts of STEM can shift to be more inclusive and representative.

Though STEM retention efforts assist students in persisting through their undergraduate programs, they may do so by teaching students of color to conform to white-dominated STEM classrooms and eventually offices, labs, and plants they will inhabit in their professional lives. As long as African Americans have been in these spaces, they have been subjected to discrimination and stereotype threat (Beasley & Fischer, 2012). Whether they are given lower-ranking tasks (e.g., cleaning equipment) or they are excluded from important conversations about research, the resulting alienation students experience does not go unnoticed. African Americans have identified STEM classrooms as chilly, especially in gatekeeper courses where faculty attempt to weed out unqualified students at an early phase (Hurtado et al., 2007). Contributions of African Americans in STEM have been ignored or over-written. Due to the complex history and diverse experiences of African American STEM students, the mere existence of these retention and student success programs is not enough. Ultimately, the focus of the retention programs and their implementation strategy matters, especially since programs run the risk of failing to adequately address the spectrum of pre-college and college factors of this population. In recent decades, psychologists have offered the grit scale as a framework to develop support programming around. With the introduction of grit as an indicator of achievement in one's academic goals (e.g., persistence through graduation), institutions have discussed how STEM retention programs can develop grit in their students.

What Is Grit?

Since arriving on the scene in 2007, grit has made a name for itself as a prominent predictor of success in professional and academic settings. It has since been a buzzword in academic and media discussions. From TED Talks to the *Harvard Business Review* to the mainstream television media, grit has made its way into our daily discussions. But what is grit? Grit can be defined as the prolonged passion and perseverance for a singularly important goal (Duckworth, 2016; Duckworth et al., 2007). According to these authors, when individuals are faced with adversity, boredom, and waning interest, gritty individuals remain committed to their goal(s). Duckworth et al. (2007) conducted multiple studies to investigate how achievement and cognitive factors such as IQ predict success. Studies included Ivy League undergraduates, West Point cadets, and National Spelling Bee participants. Study subjects completed the Grit Scale questionnaire, then their demographic and achievement information were analyzed. All in all, individuals with more grit achieved higher levels of education than their less gritty counterparts across two studies. A third study indicated undergraduates at highly selective institutions earned higher GPAs despite having lower SAT scores, suggesting grit trumps intellect. Grittier individuals made fewer career changes and grittiness proved to be a substantial predictor in program retention in two studies. However, these studies do not take into account structural inequities and other racialized life experiences. When examining the success factors of historically underserved students, and historical context must be examined rigorously, thus, the application of the grit scale calls for closer inspection.

Reliability of Grit Measures

When examining the influence of grit in academic and professional settings, a counter assessment of the measure's reliability is necessary. Who has the true authority to determine how much grit a student possesses? If we rely on the measure created by Duckworth et al. (2019), we run the risk of relying on a flawed self-assessment, leading to a subjective and potentially inaccurate account of the student's experience and capability. For starters, the Grit Scale questionnaire is a self-assessment which relies on respondents to recall situations from both recent and distant memory, rather than assessing objective facts. How can the measure account for respondents' inaccurate recollections? How does it account for respondents' biases? Take for instance a respondent whose challenges are normalized by their homogenous pre-college community (e.g., attending a lower-resourced high school). When asked to reflect on their response to challenges while growing up, they scored themselves lower on the grit scale because they examine their experience through their communal lens. They do not think of the obstacles they have overcome as particularly challenging, but rather commonplace. If placed in the same situation, a student from a different background, with little to no racialized experiences, might see these same challenges and their response to it as demonstrating more grit. The subjectivity of the self-assessment does not allow for true standardization or comparison among respondents.

Further expanding on the subjectivity of the grit measure, timing of data collection matters. The questionnaire cannot fully account for the depth and breadth of experiences that take place in a student's life and the researchers say as much. Depending on when the questionnaire is administered, students might only reflect on the challenges and scenarios within specific contexts such as academic, professional, or social settings instead of reflecting on experiences across all contexts. Each of these contexts holds equal importance in determining an individual's persistence, determination, and likelihood to succeed. Colleges and university employees have been charged with the holistic care of students; thus, the inconsistency of the measure makes grit a relatively unreliable and subjective non-cognitive factor that institutions should not rely heavily on.

Historical Context

It would be negligent to discuss African American STEM alumni without discussing the historic context which has prevented them from equitable achievement outcomes. Even after the Emancipation Proclamation, African Americans still did not fully regain their basic human rights, nor did they receive adequate or comparable education. In the Jim Crow Era, *Plessy v.*

Ferguson (1896) legalized separate but equal education, placing African American students in sub-standard classrooms with outdated, damaged materials (Allen & Jewell, 2002). With the introduction of Historically Black Colleges and Universities (HBCUs) through the Morrill Act of 1890, segregation in education legally persisted (Harper et al., 2009). HBCUs had been the only means for African Americans to engage in higher education (Allen & Jewell, 2002; Harper et al., 2009). Despite cases such as *Brown v. Board of Education of Topeka* (1954) setting precedent for integrated education, de facto segregation in education has persevered. Systemic racism in education covertly persists with de jure segregation at the institutional level wherein legislation allows for separate learning environments. Students of color and those from lower socioeconomic statuses continue to attend poorly resourced schools and districts (Baker & Robnett, 2012; Harper et al., 2009; Schneider et al., 2013), while the prevalence of white parents enrolling their students in private education has resulted in classrooms that lack the demographic makeup of the college setting (Balkin, 2002).

African Americans' historical legacy of exclusion from education, especially postsecondary and professional education, explains the disparate attributes they bring to academic settings compared to their white counterparts. Examining African Americans' triumph over oppressive and exclusionary systems gives new meaning to the experiences and knowledge African American students bring to the table. To better understand the achievement of African American students, this study utilized Harper's Anti-Deficit Achievement Framework (see Figure 7.1). Unlike other frameworks for students of color, Harper's seeks to investigate the experiences of African American males from an asset-based approach. The Anti-Deficit Achievement Framework centers on "[using] popular theories in uncommon ways" and offers an alternate lens through which the STEM experiences of successful African American males can be viewed (Harper, 2010, p. 71). Various psychological, social, and educational theories—e.g., social and cultural capital (Bourdieu, 1986), stereotype threat (Steele, 1997), attribution theory (Weiner, 1985), campus ecology theory (Moos, 1986; Strange & Banning, 2001), self-efficacy (Bandura, 1997), critical race theory (Harper et al., 2009; Solórzano & Yosso, 2002; Yosso, 2005), college retention (Swail et al., 2003; Tinto, 1993)—were used to identify three key stages in the STEM pipeline: (1) pre-college socialization and readiness, (2) college achievement, and (3) post-college persistence in STEM. Additionally, this research includes nine dimensions of achievement: (a) familial factors, (b) K-12 forces, (c) out-of-school college preparatory experiences, (d) classroom interactions, (e) out-of-class engagement, (f) experiential and external opportunities, (g) industry careers, (h) graduate school enrollment, and (i) research careers (see Figure 7.1). The broad themes and inquiries identified

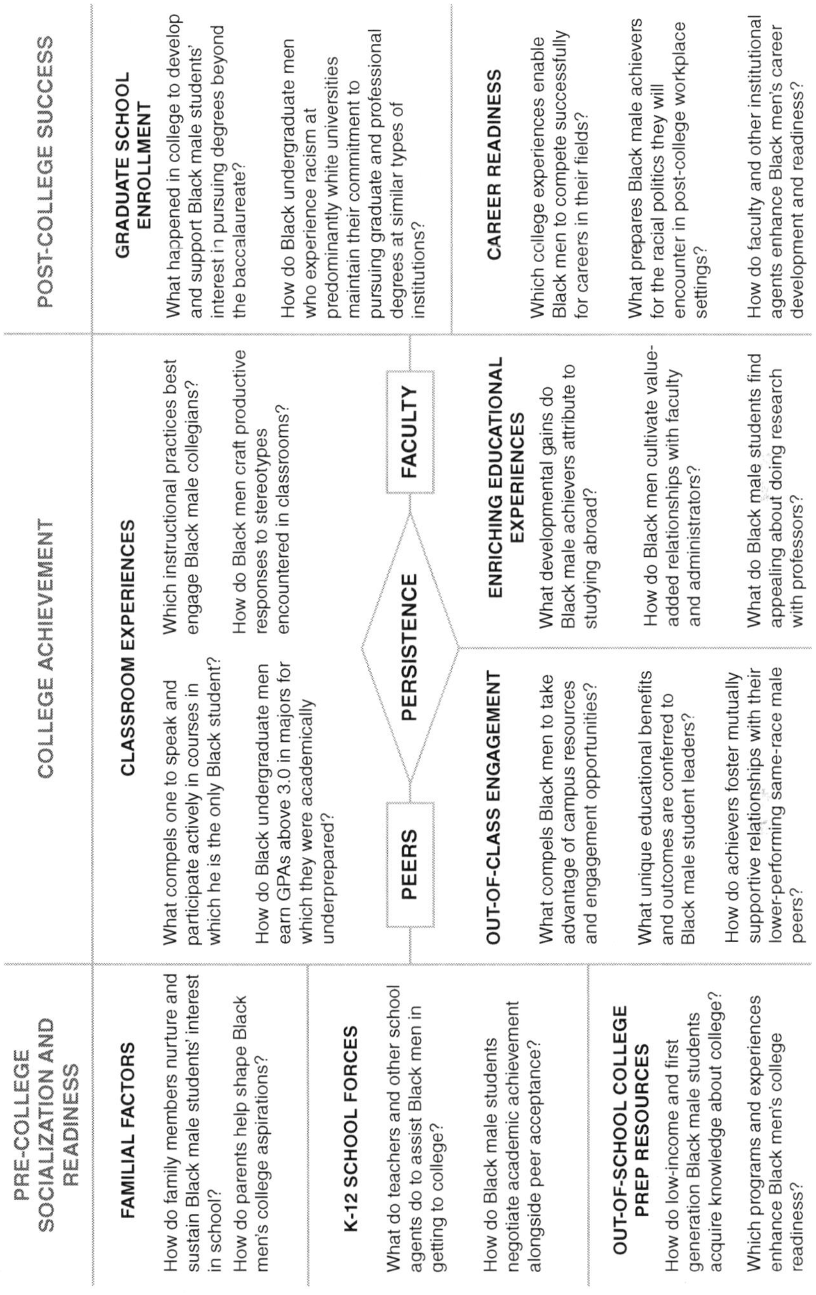

PRE-COLLEGE SOCIALIZATION AND READINESS

FAMILIAL FACTORS

How do family members nurture and sustain Black male students' interest in school?

How do parents help shape Black men's college aspirations?

K-12 SCHOOL FORCES

What do teachers and other school agents do to assist Black men in getting to college?

How do Black male students negotiate academic achievement alongside peer acceptance?

OUT-OF-SCHOOL COLLEGE PREP RESOURCES

How do low-income and first generation Black male students acquire knowledge about college?

Which programs and experiences enhance Black men's college readiness?

COLLEGE ACHIEVEMENT

CLASSROOM EXPERIENCES

What compels one to speak and participate actively in courses in which he is the only Black student?

How do Black undergraduate men earn GPAs above 3.0 in majors for which they were academically underprepared?

Which instructional practices best engage Black male collegians?

How do Black men craft productive responses to stereotypes encountered in classrooms?

PEERS ◇ PERSISTENCE ◇ FACULTY

OUT-OF-CLASS ENGAGEMENT

What compels Black men to take advantage of campus resources and engagement opportunities?

What unique educational benefits and outcomes are conferred to Black male student leaders?

How do achievers foster mutually supportive relationships with their lower-performing same-race male peers?

ENRICHING EDUCATIONAL EXPERIENCES

What developmental gains do Black male achievers attribute to studying abroad?

How do Black men cultivate value-added relationships with faculty and administrators?

What do Black male students find appealing about doing research with professors?

POST-COLLEGE SUCCESS

GRADUATE SCHOOL ENROLLMENT

What happened in college to develop and support Black male students' interest in pursuing degrees beyond the baccalaureate?

How do Black undergraduate men who experience racism at predominantly white universities maintain their commitment to pursuing graduate and professional degrees at similar types of institutions?

CAREER READINESS

Which college experiences enable Black men to compete successfully for careers in their fields?

What prepares Black male achievers for the racial politics they will encounter in post-college workplace settings?

How do faculty and other institutional agents enhance Black men's career development and readiness?

FIGURE 7.1 Harper's Anti-deficit achievement framework for research on students of color in STEM.

in the Anti-Deficit Achievement framework have been adapted to examine the collegiate and professional experiences of STEM African American males—both male and female. The following research questions guided the study and support the qualitative research methodology.

1 What do African American STEM students identify as factors contributing to their academic success at HSIs?

A How do faculty interactions and pedagogical practices influence academic success for these students?
B What campus services and extracurricular activities influence academic success?

Methodology

Participant Sample

Using a phenomenological approach, 12 individuals who identified as African American STEM alumni were interviewed. The phenomenological approach was used to help reveal the lived experiences of participants from a holistic perspective, while suspending the researcher's own preconceived ideas of the subjects' experience (Emiliussen et al., 2021). Participants were selected based on their successful STEM degree completion at one of the HSI-designated campuses within a large, public four-year comprehensive university system on the Pacific Coast. HSI-designated campuses were selected because of their rapid designation growth (Excelencia in Education, 2022). Additionally, the number of socioeconomically disadvantaged and historically underrepresented minority students they serve positively correlates with African Americans students' likelihood of enrolling at one of these institutions (Conrad & Gasman, 2015; Gasman et al., 2008; Terenzini et al., 1996). This particular comprehensive university system served as the setting for this study as more than 90% of the campuses meet the HSI designation criteria, making this university system one of the most highly HSI-concentrated systems in the country. Participants attended their respective institutions between 2008 and 2016. Full participant demographic information can be found in Table 7.1.

Data Collection, Instrumentation, and Analysis

Each participant engaged in a 60- to 90-minute one-on-one interview with the researcher. Interview questions in the standardized protocols were derived from Harper's (2010) Anti-deficit Achievement Framework. As previously outlined, this framework aims to identify sources of power instead of

TABLE 7.1 Participant demographics

Participant Name	Sex	CSU Campus	Academic College	Graduation Year
Aaron	Male	Fullerton	College of Engineering	2012
Alexandra	Female	Long Beach	College of Engineering	2010
Archer	Male	Dominguez Hills	College of Health, Human Services & Nursing	2015
Big Fear	Male	Pomona	College of Science	2015
Carlos	Male	Pomona	College of Science	2015
Chase	Male	Fresno	College of Engineering	2009
Gravin	Female	Pomona	College of Science	2013
Jack	Male	San Jose	College of Engineering	2008
Kara	Female	Pomona	College of Science	2016
Katie	Female	Dominguez Hills	College of Health, Human Services & Nursing	2016
May	Female	Fullerton	College of Health & Human Development	2013
Maya	Female	Fullerton	College of Health & Human Development	2016

identifying the downfalls to students' achievement. Examples of strengths include exploring what shapes Black students' college aspirations, how they craft productive responses to classroom stereotypes, how they foster mutually supportive relationships with lower-performing same-race peers, and what compels them to speak out in classrooms where they are the only Black person. Furthermore, it focuses on three key stages in a student's academic trajectory which are easily applied to the STEM pipeline as seen in Figure 7.1—(1) pre-college socialization and readiness, (2) college achievement, and (3) post-college persistence in STEM—and nine dimensions of achievement: (a) familial factors, (b) K-12 forces, (c) out-of-school college preparatory experiences, (d) classroom interactions, (e) out-of-class engagement, (f) experiential and external opportunities, (g) industry careers, (h) graduate school enrollment, and (i) research careers. This inquiry aimed to uncover which factors this population identified as contributing to their academic success at HSIs including faculty interactions, pedagogical practices, campus services, and extracurricular activities.

Data analysis involved qualitative interview transcription and multiple rounds of coding as described by Plano Clark and Creswell (2010). Coding gave way to a number of independent and overlapping themes (Patton, 2002). A summary of relevant findings is provided in the following section.

Researcher Positionality

Being a Black female who attended and worked at multiple HSIs, the researcher could identify with participants' sentiments and general feelings of isolation and discrimination. However, the researcher's field of study (sociology) and profession (higher education) put some distance between her and the study subjects. Additionally, the researcher attended a private undergraduate institution whose focus was on social justice and the promotion of diversity; her experiences were very likely different than many study participants. To gain a more thorough understanding of how African American STEM students may have experienced their chillier and/or more competitive STEM spaces, the researcher asked follow-up questions with the intention of closing knowledge gaps. Taking these identities into account, the researcher acknowledged her possible worldview biases in an attempt to suspend partiality from protocol development, data analysis, and research conclusions.

Findings

Each member of the study brought their own interpretation and self-reflection to the interview. In line with Harper's (2010) Anti-Deficit Achievement Framework, findings are described in three sections: pre-college factors of success, college experiences, and post-graduate involvements. Influences on students' success span decades and were present both in and out of the classroom.

Pre-College Factors Contributing to Student Success

In addition to having encouraging parents, participants made note of secondary school personnel who were instrumental in introducing them to STEM and helping them to explore the field. Students were equally impacted by the staff who highlighted STEM as a postsecondary discipline and career path. Many participants could easily recall teachers and counselors who made a difference in their academic careers. For instance, Archer and Jack recalled math and science teachers who wanted them to exceed expectations and enroll in advanced college preparatory STEM courses. When Archer indicated interest in becoming a firefighter, his counselor bluntly stated, "You could do way more. I'm looking at your grades here and you need to apply yourself." His academic achievements spoke for themselves and Jack's counselor wanted to make Jack aware of all the possible career paths, including the more rigorous ones. This counselor reignited Jack's childhood interest in medicine and created an academic plan with advanced STEM courses. Such advanced STEM coursework proved to be challenging for participants, but the intensity of the courses prepared them for postsecondary coursework in their respective STEM fields. In these two instances, the teachers' encouragement catalyzed the students' passion for STEM and opened the students to STEM engagement opportunities beyond high school. Likewise, Big Fear performed poorly during his junior year of high school but his science teacher knew of his potential and selected him to participate in an exclusive, cocurricular STEM program. Not only did this instructor believe in him, but he believed advanced STEM content might reignite Big Fear's passion for learning. Big Fear reflected on his experience in the co-curricular program through Kaiser Permanente:

> The program was offered to only 20 students out of 175 to 200 [applicants]. I was lucky enough to get picked. The teacher got to choose the students. She knew me and my ability for science. I was lucky enough for her to allow me to join that program and that honestly was one of the major reasons I decided to do a 180 [academically] and continue on with science. And what impressed me more about science, seeing what [the program] allowed us to see.

The science teacher encouraged Big Fear, and she provided him with an opportunity many of his peers did not receive—hands-on experience in the medical field. The exclusivity of the program, combined with the unique experiences and exposure to real world experiences allowed students to feel special and capable.

Similarly, other participants beamed about their exposure to STEM through out-of-class and after school programs such as math competition teams and robotics programs. Such co-curricular activities exposed Katie, Aaron, and Alexandra to STEM in a more engaging format compared to their in-class experiences. Math competitions allowed students to showcase their competitive side while engaging with a community of STEM achievers. In another example, Alexandra explained how her future in STEM was confirmed once she enrolled in a community college programming class at the age of 13: "I decided at that point I was going to take something math, science, computer science, or computer engineering-related when I got to college." Likewise, Katie's after school robotics club filled knowledge gaps created in her academic courses. Though participants' exposure to STEM varied by age, it encouraged a long-term passion for STEM and help students envision themselves in the field professionally.

College Achievement

Even as students progressed in their STEM degrees and encountered social, academic, or financial challenges, motivation to complete their degrees was two-pronged: the individual success and collective success. Participants knew their achievement was singular and representative of their individual efforts. However, most interviewees acknowledged their degree contributed to the perception of their social attributes, specifically their race and gender. Students noted being "the only Black person," "the only African American male," "one of few Black people," or "one of the only sistas" in their respective programs and even felt a responsibility to represent their race or gender well. Instead of allowing tokenism and compounding stereotyping to threaten their success, participants like Katie used this as motivation to succeed and increase the presence of African American students in STEM spaces. Obtaining her STEM degree would allow her to "be the voice to spread word, to spread knowledge, and to spread inspiration to [my] Black brothas and [my] Black sistas." Not only would she benefit from the degree for her own personal gain, but she would be a positive representation of what was possible for other African Americans, and especially African American women. Grit does not account for culturally relevant motivators such as community. The importance of representation and the communal prosperity rang true for many of the study participants.

In this regard, representation was a multi-dimensional motivator for many students. At a basic level, the students acknowledged their tokenism in STEM spaces and saw increasing their presence as beneficial long-term. However, how they were perceived in these spaces was equally as important. Achieving altruistic missions such as disproving stereotypes through tokenism and increasing representation, was a motivator for many. Participants considered overcoming tokenism and negative stereotypes in STEM classes as preparation for their graduate degree programs and/or their professional careers where they would continue to be one of few African Americans in their chosen field. First-generation college students and students from immigrant families felt a level of pressure to succeed. Upward social mobility was an immediate motivation, knowing of the sacrifices their family members and other African American scholars made for college to even be a prospect. There was a sense of pride associated with being able to repay the sacrifices of their elders.

Along with the idea of communal achievement, connecting with other African American STEM majors proved to be one of the most meaningful factors for alumni in this study. Often, participants were raised in communities with heavier concentrations of African Americans or Latino students. However, their college STEM classrooms did not mirror this demographic makeup. Thus, participants eagerly sought to create communities of their peers. The investment and commitment to college is not reflected in Duckworth and colleagues' conceptualization of grit. These communities were reproduced on college campuses in one of two ways: academic excellence practices or participating in formal STEM success and retention program.

Programmatic Support

Formal retention and student success programs were either grant-funded or university facilitated. On the other hand, student-led programs were run by students who were elected to campus leadership roles. The majority of these university-facilitated programs were open to students of all disciplines, yet they aimed to address the financial need, familial influence and social belongingness of the students they served. Student-led organizations, such as the Black Student Union (BSU) or National Society of Black Engineers (NSBE), made their purpose and target audience easily identifiable. The clear purpose served as a beacon, welcoming students to participate. These programs compensated for tokenism in the classroom by bringing the community together. While few study participants were involved in discipline-specific clubs, the national professional organization and university student success programs were ultimately held in higher regard. Unlike grit, which focuses on the individualistic traits impacting success, university-led and student-facilitated programs use the success of the community to overcome system obstacles.

Building Community

Though the reason for participants' lack of engagement with university-facilitated programs is unclear, most participants were unable to recall any programs offered by their institution at the time of the interviews. This brings the accessibility and marketing of university programs into question. The word-of-mouth advertising and explicit demographic audience in student-led programs like NSBE and BSU made them appealing. These two student-led programs helped students navigate the exclusive and predominantly white STEM classrooms, laboratories, and research teams; participants joined organizations like the NSBE, BSU, and even some major-specific clubs. Uniquely, NSBE served as a networking opportunity for African American students of all disciplines, despite originally being founded to serve engineers. As an added perk, members gained access to a national network of STEM enthusiasts of color and other Black professionals. Aaron's college experience was defined by what he learned outside of the classroom. True knowledge acquisition came from learning "how to forge relationships, experiences and things of that nature. Part of that got developed because I joined NSBE." For many students at Erin's school, joining NSBE was an expectation for Black students: "At our school it's kind of like a gang. We were only 3.5% Black at the school. If you're not an athlete, you are definitely joining NSBE." Whether networking was taking place for purely academic purposes or to expand one's professional network and future job prospects, students were aware they would need the community's support to succeed. Thus, making connections early and often was appealing. Similarly, discipline-specific programs allowed participants to engage with others interested in improving their grades. This shared goal speaks to the importance of community for students of color.

Formalized communities, student-run or university-facilitated, were not the only mechanisms for students to connect with peers, and some students opted out of formalized programs altogether, and sought less formal opportunities to connect with their peers. Participants used their belongingness to traditionally underserved groups (e.g., African American, female, first-generation, low-income, single-parent households, etc.) to identify and convene with like others and build community on campus. They collectively strategized how to pass gatekeeper and major courses, held one another accountable, and remained a core source of support for each other through graduation, all while keeping their collective and individual long-term goals in mind. These connections were made both in and out of the classroom and students relied heavily on the knowledge of their predecessors. Whether they were sharing textbooks, engaging in group study, or discussing components of a successful job or graduate school application, students leveraged the social capital of their college network to access resources. Even for students who had more egocentric, individualistic reasons for pursuing STEM, they remained aware they needed to rely on others to cross the finish line and found strength in their traditionally underserved identities. Where the grit scale focuses solely on the individual's qualities, participants leveraged communal resources to succeed. The collectivist orientation demonstrated by these participants is unaccounted for by the grit scale and subsequent programming efforts developed from it.

Representation and Confronting Negative Stereotypes

As demonstrated by the informal communities formed by students of color, not only were students' representations of Blackness in these exclusive STEM spaces, but they represented their gender/sex as well. Accordingly, being one of few African Americans in her computer science program, Kara noted the responsibility of needing to be "as close to the best as [she] could be." She knew she might be the only African American computer science student her peers and professors encountered in their lives. Not to mention, she might be the only African American female at future job sites. Kara felt the burden of paving the way for future generations. For students like Archer, being one of the few African American STEM students on campus made degree completion even more dire. He described the exclusivity of being a Black STEM student as "coming with a bit of 'machoness.'" The exclusivity of the role made him somewhat of a celebrity in his own right and he channeled this visibility into motivation. He liked the attention it came with and saw being one of only a couple African Americans in his classes as an opportunity to prove prejudices wrong. He would not allow himself to fail since he was representing his community in such a high-visibility role. For many participants, completing their bachelor's STEM degree was simply a means to an end. Even during their most trying moments, students derived strength from this long-term goal. Whether participants pursued a bachelor's in STEM with the hopes of becoming medical professionals, engineers, researchers or public health professionals, they knew a degree was a necessary part of their career path and did not let obstacles divert their attention or efforts.

By being token members of their racial communities in STEM spaces, students were presented with blatant and covert assumptions about Blackness. Participants confronted negative stereotypes both in and out of their STEM courses. General inaptitude or inability to succeed in the challenging field of STEM were stereotypes typically attributed to participants' race and/or gender. The participants were split on how they dealt with negative stereotypes. Some participants verbally confronted their aggressors in the moment, while others took a less confrontational approach and used academic performance as a means to dispel negative stereotypes. Carlos was working on a group project with a white student and she was impressed with his performance on the project. She remarked, "You know you aren't a normal Black person," suggesting that African Americans are not "normally" knowledgeable in STEM. Carlos responded, "Well, your perception of Black people is wrong." When Carlos' academic performance was not enough to speak for itself, he did not hesitate to correct those around him.

Likewise, Archer was not bashful about correcting peers when they made broad, incorrect generalizations about African American and low-income people in course discussions. As previously mentioned, representation was a strong motivator for many of the participants in this study. Though increasing representation paved a path for future African American STEM aspirants, it also served as a means for changing the dialogue and research of STEM. In a class conversation about public health, one of Archer's classmates blamed low-income communities for their own poor health outcomes. As someone who grew up in a lower resourced neighborhood, Archer took it upon himself to offer an alternate perspective to this common narrative:

You're going to see more liquor stores and other stuff like in [a low-income neighborhood] as opposed to if you go to [a wealthy neighborhood]— I'm going to see Equinox and 24 Hour Fitness and a hiking trail. I'm going to see all these different amenities. Don't tell me that! Those are some of the arguments I would have with people in these classes. They just don't know. First of all [they] can't even comment because they're scared to step into that [low-income neighborhood] anyway.

By educating his peers on their flawed conclusions, Archer dispelled the negative stereotypes about his community. While this direct approach was not related to his academic or professional outcomes, he felt he had a role to play as the only member of his community in this space. This underscores the impact of representation in STEM and dialogue and exposure challenges historically held "facts" should be reexamined.

In one of the most unique cases, Kara was diagnosed with a learning disability in college and noted feelings of isolation before, and especially after, the diagnosis. As a heavyset individual among a cohort of physically fit, current or former athletes, Kara never fit in with her athletic training peers. When Kara contemplated changing majors in her junior year, she "would go back to the pride aspect of wanting to complete [the athletic training degree] especially with my learning disability." Not only did Kara want the degree for herself, she felt she had something to prove as an individual with a disability on top of her other marginalized identities. Not only did she lack peer support, but she could not rely on her instructor either for support either. Faculty did not fully understand her disability and how it impacted her ability to retain information, resulting in comments like, "This is stuff you should have remembered from the second week." In her words, "I didn't feel comfortable talking to him and trying to get help from him. We didn't have tutoring or anything like that for these specific like classes, so I just avoided him." Carrying the burden of being a minority in her program, Kara was further taxed by both a learning disability and unsupportive faculty. Alienation and isolation left her exhausted by the end of her program. These stories exemplify how students of color exhibit perseverance in the face of challenges.

Faculty Involvement

Similar to experiences at the K-12 level, participants took note of faculty who nurtured and supported their personal growth and academic achievement. Contrarily, they recalled a stark difference between faculty who took little to no interest in their achievements and faculty who went above and beyond to provide individualized resources, unique pedagogical approaches, and memorable moments of challenge and support. The participants did not allow the lack of support or indifference from some faculty to overshadow the resources provided by supportive faculty.

While the grit scale does not account for structural and external factors such as the demeanor of instructors of staff, Gavin and Maya underscore the importance of the demeanor and pedagogical practices as being influential and memorable to their success. Instructors with credibility in the industry were given higher value because they provided examples beyond what the textbook could. As Gavin described it, the most impactful instructors were not the ones who had years of teaching experience. Instead, they took time to review material when the class performed poorly on tests and assignments. They also provided real-world experiences because they "literally just left their own office, they had their own practice, or had done business before, and then they came back after they retired." Similarly, Maya recalled professors who went out of their way to reinforce STEM concepts and engage students outside of class:

> They made effort to really get on the same level as their students and help us understand what they are trying to teach us. They made themselves available and I can only speak for [my school] but they made themselves extremely available. If there was something you did not understand, you can come to them, whether it's after classes or during office hours. I probably only went to office hours a handful of times when I couldn't grasp [a concept] and my classmates couldn't grasp it either. If I asked [my classmates] for help but they didn't get it either, I was going to go straight to the professor to get something I needed. I mean as far as my major is concerned, they were really passionate about the subject.

Not only does Maya speak to the availability and intentionality of her professors but she speaks to her resourcefulness in seeking out answers from multiple sources. These two students took ownership of their learning and academic achievement while acknowledging instructors who served as resources. These instructors did not put limits on the students' abilities; rather, they provided them with the tools they needed to be successful.

Post-Graduate Involvements

At the time of this study, the alumni were involved in a variety of professional and academic pursuits. Participants had an astounding 75% retention rate in the STEM field. More specifically, participants were working or pursuing advanced degrees in engineering, research, public policy, public health, and healthcare. Those who chose to pursue careers outside of STEM entered professions such as transportation security and finance while others had yet to start their professional careers and sought higher professional and postsecondary degrees outside of STEM. For participants providing direct services to the community, namely healthcare and public health, they noted altruism as a means of persisting through adversity. While he waited to apply to medical school, Big Fear worked as an in-home caregiver for elderly and disabled individuals. He noted how special this work was because it allowed him to help another human being who could not return the favor.

A consistent theme among participants was the idea of collegiate education being a means to an end. Participants were not shy about revealing the difficulties and rigor of their STEM courses and in hindsight they could see the value of the STEM degree following graduation. For example, Katie was disgruntled because college was a necessity to establish credibility in her field, but she noted how it helped her more than she had anticipated:

> I think if it wasn't for my education. I wouldn't be as confident as I am, honestly. I think education truly brought me a lot confidence and knowing that people know I know exactly what I'm talking about. I'm not just selling them fluff. I'm selling them real life.

Whether students remained in their respective STEM field after graduating or they pursued other professional avenues, none of them regretted pursuing a STEM degree. They knew the degree offered them flexibility and security. It was worth pushing through the challenges to obtain the degree.

Discussion

As students who were historically left out of higher education and STEM, African American students come with their own unique strategies of success. As mentioned by the blog Black and Smart (2015), African Americans have historically exhibited perseverance, resilience, optimism, confidence and creativity, thus, they don't need to have grit. The alumni in this study are no different. By the time these students arrive in college, they have surpassed the expectations, likely experienced racism and/or microaggressions, yet they remain committed to academic achievement in spaces where they have few examples to follow compared to white and Asian American counterparts. They have developed their own approach to dealing with structural obstacles and institutions should recognize, applaud, and encourage students to repurpose these methods in higher education as necessary.

The myth of grit can be prescriptive as tactics for developing grittier students fail to acknowledge students' previous methods of overcoming obstacles. Students may need the assistance of advisors, counselors, and respected staff members when connecting the dots between students' previous practices and their application collegiate scenarios.

Higher education is experiencing an enrollment and retention crisis "post-pandemic." With fewer students attending college, it is imperative that institutions provide a higher level of service to the students who choose to enroll—this includes personalized services and advising. Using the grit scale to tell students of color they are inadequate despite their academic achievement will not be acceptable. Instead of forcing the grit narrative onto these successful, determined, and committed students, resources can be spent helping students uncover how they have addressed obstacles in the past. With years of undergraduate and post-graduate coursework ahead of them, grades and high school graduation can seem like a means to an end for aspiring STEM high school students. Celebrating the accomplishment of completing high school and taking time to reflect on the challenges they have overcome is one way to reframe these experiences.

Pre-College Factors and the Application Process

College applications do not paint a holistic picture of the students under evaluation. Since students do not go through their K-12 education in a vacuum, structural factors should also be taken into consideration. Failing to take this into account may erase vital parts of students' experience and identity.

Ignoring such experiences can lead institutions of higher education to make incorrect assumptions about its student body. Just because students do not illustrate their grittiness the same way Duckworth and colleagues describe, does not make their experiences any less valid. Expecting students to portray their strength and perseverance in a high-brow, scholarly rhetoric is unreasonable. Instead, educators and higher education leaders can reconsider what questions are being asked in the application process—specific questions can focus on helping institutions learn more about the students they admit. This approach moves away from asking generic essay questions where students might anticipate a correct or incorrect answer to the questions. The approach intends to incite meaningful storytelling from students rather than a canned response to a deficit-based essay prompt. Applications should not be the only measure of students' qualification. Academic factors and performance tasks may still be essential for many schools, though questionnaires and performance tasks have serious limitations as detailed by Duckworth and Yaeger (2015). Learning more facts about students in the application process will require colleges and universities to be more intentional in designing programs that meet the needs of students from all backgrounds.

Learning and Growing in College

Students may not have the vocabulary to identify the strategies employed in their academic success, however, study participants regularly displayed components of grit (e.g., commitment, perseverance, resilience, etc.) while pursuing postsecondary degrees. Students remained steadfast in their pursuits as they verbally addressed racism and microaggressions and refused to allow financial setbacks and extreme circumstances to prevent them from achieving their goals. Additionally, students entered their respective STEM disciplines knowing they would be one of few (if not the only) African American students in the space. Despite the challenges of tokenism and a generally challenging curriculum, students kept their end goal in mind—and they did not need a grit-building program to do so.

School-sponsored student success programs gave students a leg up by providing them with key resources like funding, access to early registration, test prep materials, and designated staff or faculty members to connect with. One of the most valuable resources they gave students was a network of like-minded peers. Universities should reconsider how they brand university-facilitated programs and be more intentional with how and where they advertise such opportunities. While we do not expect that every student of color should apply for all programs they are eligible for, all students of color should be aware of the offerings and benefits of programs offered by their school.

As evidenced by students who did not participate in these student success programs and formal communities, students found a way to create community with like peers. Though identifying like-minded peers may have been more challenging for students who did not participate in these programs, they still connected with other African American STEM peers and attributed this social network to their overall success in the field. Universities can capitalize on the self-facilitated community building that students of color are already doing. Institutions can create more inclusive campus environments and show support by removing barriers such as restrictions on when the space can be used and by whom (e.g., allowing lay persons to use the spaces rather than limiting use to registered student organizations).

Opportunities for Further Exploration

While this study did not aim to assess the post-collegiate lived experiences of African American STEM students, information about participants' current professions was collected. An astounding 75% of the STEM alumni in this study continued on to STEM careers following graduation. Though 100% retention would be ideal, participants' retention in STEM far exceeds the national average of 28% retention (Cheeseman Day & Martinez, 2021). While participants' retention cannot be assumed to represent outcomes for most or all African American STEM degree recipients at HSIs, it does warrant further exploration. Thus, future research could benefit from a longitudinal analysis, following the journeys of these alumni. Specifically, future studies would investigate whether these individuals return to STEM careers and what factors participants identify as contributing to their decision to leave or remain in STEM.

Conclusion

Institutions must have curiosity and concern over how students will overcome obstacles in college and persist through degree completion. It is also reasonable for institutions to help students develop skills so they can overcome forthcoming adversity in college. However, institutions may miss the mark in determining who has grit and who needs to develop it when they rely on grit measures to determine a student's likelihood of success in college and beyond. Colleges and universities can best serve their students by getting to know learners individually. Additionally, they should refrain from blanketly assuming that students from historically underrepresented, underserved populations lack grit. As exemplified by reflections from the study sample, students can identify factors of motivation and how they contributed to their long-term persistence. They may not have the academic vernacular to describe the phenomena they experience, but they demonstrate long-term commitment and perseverance toward their passion.

Once institutions have a better understanding of the students they serve, they can better tailor resources and opportunities to meet the needs of these students. Students of color, especially African American students, have demonstrated passion and commitment simply by arriving at a postsecondary institution and in a STEM classroom. By asking them to participate in activities aimed at increasing their fortitude and resilience, programs continue to use a deficit-based approach and create a potentially negative relationship between the students and the institution by instilling doubt. Celebrating the accomplishments of these students and helping them to reframe and apply proven methods of persistence and success is a more meaningful use of staff–student and faculty–student interactions.

When considering how to prepare students for postsecondary success, institutions should be wary of the myth of grit as it influences who is labeled as a "student in need" and how subsequent interventions are administered. It is imperative that higher education take a holistic approach to student success, especially with students of color. Not only does ignoring these students' pre-collegiate experiences and success make them feel disregarded, it dismisses part of their identity altogether. As colleges and universities consider how STEM degree attainment positively assists these students after graduation (e.g., job security, upward social and economic mobility, etc.), they have a unique opportunity to prepare students for the challenges of the workforce by helping students to capitalize on their strengths in new environments.

References

Allen, W. R., & Jewell, J. O. (2002). A backward glance forward: Past, present, and future perspectives on historically Black colleges and universities. *The Review of Higher Education, 25*(3), 241–261. https://doi.org/10.1353/rhe.2002.0007

Baker, C. N., & Robnett, B. (2012). Race, social support and college student retention: A case study. *Journal of College Student Development, 53*(2), 325–335. https://doi.org/10.1353/csd.2012.0025

Balkin, J. M. (2002, Spring). Would African Americans have been better off without Brown v. Board of Education. *Journal of Blacks in Higher Education, 35*, 102–104. https://doi.org/10.2307/3133871

Bandura, A. (1997). *Self-efficacy: The exercise of control*. Freeman.

Beasley, M. A., & Fischer, M. J. (2012). Why they leave: The impact of stereotype threat on the attrition of women and minorities from science, math and engineering majors. *Social Psychology of Education, 15*(4), 427–448. https://doi.org/10.1007/s11218-012-9185-3

Black & Smart. (2015, April 22). Now I need to have grit? *Black & Smart*. https://blackandsmart.wordpress.com/2015/04/22/now-i-need-to-have-grit/

Bourdieu, P. (1986). The forms of capital. In J. Richardson (Ed.), *Handbook of theory and research for the sociology of education* (pp. 241–258). Greenwood.

Cheeseman Day, J., & Martinez, A. (2021, October 8). *STEM majors earned more than other stem workers*. Census.gov. https://www.census.gov/library/stories/2021/06/does-majoring-in-stem-lead-to-stem-job-after-graduation.html

Conrad, C., & Gasman, M. (2015). *Educating a diverse nation; Lessons from minority-serving institutions*. Harvard University Press.

Duckworth, A. (2016). *Grit: The power of passion of perseverance*. Scribner/Simon & Schuster.

Duckworth, A. L., Peterson, C., Matthews, M. D., & Kelly, D. R. (2007). Grit: Perseverance and passion for long term goals. *Journal of Personality and Social Psychology, 92*(6), 1087–1101. https://doi.org/10.1037/0022-3514.92.6.1087

Duckworth, A. L., Quirk, A., Gallop, R., Hoyle, R. H., Kelly, D. R., & Matthews, M. D. (2019). Cognitive and noncognitive predictors of success. *Proceedings of the National Academy of Sciences, 116*(47), 23499–23504. https://doi.org/10.1073/pnas.1910510116

Duckworth, A. L., & Yaeger, D. S. (2015). Measurement matters: Assessing personal qualities other than cognitive ability for educational purposes. *Educational Researcher, 44*(4), 237–246. http://www.jstor.org/stable/24571517

Emiliussen, J., Engelsen, S., Christiansen, R., & Klausen, S. H. (2021). We are all in it!: Phenomenological qualitative research and embeddedness. *International Journal of Qualitative Methods, 20*(1). https://doi.org/10.1177/1609406921995304

Excelencia in Education. (2022, March 1). *HSI 2020–2021: Excelencia in education*. HSI 2020–2021 | Excelencia in Education. https://www.edexcelencia.org/research/series/hsi-2020-2021

Gasman, M., Baez, B., & Turner, C. S. V. (Eds.). (2008). *Understanding minority-serving institutions*. SUNY Press.

Gonzalez, H. B., & Kuenzi, J. J. (2014). *Science technology, engineering and mathematics (STEM) education: A primer* (CRS Report No. R42642). http://stemedcaucus2.org/wp-content/uploads/2015/01/CRS_R42642_STEMPrimer.pdf

Harper, S. R. (2010). *Black male student success in higher education: A report from the National Black Male College Achievement Study.* University of Pennsylvania, Graduate School of Education: Center for the Study of Race and Education.

Harper, S. R., Patton, L. D., & Wooden, O. S. (2009). Access and equity for African American students in higher education: A critical race historical analysis of policy efforts. *Journal of Higher Education, 80*(4), 389–414.

Hill, S. T., & Green, M. M. (2007). Science and engineering degrees, by race/ethnicity of recipients: 1995–2004 [Table]. https://www.nsf.gov/statistics/2015/nsf15321/

Hurtado, S., Han, J., Sáenz, V., Espinosa, L., Cabrera, N., & Cerna, O. (2007). Predicting transition and adjustment to college: Biomedical and behavioral science aspirants' and minority students' first year of college. *Research in Higher Education, 48*(7), 841–887. https://doi.org/10.1007/s11162-007-9051-x

Moos, R. H. (1986). *The human context: Environmental determinants of behavior.* Krieger.

National Center for Education Statistics (NCES). (2022a). *Postbaccalaureate enrollment.* U.S. Department of Education, Institute of Education Sciences. https://nces.ed.gov/programs/coe/indicator/chb

National Center for Education Statistics (NCES). (2022b). *Undergraduate enrollment.* U.S. Department of Education, Institute of Education Sciences. https://nces.ed.gov/programs/coe/indicator/cha

Olson, S., & Riordan, D. G. (2012). Engage to excel: producing one million additional college graduates with degrees in science, technology, engineering, and mathematics. Report to the president. *Executive Office of the President.*

Patton, M. (2002). *Qualitative research and evaluation methods.* Sage.

Plano Clark, V., & Creswell, J. (2010). *Understanding research: A consumer's guide* (2nd ed.). Merrill/Pearson Educational.

Schneider, B., Broda, M., Judy, J., & Burkander, K. (2013, Winter). Pathways to college and STEM careers: Enhancing the high school experience. *New Directions for Youth Development, 2013*(140), 9–29. https://doi.org/10.1002/yd.20076

Solórzano, D. G., & Yosso, T. J. (2002). Critical race methodology: Counter-storytelling as an analytical framework for education research. *Qualitative Inquiry, 8*(2), 23–44. https://doi.org/10.1177/107780040200800103

Steele, C. M. (1997). A threat in the air: How stereotypes shape intellectual identity and performance. *American Psychologist, 52*(6), 613–629. https://doi.org/10.1037//0003-066x.52.6.613

Strange, C. C., & Banning, J. H. (2001). *Educating by design: Creating campus learning environments that work.* Jossey-Bass.

Swail, W. S., Redd, K., & Perna, L. (2003). *Retaining minority students in higher education.* Jossey-Bass.

Terenzini, P. T., Springer, L., Yaeger, P. M., Pascarella, E. T., & Nora, A. (1996). First-generation college students: Characteristics, experiences, and cognitive development. *Research in Higher Education, 37*(1), 1–22. https://www.jstor.org/stable/40196208

Tinto, V. (1993). *Leaving college: Rethinking the causes and cures of student attrition.* University of Chicago Press.

U.S. Bureau of Labor Statistics. (2022). *Employment in STEM occupations.* https://www.bls.gov/emp/tables/stem-employment.htm

U.S. Census Bureau. (2021a). *Improved race and ethnicity measures reveal U.S. population is much more multiracial.* https://www.census.gov/library/stories/2021/08/improved-race-ethnicity-measures-reveal-united-states-population-much-more-multiracial.html

U.S. Census Bureau. (2021b). *QuickFacts United States* (V2021) [Data set].

U.S. Department of Education, Civil Rights Data Collection. (2009). State and National Estimates [Data file]. http://ocrdata.ed.gov

Vakil, S., & Ayers, R. (2019). The racial politics of STEM education in the USA: interrogations and explorations. *Race Ethnicity and Education, 22*(4), 449–458, https://doi.org/10.1080/13613324.2019.1592831

Weiner, B. (1985). An attribution theory of achievement motivation and emotion. *Psychological Review, 92*(4), 548–573. https://doi.org/10.1037/0033-295X.92.4.548

Yosso, T. (2005). Whose culture has capital? A critical race theory discussion of community cultural wealth. *Race Ethnicity and Education, 8*(1), 69–91. https://doi.org/10.1080/1361332052000341006

8

BEYOND THE BOOTSTRAPS MENTALITY

The Fallacy of Grit as a Measure of Success for Black and Latine/x Men in California Community Colleges

Julio Fregoso

When grit models are applied to higher education, measures for understanding success are often limited to the ways in which *traditional* college students develop, learn, and acquire knowledge through a college education (Deil-Amen, 2015). Measures of grit inherently prioritize the fetishizations of Black and Brown perseverance, while ignoring the need to delve deeper into the historical legacies of racism, settler colonialism, imperialism, and capitalism (Almeida, 2016). Such traditional college student norms for measuring learning implicitly use the experiences of white male college students as benchmarks for achievement, development, and college student success (Deil-Amen, 2015). Attempting to apply this schema to Black and Latine/x community college male enrollers in California Community Colleges (CCCs) inherently comes from a deficit-based perspective. Deficit perspectives within the context of college students' success refer to the attempts to ascribe blame on respective communities, families, and other marginalized social identities, most prominently race, gender, and socioeconomic status, for the (potential) academic problems students face (Peck, 2020). These deficit perspectives, masked under student support and development, have detrimental impacts toward college completion, sense of belonging, and validation (Long, 2016). In this chapter, I extend the conversation on Black and Latine/x men in California Community colleges beyond the bootstrap explanations of their transfer aspirations.

Grit, as a measure applied toward college students, inherently relies on greater agency (and onus) of students overcoming obstacles (Almeida, 2016), leaving them with feelings of failure. Essentially, scholars inadvertently position themselves to not only see why students are *failing* or

DOI: 10.4324/9781003332497-10

successfully meeting educational outcomes but move forward with findings that may create spaces catered toward fostering resilience in students, when institutions, state, and federal stakeholders should be brought into the conversation to advance student-centered policies (Almeida, 2016). The difference at hand is that racialized minorities, often Black and Latine/x students, face challenges that are rooted in their marginalized identities; one notable identity is in relation to their socioeconomic status. Students' *inability* to *pull themselves up by their* bootstraps may be treated as students not trying hard enough and being at fault for their difficult experiences navigating college. When in fact, structural inequality, poverty, and racism are typically what constrain racially minoritized college students from achieving successful outcomes like degree completion, persistence, and experiencing a healthy campus climate (Hurtado et al., 2012).

Segregation and Structural Inequality

The history of U.S. racial segregation and other policies explicitly passed to create structural inequality is inherently intertwined to concepts of grit. Forceful segregation due to housing policies became inextricably linked to the demographics of local schools which resulted in unequal funding and distribution of resources (Rothstein, 2017). These efforts by the U.S. federal government underwrote the mass development of racially exclusive white suburbs and other landscapes that forced Black and Brown bodies away from white families and the resources available to them (Rothstein, 2017). Such U.S. federal policies on segregation map a *geography of opportunity* that either hinders or bolsters opportunities for people pursuing postsecondary education. A geography of opportunity speaks to both educational and occupational attainment through a geographical perspective that analyzes the level of proximity a person has between workforce and educational experiences in relation to their place of residence (Dache-Gerbino, 2018; Turley, 2009). These studies demonstrate how race and racism shape the spaces that people of color occupy; specifically, it can be used to demonstrate not only the educational inequity one sees through resource allocation of K-12 schooling but also the type of postsecondary opportunities that are within geographic region of such landscapes. Research has also demonstrated that students of color who reside in low-income areas are part of a geographic *mismatch*, in that they do not reside in areas where postsecondary education systems are readily accessible (Reyes et al., 2019). In the case of California, University of Southern California (USC) is an example of a prominent university whose student body does not match that of its most proximate surrounding neighborhood.

Champions of grit concepts see perseverance from disparate circumstances as key points for research discussions and implications (Almeida, 2016); yet their perspectives disregard the history of marginalized students and how their upbringing is often tied to structural inequalities and racial segregation practices. This is a crucial point that proponents of grit measurements almost entirely miss (Almeida, 2016). The lack of consideration of such troubling history in turn influences deficit narratives of students of color; particularly those from low-income backgrounds into thinking that the level of success acquired by marginalized folks is strictly tied to the amount of *push through* marginalized students embark on. Given how the racial and ethnic critical mass begin their postsecondary journeys at the community college (Barney & Higginson, 2017), a brief history on the development of community colleges and how it is also intertwined with grit and racist U.S. policies merits further discussion.

Community Colleges

Considering the spatial displacement and need for technical training in lieu of racist redlining practices, the rise of community colleges was pivotal in the educational and technical training for racially minoritized peoples (Long, 2016). Expansion of the community college system throughout the 20th century also amplified concerns over issues on access and equity for racial and ethnic minorities who needed support the most (Bahr & Gross, 2016).

Long's (2016) work on racism in the community college provides context on the prevalence of racism and its negative impact on student success outcomes. Long (2016) posits that educational racism is manifested overtly or covertly within a system of educators (and education as a whole) that may benefit or inhibit/punish a student contingent upon their race, culture, ethnicity, socioeconomic status, and/or ideologies. This inherent systemic bias presents itself as a construction of expectations, rules, and cultural norms based on an educational model that benefits the middle- and upper (white)-class state of mind in America. College learning and discourse has long had its roots planted in modes of instruction that are not reflected in ways that non-white students learn (Deil-Amen, 2015). Examples include diverse learning environments (Hurtado et al., 2011), peer support and engagement (Hall et al., 2011), and collectivist orientations (Arevalo et al., 2016). This type of learning as capital is passed down from one generation to the next, allowing future (privileged) students to embody the college student norm while first-time (often low-income or minoritized) college students have not gotten such opportunities to learn and excel at rates similar to their white peers. The expectations, cultural norms, and rules also coincide with the ideology behind the traditional college student, where such students hold the economic, cultural, and social capital needed to be successful within a higher education setting (Deil-Amen, 2015). Such students are considered prepared for college level rigor and have the privilege to be enrolled full-time (Deil-Amen, 2015), which further provides several advantages to disproportionately white and wealthier students via private tutors, academic coaches, and attendance at high schools with support structures to facilitate college access. Further, there are racial differences in how and why students transfer from a community college to four-year institutions (Crisp & Nuñez, 2014). It is with these systemic biases that faculty, staff, and other personnel serve their students (Deil-Amen, 2015; Long, 2016).

These practices reinforce deficit ideologies by positioning community college personnel to reward behaviors they may qualify as "grit," such as taking initiative, raising their hand in class, seeking faculty during office hours, or any other construction around *hard work* that appeases the implicit biases of staff, faculty, and administration (Long, 2016). This study, as the findings will discuss, appears to show that Black and Latinx males often attempt to emulate efforts deemed as successful college habits, yet find it difficult to meet the educational outcome under investigation.

The purpose of this study was to explore what factors shape, sustain, or inhibit the transfer aspirations of Black and Latinx men enrolled in California Community Colleges (CCC). The study challenges concepts of grit by reminding scholars, practitioners, and policymakers of the inapplicability of grit toward such demographics. Community college enrollers not only must have navigational prowess but must have their needs of support met by postsecondary institutions.

A Landscape of Black and Latine/x Male College Enrollers

African American and Latine/x men have proportionally low enrollment in higher education, compared to white male college students. For example, The National Center for Education Statistics (NCES) noted that in the Fall of 2021, African American males represented 4.2% of all students enrolled in Title IV degree-granting institutions (NCES, 2023). In addition, Latine/x men had a postsecondary enrollment of 7.4% for the 2021–2022 academic year (2023). This demonstrates the significantly low enrollment of such men of color, since the NCES reported an enrollment of 20.5% for white male students that same year (2023). Within a CCC context, 34.4% of enrollers were male in Fall of 2022; within this subpopulation, 3.2% were Black men, over half of male enrollers were *Hispanic* (California Community Colleges Chancellors office [CCCCO], 2023) at 55%, while white men represented 15.7% of Fall 2022 enrollment. In addition to the low enrollment rates of men of color in colleges and universities in the United States, research on the students show patterns of low performance while enrolled in their respective institutions (Cuyjet, 2006; Harper, 2009; Harris et al., 2010; Hilton et al., 2012; NCES, 2014; Noguera, 2003; Palmer & Strayhorn, 2008; Sáenz & Ponjuan, 2011).

It is only recently that these men of color have been granted audience and attention from scholars. Despite their low enrollment numbers across different segments of higher education, African American and Latine/x males are disproportionately overrepresented in California Community Colleges (CCCs) in comparison to other public sectors of higher education; of the 216,685 Black undergraduates enrolled in higher education in California in 2018, 64% were at community colleges, 9% at CSUs, and 3% at CCCs (Campbell et al., 2021). Unfortunately, out of the 73% of African American men and 70% of Latine/x males enrolled in CCCs, less than one quarter of each student population actually returns within the following two to five years of enrollment (Campaign for College Opportunity, 2014; Vasquez-Urias, 2012; Wood & Turner, 2011) This rate of persistence within CCCs from such student populations demonstrates the disparities and call for attention amongst such men of color enrolled at the CCC level.

Research on the experiences of men of color (Cooper, 2010; Laanan, 2003; Martinez & Cervera, 2012) have consistently documented the difficulty that African American and Latine/x males have in navigating their early college years. Yet, researchers rarely examine such marginalized groups' degree aspirations in a context of social justice and equity that moves further away from traditional notions of grit.

Theoretical Framework

The framework chosen to guide this study is Carter's (2002) model for degree aspirations for Black and Latine/x students in higher education; this framework uses decades of research that is still useful in the new millennia, given the ever so present completion gaps and systemic racist practices still at play across colleges and universities in the U.S. Carter argues that students' degree goals and similar college-going behaviors are derivative from their own individual circumstances and backgrounds and their socializing influence to make such institutional choices. Within the framework, Carter discusses a myriad of variables that predict degree aspirations of such student populations. Carter's framework is stratified into four main categories offering several predictor variables within such areas: pre-college characteristics; initial aspirations and goals; institutional experiences/external-to-campus involvement; and academic achievement. This framework helps measure degree aspirations for Black and Latine/x students, and men of color in particular, given the depth and breadth of concepts and experiences to consider for such a demographic. Because Carter's work considers the systemic barriers set in place that impact Black and Latine/x students today, having this model as a guided framework can serve well to challenge concepts of grit that fail to truly understand community college men of color.

Degree Aspirations for Men of Color

Literature on the degree aspirations for men of color in a postsecondary context is scarce. The literature that is available, observes personal goals (Wood & Palmer, 2013a), the likelihood of transferring (Wood & Palmer, 2013b), and institutional characteristics relevant to aspirations in community colleges (Vasquez-Urias, 2012). Although the literature does not observe educational aspirations of men of color specifically, findings from such studies may provide important experiences conducive to men of color's degree aspirations at two-year colleges.

Degree aspirations for African American men. Wood and Palmer (2013a, 2013b) highlight findings of Black men's personal and transfer goals that may be conducive to positive student outcomes. Scholars found that the need to be a community leader, having children, and being financially well off were significantly greater amongst African American men than other males observed in the study (Wood & Palmer, 2013a). In regard to transferring, African American men reported greater likelihood to enroll in four-year colleges as their exposure to diversity increased (Wood & Palmer, 2013b). Secondly, their willingness to seek help from on-campus services was a significant factor related to a greater response rate of one's willingness to transfer (2013b).

Degree aspirations for Latine/x males. Since literature on degree aspirations for Latine/x males is scant, Laanan's (2003) study on two-year degree aspirations provides the appropriate background to preface the discussion for educational aspirations of Latine/x males. The author's findings state that one's precollege experiences, along with their initial goals may shape their level of aspirations leadings toward eventual degree attainment (Laanan, 2003). The limited research that discusses Latine/x male aspirant issues in higher education (Sáenz & Ponjuan, 2008) does so in a four-year university setting, but does not include the experiences of Latine/x male aspirants in two-year colleges, further highlighting the need to investigate this issue.

Carter's (2002) model reminds consumers of research of the importance of taking into consideration the structural and systemic barriers Black and Latine/x men face while navigating higher education. For Black and Latine/x men enrolled in community colleges, a more nuanced discussion on their experiences while enrolled at the CC merits further discussion, given the literature above that highlights the entanglement of oppression that these students face as enrollers in two-year higher education systems (Long, 2016).

Finances and Family

Research has demonstrated the deterring effects that socioeconomic status may have on students of colors' degree and career goals (Carnevale & Strohl, 2013; Carter, 2002; Dougherty, 1987; Dowd et al., 2008; Laanan, 2003; O'Connor, 2009; Strayhorn, 2010). O'Connor (2009) noted that African American and Latine/x students enrolled in community colleges were in the lowest average socio-economic status (SES) strata in comparison to other student populations. A typical reported pattern found in O'Connor's study is that Latine/x students with a lower-than-average SES also reported having larger families within one household than any other student population participating in the study. Such family size and low SES may be related to students' lower degree aspirations than their higher-SES student counterparts, since having the added stressors of financially supporting other family members puts these students at a disadvantage (O'Connor, 2009).

"Traditional" Students

Traditional age students (usually aged between 18 and 24) in postsecondary education tend to have higher degree aspirations whether enrolled at either two- or four-year colleges than non-traditional age students (Carter, 2002). The longer Black men delay their enrollment in a community college setting, the more difficult it may become to navigate their initial experience on campus, influencing their current attrition rates (Wood & Palmer 2013a; Wood & Williams, 2013). These experiences are not meant to state that being older in itself is what perpetuates attrition rates; rather, the way non-traditional students are perceived by support staff and faculty is what contributes to their attrition (Deil-Amen, 2015; Lundberg et al., 2018). These experiences are not limited to Black men, as Latine/x men and most other older adult community college students face similar institutional barriers that contribute toward their attrition and belonging on campus (Steinhauer & Lovell, 2021).

Career Goals

Men of color benefit from career development through student–faculty interactions (Mejia-Smith & Gushue, 2017; Wood & Newman, 2017). These efforts of course must be grounded in equity and social justice to minimize deficit ways of thinking to allow for men of color to gain career development while having their racial, ethnic, and cultural identities affirmed (Lundberg et al., 2018; Mejia-Smith & Gushue, 2017). When faculty or staff engage in deficit ways of thinking (even when trying to support minoritized youth), they often engage in microaggressive strategies that impact the way students perceive themselves (e.g., race lighting in academic settings) (Mejia-Smith & Gushue, 2017; Wood & Newman, 2017). These experiences are often treated as a career barrier by students in which they perceive these events to minimize their potential in economic mobility and advancement (Mejia-Smith & Gushue, 2017; Wood & Newman, 2017). When they do receive career support and are validated, the support received in turn impact intrinsic motivators to either pursue more formal learning or strengthen knowledge on a particular trade (Lundberg et al., 2018; Mejia-Smith & Gushue, 2017).

Institutional Contexts

African American and Latine/x men in the community college report negative college experiences that involve alienation premised on racial isolation and other forms of marginalization (Perrakis, 2008). These experiences have led to feelings of loss of their kinship connection toward their culture and cultural identity development, including a collectivist orientation, as it conflicts with the dominant, individualistic culture that encourages repression of identities along with the lived experiences of marginalized students (Deil-Amen, 2015; Long, 2016; Lundberg et al., 2018; Perrakis, 2008). These cultural disconnects are associated with high levels of attrition from the community college (Liang et al., 2011; Perrakis, 2008).

External Context

The external contexts surrounding men of color throughout their postsecondary experience may influence their engagement within community colleges (Harris & Wood, 2013). External influences such as work and family responsibilities are salient forces that not only have an impact on degree aspirations, but overall ability and opportunities to excel in higher education (Carter, 2002). Working was conducive for student success when such work aligned with their educational or professional pursuits (Wood et al., 2011) yet the tipping point for work responsibilities deterring students from their career and academic pursuit is working 25 hours or more per week (Wood et al., 2011). Given the number of students who work full-time or multiple jobs, this is a structural challenge for students seeking to transfer.

Family responsibilities have been known to deter student enrollment for African American and Latine/x males while enrolled in higher education (Harris & Wood, 2013). African American and Latine/x men were more likely to leave after their first year in college, due to family responsibilities (Harris & Wood, 2013). This likelihood of leaving due to family obligations became less likely during these men of color's third year at the college (Harris & Wood, 2013). This also highlights the needs men of color have during the early years in college, which may be critical to their continued enrollment. Students' motivation to succeed in order to impress family members was noted to be pertinent toward student success (Strayhorn, 2010; Wood, 2011). This level of motivation increases students' satisfaction within their program of study, specifically among Black males (Strayhorn, 2010). Wood (2011) notes that such motivation is carried through as a family responsibility for African American males. Black males defined family members as children, immediate family members, non-biological family members, and ancestors (Wood, 2011).

Academic Achievement

There have been several response programs that attempt to mediate the issue of high attrition rates of African American and Latine/x males. Generally speaking, programs considered *high-impact practices* have been known to not only close completion gaps but contribute toward a more fruitful-academic experience for marginalized students (Long, 2016). High-impact practices like learning communities or experiential learning are found to contribute to their academic and career development in ways that also affirm their racial and ethnic identities (Barnes & Piland, 2011; Garcia, 2019, 2023; Garcia, 2023; Jehangir, 2009; Laanan et al., 2013).

Overall, there are many structures in place and at play that ultimately hinder the experiences of Black and Latine/x men enrolled in CCCs. From system barriers rooted in historical legacies of U.S. racism and marginalization, toward microaggressive and deficit ways of *supporting* men of color, to mis-guided measurements of Grit that appear to not contextualize these experiences for better informed implications for research. The literature highlighted above is a reminder on how short-sighted and dangerous concepts of Grit can be toward Black and Latine/x men.

Method

Sample

Secondary data from the Community College Survey of Student Engagement (CCSSE) were analyzed from a three-year cohort ending in 2014 (2012–2014). The survey was developed by the CCSSE department housed at the University of Texas, at Austin, and serves as a benchmarking instrument in efforts to establish national trends regarding educational performance and practice by technical and community colleges. CCSSE administers their survey to students in randomly selected, credit courses in participating community colleges. Disaggregated data with no unique student or institutional identifiers were requested for African American and Latine/x men enrolled in California's community colleges. The total sample size analyzed for this study was 6,279: 5,216 of survey respondents identified as a "Hispanic, Latino, or Spanish" males, and the remaining 1,063 identified as African American or Black, Non-Hispanic. There were no additional inquiries to CCSSE on including multi-racial students that have identified as both Black and Latino, which is a noted limitation in this study.

CCSSE Benchmark Scores

CCSSE benchmarks provide ways to compare performance of similar institutions in attempts to identify areas for improvement and provide implications that promote best practices to further engagement strategies for students in participating institutions. The CCSSE benchmarks scores used in this study are active and collaborative learning, student effort, academic challenge, student–faculty interaction, and support for learners.

Measures of Degree Aspirations

For this study, *Transfer Aspirations* is measured by students' self-reported data from the CCSSE instrument that transferring to a four-year college or university was seen as their primary goal for attending a California community college. This was measured by an item that asked students to clarify if transferring to a "4-year college or university" was "not a goal," a "secondary goal," and lastly a "primary goal." Recodes were created into two values where the dependent measure was dichotomous, in that reference value was "not a goal" and "secondary goal" while comparing the higher value of "primary goal." Combined values of "not a goal" and "secondary goal" were still less than that of "primary goal." This was part of the reason the researcher chose to combine such values together. The overarching research was to ensure that analyses considered comparisons in those that originally identified community college as being an educational setting that can prepare them for transfer. Thus, isolating transfer to a four-year college or university as a "primary goal" was necessary to consider for this study.

Analyses

Descriptive statistics, exploratory factor analyses, and logistic regressions were the primary modes of analyses for this study.

Descriptive Statistics

The following table highlights important descriptive statistics that paint a portrait of Black and Latine/x enrollers at the time the CCSSE instrument was implemented across 2012–2014.

The table provides a detailed insight into the transfer aspirations of Black and Latine/x community college enrollers in California, segmented by demographic characteristics. The data suggests that a higher proportion of non-first-generation enrollers (78.7%) considered transferring to a four-year college or university as their primary goal, compared to first-generation enrollers at 72.7%. Interestingly, the results also reveal that a significantly higher percentage of non-traditional college students aged 25 or over (59%) had transfer aspirations as their primary goal compared to traditional college students aged 18–24 (77.9%). Additionally, enrollers who used spousal or parental support (77.3%) or grants and scholarships (74.9%) to finance their education had transfer aspirations as their primary goal at a higher rate than those who did not. The data also suggests that institutional size played a role with a higher percentage of enrollers in smaller colleges (32.9%)

TABLE 8.1 Demographic Distribution by Transfer Aspirations: Black and Latine/x CA Community College Enrollers

Transfer Aspirations to a Four-Year College or University	Transfer: "Not a Goal" or "Secondary Goal"	Transfer: "Primary Goal"
Non First-Gen Enrollers	21.3%	78.7%
First-Gen Enrollers	27.3%	72.7%
Traditional College Students (ages 18–24)	22.1%	77.9%
Non-Traditional College Students (ages 25 or greater)	41%	59%
Did not use Spousal or Parental Support to Finance CC	29.8%	70.2%
Used Parental or Spousal Support to Finance CC	22.7%	77.3%
Did not use Grants & Scholarships to Finance CC	27.6%	72.4%
Used Grants & Scholarships to Finance CC	25.1%	74.9%
Institution size: Small	32.9%	67.1%
Institution size: Medium	29.9%	70.1%
Institution: Large	26.9%	73.1%
Institution: Extra-Large	23.6%	76.4%

Note. This table explains demographic characteristics distributed by participants' responses toward transferring to a four-year college or university. As it is with this table and the overall analyses for this study, both Black and Latine/x men from this study were aggregated.

choosing not to prioritize transfer aspirations compared to those in larger colleges (23.6%). Overall, the findings highlight the importance of considering demographic characteristics such as generational status, age, financial support, and institutional size when designing programs and interventions aimed at increasing the transfer aspirations and success of Black and Latine/x community college enrollers in California.

Exploratory Factor Analyses (EFA)

Exploratory factor analyses were completed on items pertaining to one survey question from the CCSSE instrument. The survey question ran for an exploratory factor analyses asked, "How much has your experience at this college contributed to your knowledge, skills, and personal development in the following areas?" Cronbach's alphas were also calculated to determine the reliability of the factor listed in Table 8.2. The factor held a Cronbach's alpha of .846 with individual factor item loadings at .500 or greater, which meets the threshold on the reliability and validity of the data reduction technique as one continuous scale to measure overall quality of experiences contributed by the college (Cronbach, 1951). These select variable items with interrelationships found with an EFA data reduction technique were computed as single variables to be considered for the logistic regression analyses ran for African American and Latine/x males. Scales were calculated to have one continuous value that can uniquely capture a particular sentiment or theme found with items merged together through a data reduction technique. All items under the "Academic, Cognitive, and Technical Skills" factor that was used as a variable to control in the model are indicative of what scholars consider successful habits to obtain in college (Hurtado et al., 2012). See Table 8.2 for a complete descriptive table on items used for the factor.

Logistic Regression

Logistic regression analyses were completed in efforts to test the application of Carter's (2002) theoretical framework on African American and Latine/x males' associate degree and transfer aspirations, within California community colleges. Using a forced entry method for logistic regressions, variables were assessed within one block to see levels of predictive ability between the predictive variables and the study's categorical outcomes (transfer aspirations). One logistic regression model was computed to observe the effect that the predictor (independent) variables had on dependent (categorical outcomes) variables.

TABLE 8.2 Factor Loading and Reliability for Independent Variables by All Respondents

Item[a]	All Responses
	n = 6,279 (alpha) Factor Loading
Academic, Cognitive, and Technical Skills	*0.846*
Experiences contributing toward writing clearly and effectively	0.784
Experiences contributing toward speaking clearly and effectively	0.779
Experiences contributing toward thinking critically and analytically	0.773
Experiences contributing toward acquiring a broad general education	0.647
Experiences contributing toward solving numerical problems	0.619
Experiences contributing toward using computing and information technology	0.565

[a] Four-point scale: Very little = 1 to Very much = 4.

Findings

Twelve variables held statistical significance for Black and Latine/x males aspiring to transfer to a four-year college or university. Items that fall under specific categories for Carter's (2002) model for degree aspirations are detailed in Table 8.3). Any Odds Ratio (OR) less than 1 is considered to be a negative predictor that detracts students from wanting to aspire toward transferring to a four-year college or university, while any OR with a value of 1 or greater are experiences that contribute odds in Black and Latinx students wanting to transfer to a four-year college or university. For this study, the author used more than one categorical value as a reference when examining change in odds for the institutional size variable once controlled for in the model. When examining "small" institutions (less than 4,500 students), all other categorical references of "medium" (4,500–7,999)- and "large" (8,000–14,99)-sized institutions that students may have chosen were used as references in the same variable for "small" and vice versa for other institutional measures (Roman et al., 2010). This was done to not only examine how enrollment in one institution impacted odds of the outcome in comparison to the other, but to truly examine if enrollment in one particular institution did fair better than others combined. Additionally, one can minimize the potential for multicollinearity and other collinearity diagnostics if institutional measures were parsed in the binary.

Pre-College Characteristics

Findings from this study note that pre-college characteristics were salient in predicting the transfer aspirations of Black and Latine/x men at CCCs. Students who were flagged for being first-generation and reported their age to be 25 or greater had their odds significantly detracted in aspiring to transfer to a four-year college or university. In addition to reporting their identity salience and how it impacts their education, their ways to fund higher education expenses proved to increase odds in aspirations. For men of color in this study, greater odds toward transferring from the community college were found when they reported to receive financial support from their parent(s) or spouse, receive gift-aid (aid that does not need to be repaid), and use their own personal income to support community college expenses.

Academic Achievement and External/Institutional Indicators of Success

The bulk of the variables situated around Carter's (2002) model meant to assess climate experiences in relation to their outcome were significant in predicting odds for transfer. Institutional characteristic variables had two significant predictors that detracted odds of the outcome, one of which was students' self-reported enrollment in "small" community college institutions; another detailed their experiences in community college and the impact it had on having clearly defined career goals also served as a deterrent for transfer aspirations. The academic, cognitive, and technical skills factor along with CCSSE benchmarks of Academic Challenge, Student Effort, and Support for Learners also contributed to ways in which students aspired toward a four-year college or university degree. All but *Support for Learners* were positive predictors of transfer aspirations (see Table 8.3).

Discussion

Transfer Aspirations

Carter's (2002) model for degree aspirations for Black and Latinx male students accounts for potential systemic barriers that may detract students from aspiring to earn a degree or transfer to a four-year college or university. Though such work has accounted for structural forces at play, this framing

TABLE 8.3 Logistic Regression Results Predicting Transfer Aspirations to a Four-Year College or University

Predictors	Transfer Aspirations		
	Odds Ratios	std. Beta	p
Pre-college Characteristics (Carter, 2002)			
First-Generation College Students (ref: non-first gen students)	0.72	0.85	***
Non-traditional students (ref: "traditionally aged" students)	0.49	0.73	***
Personal Income (ref: Not a source of income)	1.22	1.08	**
ParentsORspouse $$ (ref: Not a source of income)	1.20	1.1	**
Grants & Scholarships (ref: Not a source of income)	1.27	1.13	***
External Contexts (Carter, 2002)			
Employer Contributions (ref: Not a source of income)	0.96	0.99	
Withdrawing due to Lack of Finances (ref: Not Likely to Withdraw)	1.07	1.03	
Withdrawing due to Working Full Time (ref: Not Likely to Withdraw)	0.84	0.92	*
Withdrawing-Caring for Dependents (ref: Not Likely to Withdraw)	0.89	0.94	
Institutional Characteristics (Carter, 2002)			
Institutional Size: small (ref: All non-"small" institutions")	0.47	0.87	***
Institutional Size: medium (ref: All non-"medium" institutions)	0.84	0.95	
Institutional Size: large (ref: All non-Large institutions)	0.92	0.96	
Initial Goals & Academic Achievement (Carter, 2002)			
Goals: Change Careers (ref: Not a Goal)	0.80	0.9	**
Academic, Cognitive, Technical Skills factor (continuous)	1.14	1.1	*
Academic Challenge (continuous)	1.01	1.29	***
Student–Faculty interaction (continuous)	1.00	1.02	
Student Effort Benchmark (continuous)	1.00	1.11	*
Support For Learners (continuous)	0.99	0.88	**

*$p<0.05$., ** $p<0.01$., *** $p<0.001$.

while keeping grit concepts in mind may signal a different interpretation of results highlighted in Table 8.3). A grit narrative might focus on pre-college characteristics and use first-generation and non-traditional student controls to indirectly highlight men of color's *inability* to aspire toward higher learning. These measures could indirectly point toward stereotype threat and mis-interpretation of their intrinsic motivators and passions for pursuing higher education (Almeida, 2016). If findings from these studies are viewed in such light, other controls like *Support for Learners* will be taken as a signal that Black and Latinx men choose not to reciprocate and be open toward academic support in college, when greater marginalizing forces are actually at play. Nurturing and sustaining educational aspirations for Black and Latinx students takes intentionality on behalf of the institutions (Garcia et al., 2019). Findings from this study not only demonstrate that CCCs have been a disservice to Black and Latine/x enrollers, but additionally imply navigating in a manner filled with implicit biases that contribute to the barriers and achievement gaps in comparison to their white student counterparts. These same harmful biases also parallel concepts of grit.

Non-Traditional College Students

Students who identified as first-generation, along with being 25 years or older (coded as "non-traditional students"), detracted odds from aspiring to transfer to a four-year college or university. Carter's (2002) framework discusses that a parents' low educational levels may have an impact on African American and Latine/x students' degree aspirations. Black and Latine/x males' report on age being a negative factor on transfer aspirations (for all participants and individual unique regressions) corroborates with prior research (Hagedorn et al., 2002; Perrakis, 2008; Wood & Williams, 2013) discussing the difficulties non-traditional students of color have in persisting throughout community college. Scholars have stated that the longer men of color delayed their enrollment within a community college setting, the more difficult it had become for such males to navigate their pathway through two-year institutions (Hagedorn et al., 2002; Perrakis, 2008; Wood & Williams, 2013). This of course, has nothing to do with them being physically older males, but more so with the implicit biases that men of color face that are indirectly tied to measures of grit. Grit proponents base their claim on intrinsic motivation and ways that institutions can support and further nurture such *passion* for students in ways that support their holistic development in college (Almeida, 2016). When institutional agents (Stanton-Salazar, 2011) are exposed to nontraditional student enrollers, their perceptions of life stages may have a greater influence when devising strategies for support that are biased. A popular way these biases manifest is

through the *cool out* method of community college enrollers in which institutional agents might challenge students' aspirations and *assist* them with
actions that are perceived to be more *doable*. One popular example is dis-
couraging students from transferring to a four-year college or university,
choose a specific vocation that requires less education, or even redirect them
away from the community college experience altogether (Jain et al., 2011).

Grit measures often surround notions that students must develop a har-
monious passion based on their willful participation in activities that bring
one's happiness (Almeida, 2016; Stoeber et al., 2011). This in turn is not
only contradictory toward Carter's (2002) discussion around intrinsic
motivators for Black and Latinx students, but inherently leaves the onus on
students for having *minimal* motivation to transfer to a four-year college or
university, when there are structural forces at play that warrant further discussion, and especially, when Black and Latine/x male, first-generation or
non-traditional students are less likely to aspire toward transferring to a
four-year college or university.

Financing Educational Costs

The bulk of variables measuring educational costs were positive predictors
supporting transfer aspirations (see Table 8.3). For covering educational
costs, grants and scholarships appeared to be the strongest predictor that
supported transfer aspirations for Black and Latine/x males. Students who
come from lower-SES backgrounds have a greater likelihood to apply for
(and receive) federal financial aid (in the form of grants and scholarships),
contributing to their educational experiences and overall degree aspirations
(Wood & Palmer, 2013a). Students can have passions, motivators, and *gusto*
to want to further themselves educationally; yet when structures and support systems are not in place to increase retention and solidify educational
gaps, educational goals and aspirations may be difficult to come to fruition.

Withdrawing from College

Black and Latine/x men reported that they were less likely to have transfer
aspirations as the likelihood to withdraw due to working full-time increased
in student responses. This finding held significance across regressions ran
for all participants and individual sub-populations within the dataset. Wood
et al. (2011) noted that employment maintained a negative perception of
community college students of color if such work limited their educational
pursuits.

Being pulled away from college because of work can be easily interpreted
as students placing less value in a college education in comparison to current,

fast money. Grit understandings may fail to see the connection between family responsibilities for nontraditional students along with historical implications that have positioned minoritized families to galvanize individual earnings just to make ends meet. Marginalized students and their families often reside in areas where there are minimal geographies of opportunity that support social and economic mobility (Deil-Amen, 2015). Black and Latine/x men from this study want to succeed. They want to transfer to a four-year college or university more times than not. The findings here reflect the institutional and systemic barriers at play that are hidden in the auspices of whiteness and white supremacy in addition to grit as a value associated with SES and students of color.

Challenge and Support

Findings that highlight students' efforts to be successful in college yielded contradictory results. Blocked regressions were conducted to note how other variables were either moderated or suppressed as further items that fit Carter's (2002) framework were accounted for in the model. A suppressor effect did in fact occur, when the "support for learners" CCSSE benchmark was introduced in the last block of the model. The variable that had a suppressor effect was the EFA variable on academic, cognitive, and technical skills factor. The EFA factor examined the experiences of Black and Latine/x males to assess how this has contributed to their knowledge development within acquiring a broad general education; writing effectively, speaking clearly and effectively; thinking critically and analytically; using technology; and solving numerical problems. These are typically seen as successful habits that have been prevalent in positive educational outcomes for students (Hurtado et al., 2012).

Tensions in men of color and their support in college can be observed through the negative predictor of *support for learners* as it is suppressed by the true effect of the *academic, cognitive, and technical skills* factor. The support for learners CCSSE benchmark is intended to measure holistic support that takes into consideration students' identities that have been traditionally marginalized, while also accounting for academic and career counseling. Correlations revealed that independent measures of support for learners and academic, cognitive, and technical skills were negatively correlated to each other, while each item (respectively) were negatively and positively correlated with the outcome measure. This means that students' positive experiences in their respective institutions that supported their growth around academic, cognitive, and technical skills would have been an even greater predictor increasing transfer aspirations, had it not been for their experiences in receiving support at the CCCs that detracted such odds for aspirations.

Such findings corroborate implicit biases that could be happening when institutional agents are attempting to *support* men of color. Given how being first-generation and non-traditional had a moderating effect when support for learners was introduced, this could further be interpreted as students who do not fit the traditional mold of college students (Deil-Amen, 2015); and that their interactions within campus support systems led to a greater potential for such a demographic to be *cooled* out from the community college system. So, if student services professionals and instructional support had not been adamant in "cooling" out students, men of color's perceptions of overall institutional support with academic development would have been a greater predictor for transfer aspirations than it is now.

Applying grit as a measure for success in determining how they can *persevere* with their *passions* for transferring to a four-year institution would limit our collective understanding of what men of color in community colleges face and heighten the implications in supporting Black and Latine/x men through the transfer process by placing the greater onus on students' ability to transfer. Such findings support a call for further investigations for current support strategies and the level of cultural relevance it has on serving the students' demographics.

Unfortunately, this study had predictors that revealed detracted odds for students aspiring toward transferring to a four-year college or university. These negative predictors are either directly related toward historical legacies of racism and oppression (i.e., first-generation, or non-traditional student status) or are stereotypes and implicit biases that were established to rationalize the disparate circumstances minoritized students face under the cloak of white supremacy. Nonetheless, these findings should provide a space for future scholars, practitioners, and policy stakeholders to engage in dialogue premised on social justice and equity. Conversations around the support and plight of men of color must be met with actionable items that truly uplift, affirm, and support their racialized identities.

References

Almeida, D. J. (2016). Understanding grit in the context of higher education. In *Higher education: Handbook of theory and research* (Vol. 31, pp. 559–609). Springer.

Arevalo, I., So, D., & McNaughton-Cassill, M. (2016). The role of collectivism among Latino American college students. *Journal of Latinos and Education*, 15(1), 3–11.

Bahr, P. R., & Leigh Gross, J. (2016). Community colleges. In M. N. Bastedo, P. G. Altbach, & P. J. Gumport (Eds.), In *American higher education in the 21ˢᵗ century: Social, political, and economic challenges* (4th ed., pp. 462–502). Johns Hopkins University Press.

Barnes, R. A., & Piland, W. E. (2011). Impact of learning communities in developmental English on community college student retention and persistence. *Journal of College Student Retention: Research, Theory & Practice, 12*(1), 7–24.

Barney, D. C., & Higginson, K. (2017). Student voices for why college students take physical activity classes when it is not required for graduation. Asian Journal of Physical Education and Recreation, *23*(1), 6–14.

California Community College Chancellor's Office. (2023). California Community Colleges: Enrollment by gender, age, and ethnicity. [Data set]. CCCCO Datamart. https://datamart.cccco.edu/

Campbell, T., Reddy, V., & Siqueiros, M. (2021). The State of Higher Education for Black Californians: Examining Disparities in College Opportunity by Gender for Black Californians. *Campaign for College Opportunity.* https://files.eric.ed.gov/fulltext/ED618539.pdf

Carnevale, A., & Strohl, J. (2013). White flight goes to college. *Poverty & Race, 22*(5), 1–13.

Carter, D. F. (2002). College students' degree aspirations: A theoretical model and literature review with a focus on African American and Latino students. In J. C. Smart (Ed.), *Higher education: Handbook of Theory and research* (Vol. 17, pp. 129–171). Agathon Presss.

Cooper, M. (2010). *Student support services at community colleges: A strategy for increasing student persistence and attainment.* White House Summit on Community Colleges.

Crisp, G., & Nuñez, A. M. (2014). Understanding the racial transfer gap: Modeling underrepresented minority and nonminority students' pathways from two-to four-year institutions. *The Review of Higher Education, 37*(3), 291–320.

Cronbach, L. J. (1951). Coefficient alpha and the internal structure of tests. *Psychometrika, 16*(3), 297–334.

Cuyjet, M. J. (2006). African American college men: Twenty-first century issues and concerns. In M. J. Cuyjet (Ed.), *African American Men in College* (pp. 3–23). Jossey-Bass.

Dache-Gerbino, A. (2018). College desert and oasis_ A critical geographic analysis of local college access. *Journal of Diversity in Higher Education, 11*(2), 97.

Deil-Amen, R. (2015). The 'traditional' college student: A smaller and smaller minority and its implications for diversity and access institutions. In M. W. Kirst & M. L. Stevens (Eds.), *Remaking college: The changing ecology of higher education* (pp. 134–168). Stanford University Press.

Dougherty, K. J. (1987). The effects of community colleges: Aid or hindrance to socioeconomic attainment? *Sociology of Education, 60,* 86–103.

Garcia, G. A. (2019). *Becoming Hispanic-serving institutions: Opportunities for colleges and universities.* Johns Hopkins University Press.

Garcia, G. A. (2023). *Transforming Hispanic-serving institutions for equity and justice.* Johns Hopkins University Press.

Garcia, G. A., Núñez, A. M., & Sansone, V. A. (2019). Toward a multidimensional conceptual framework for understanding "servingness" in Hispanic-serving institutions: A synthesis of the research. *Review of Educational Research, 89*(5), 745–784.

Hagedorn, S. L., Maxwell, W., & Hampton, P. (2002). Correlates of retention for African American males in the community college. *Journal of College Student Retention, 3*(3), 243–263.

Hall, W. D., Cabrera, A. F., & Milem, J. F. (2011). A tale of two groups: Differences between minority students and non-minority students in their predispositions to and engagement with diverse peers at a predominantly white institution. *Research in Higher Education, 52*, 420–439.

Harper, S. R. (2009). Race, interest convergence, and transfer outcomes for Black male student athletes. *New Directions for Community Colleges, 147*, 29–37.

Harris, F., & Wood, J. L. (2013). Student success for men of color in community colleges: A review of published literature and research, 1998–2012. *Journal of Diversity in Higher Education, 6*(3), 174–185.

Harris, F. III, Bensimon, E. M., & Bishop, R. (2010). The equity scorecard: A process for building institutional capacity to educate young men of color. In C. Edley, Jr., & J. Ruiz de Velasco (Eds.), *Changing places: How communities will improve the health of boys of color* (pp. 277–308). University of California Press.

Hilton, A. A., Wood, J. L., & Lewis, C. W. (Eds.). (2012). *Black males in postsecondary education: Examining their experiences in diverse institutional contexts*. Information Age Publishing.

Hurtado, S., Alvarez, C. L., Guillermo-Wann, C., Cuellar, M., & Arellano, L. (2012). A model for diverse learning environments: The scholarship on creating and assessing conditions for student success. In J. C. Smart & M. B. Paulsen (Eds.), *Higher education: Handbook of theory and research* (Vol. 27, pp. 41–122). Springer.

Hurtado, S., Cuellar, M., & Wann, C. G. (2011). Quantitative measures of students' sense of validation: Advancing the study of diverse learning environments. *Enrollment Management Journal*, 53–71.

Jain, D., Herrera, A., Bernal, S., & Solórzano, D. (2011). Critical race theory and the transfer function: Introducing a transfer receptive culture. *Community College Journal of Research and Practice, 35*(3), 252–266.

Jehangir, R. R. (2009). Cultivating voice: First-generation students seek full academic citizenship in multicultural learning communities. *Innovative Higher Education, 34*(1), 33–49. https://doi.org/10.1007/s10755-008-9089-5

Laanan, F. S. (2003). Degree aspirations of two-year college students. *Community College Journal of Research & Practice, 27*(6), 495–518.

Laanan, F. S., Jackson, D. L., & Stebleton, M. J. (2013). Learning community and nonlearning community students in a midwestern community college. *Community College Journal of Research & Practice, 37*(4), 247–261. https://doi.org/10.1080/10668920903505023

Liang, C. T., Salcedo, J., & Miller, H. A. (2011). Perceived racism, masculinity ideologies, and gender role conflict among Latino men. *Psychology of Men & Masculinity, 12*(3), 201.

Long, A. (2016). *Overcoming educational racism in the community college: Creating pathways to success for minority and impoverished student populations*. Stylus Publishing.

Lundberg, C. A., Kim, Y. K., Andrade, L. M., & Bahner, D. T. (2018). High expectations, strong support: Faculty behaviors predicting Latina/o community college student learning. *Journal of College Student Development, 59*(1), 55–70.

Martinez, S., & Cervera, Y. (2012). Fulfilling educational aspirations: Latino students' college information seeking patterns. *Journal of Hispanic Higher Education, 11*(4), 388–402.

Mejia-Smith, B., & Gushue, G. V. (2017). Latina/o college students' perceptions of career barriers: Influence of ethnic identity, acculturation, and self-efficacy. *Journal of Counseling & Development*, 95(2), 145–155.

National Center for Education Statistics. (2014). Education indicators for the white house social statistics briefing room (SSBR). *Postsecondary Remedial Education*. http://nces.ed.gov/ssbr/pages/remedialed.asp?IndID=15

National Center for Education Statistics. (2023). Summary trends: Enrollment trends in postsecondary education. enrollment trends by race/ethnicity and gender. https://nces.ed.gov/ipeds/SummaryTables

Noguera, P. A. (2003). The trouble with Black boys: The role and influence of environmental and cultural factors on the academic performance of African American males. *Urban Education*, 38, 431–459. https://doi.org/10.1177/00420859030380 04005

O'Connor, N. (2009). Hispanic origin, socio-economic status, and community college enrollment. *The Journal of Higher Education*, 80(2), 121–145.

Palmer, R. T., & Strayhorn, T. L. (2008). Mastering one's own fate: Non-cognitive factors with the success of African American males at an HBCU. *National Association of Student Affairs Professionals Journal*, 11, 126–143.

Peck, F. (2020). Towards anti-deficit education in undergraduate mathematics education: How deficit perspectives work to structure inequality and what can be done about it. *Primus*, 31(9), 940–961.

Perrakis, A. I. (2008). Factor promoting academic success among African American and White male community college students. *New Directions for Community Colleges*, 142, 15–23.

Reyes, M., Dache-Gerbino, A., Rios-Aguilar, C., Gonzalez-Canche, M., & Deil-Amen, R. (2019). The "Geography of Opportunity" in community colleges: The role of the local labor market in students' decisions to persist and succeed. *Community College Review*, 47(1), 31–52.

Roman, M. A., Taylor, R. T., & Hahs-Vaughn, D. (2010). The retention index of the community college survey of student engagement (CCSSE): How meaningful is it? *Community College Journal of Research and Practice*, 34(5), 386–401. https://doi.org/10.1080/10668920701382484

Rothstein, R. (2017). *The color of law: A forgotten history of how our government segregated America*. Liveright Publishing.

Sáenz, V. B., & Ponjuan, L. (2008). The vanishing Latino male in higher education. *Journal of Hispanic Higher Education*, 8(1), 54–89. https://doi.org/10.1177/15381927 08326995

Sáenz, V. B., & Ponjuan, L. (2011). Men of color: Ensuring the academic success of Latino Males in higher education. *Institute for Higher Education Policy*. https://files.eric.ed.gov/fulltext/ED527060.pdf

Stanton-Salazar, R. D. (2011). A social capital framework for the study of institutional agents and their role in the empowerment of low-status students and youth. *Youth & Society*, 43(3), 1066–1109.

Steinhauer, A., & Lovell, E. D. N. (2021). Non-traditional community college students' academic pursuits: Time, connectedness, support, wages and research. *Community College Journal of Research and Practice*, 45(3), 223–226.

Stoeber, J., Childs, J. H., Hayward, J. A., & Feast, A. R. (2011). Passion and motivation for studying: Predicting academic engagement and burnout in university students. *Educational Psychology*, *31*(4), 513–528.

Strayhorn, T. (2010). When race and gender collide: Social and cultural capital's influence on the academic achievement of African American and Latino males. *The Review of Higher Education*, *33*(3), 307–332.

The Campaign for College Opportunity. (2014). *Higher education in California: A primer on the state's public colleges & universities*. http://www.collegecampaign. org/files/3013/9423/6960/2014_Higher_Ed_Primer_Final.pdf

Turley, R. N. L. (2009). College proximity: Mapping access to opportunity. *Sociology of Education*, *82*(2), 126–146.

Vasquez-Urias, M. (2012). The impact of institutional characteristics on Latino male graduation rates in community colleges. *Annuals of the Next Generation*, *3*(1), 1–12.

Wood, J. L. (2011). Falling through the cracks: An early warning system can help keep Black males on the community college campus. *Diverse Issues in Higher Education*, *28*(18), 24.

Wood, J. L., Hilton, A. A., & Lewis, C. (2011). Black male collegians in public two-year colleges: Student perspectives on the effect of employment on academic success. *National Association of Student Affairs Professionals Journal*, *14*(1), 97–110.

Wood, J. L., & Newman, C. B. (2017). Predictors of faculty–student engagement for Black men in urban community colleges: An investigation of the community college survey of men. *Urban Education*, *52*(9), 1057–1079.

Wood, J. L., & Palmer, R. T. (2013a). Understanding the personal goals of Black male community college students: Facilitating academic and psychosocial development. *Journal of African American Studies*. https://doi.org/10.1007/s12111-013-9248-3

Wood, J. L., & Palmer, R. T. (2013b). The likelihood of transfer for Black males in community colleges: Examining the effects of engagement using multilevel, multinomial modeling. *Journal of Negro Education*, *82*(3), 272–287.

Wood, J. L. & Turner, C. S. V. (2011). Black males and the community college: Student perspectives on faculty and academic success. *Community College Journal of Research & Practice*, *35*, 135–151.

Wood, J. L., & Williams, R. (2013). Persistence factors for Black males in the community college: An examination of background, academic, social, and environmental variables. *Spectrum: A Journal on Black Men*, *1*(2), 1–28.

PART III

Educational Practices Supporting Achievement

9

RETURNING TO CAMPUS

Equity-Minded Approaches to Degree Completion

Sabrina K. Sanders and Su Jin Gatlin Jez

I've been wanting to come back to school, but I didn't know how. The pandemic was really difficult to me. I'm a single mom with a one-year-old and it was impossible to be there for my child while engaging in my classes virtually. I tried everything I could do, but I just got so behind, I just stopped attending. I was so embarrassed, I tried everything, I really did. I didn't think it was possible to come back to finish my degree.

– Returning Student

The Georgetown Center on Education and the Workforce projects that by 2027, 70% of employment opportunities will require a degree or credential, far more than the 52% of Americans ages 25 through 64 that possess a degree or high-value credential today (Lumina Foundation, n.d.). It is imperative that we focus on degree completion for underrepresented populations if we are to build a skilled workforce to meet the needs of our country (IHEP, 2011).

In this chapter, we (a) discuss the imperative for addressing the "some college, no degree population" (SCND) in the context of the postsecondary student success agenda, (b) highlight promising practices of degree completion programs, and (c) document recommendations that will address the barriers of traditional institutional systems to promote access and equitable outcomes for SCND students as they return to college. Through this discussion, this chapter challenges notions of grit by reconsidering how we define the efforts of persistence and retention when considering student success for returning students.

DOI: 10.4324/9781003332497-12

Postsecondary education in the four-year sector has traditionally focused its priorities on first-time freshmen and, to a lesser extent, on transfer students. Due to today's shortage of workers with a college degree to meet the labor demands of the state (California's Future Higher Education, 2018) and increasing jobs requiring a bachelor's degree (California Competes, 2018), the United States faces a critical need to prioritize degree completion for an often-ignored population of students—those with some college, no degree. Compared to the traditional student continuing their formal education directly from high school, this population of 39 million students nationally who attended community college or university, earned units but have yet to earn a degree (Causey et al., 2022), bring a breadth of experiences and knowledge, hold different objectives for their education, and have distinctive needs from their institutions than what is provided for traditional students.

Each year, millions of high school graduates join the ranks as new, first-year students across the country with dreams of a college degree (Hanson, 2021). Postsecondary institutions have focused their efforts on the traditional student enrollment pathway, which is an incoming first-year student arriving from high school or as a transfer student from the community college. Unfortunately, many of them never cross the finish line. The details vary and through the course of time, higher education administrators, researchers, and advocates have been researching the challenges of degree completion, responding through innovation and strategic planning to improve student success while addressing institutional systems and barriers to degree completion for SCND students. Currently, about 50% of students complete their degrees (Hanson, 2021).

Grit as a Concept for Student Success?

Duckworth's (2013) Ted Talk, "Grit: The Power of Passion and Perseverance," discussed what students require to succeed. Her research as a psychologist in predicting student success correlates to the innate amount of grit a student possesses. Duckworth defines grit as:

[P]assion and perseverance for very long-term goals. Grit is having stamina. Grit is sticking with your future, day in, day out, not just for the week, not just for the month, but for years, and working really hard to make that future a reality. Grit is living life like it's a marathon, not a sprint.

The concept of grit intersects with the values that each student has the ability to accomplish what they desire through hard work and commitment, forming a belief pattern that a college student who does not persist lacks such focus.

Such conceptualizations and understanding of student behavior are rooted in a deficit-thinking model and are not a reliable measure as defined by Duckworth (Credé et al., 2017). This deficit mindset explains the perceived failure as a result of the student's shortcomings and limitations, not the structures that the student faces in persevering or the obstacles that must be overcome when "sticking with your future." Consequently, many students internalize societal pressures of feelings of inadequacies or failure. A student who is tasked with caring for family and managing a career may be challenged with balancing those responsibilities, unable to prioritize their education among other competing priorities. It is not without struggle, but different challenges are evident in completing college when you are financially secure, have no dependent or elder care responsibilities, and are educated in an environment where you feel a sense of belonging and have trust in the faculty and staff. In comparison, students who may be independent without stable housing, caring for children or an elderly family member, or facing financial hardships are trying to complete their degree under fundamentally different circumstances. The demographics of SCND students typically include students who last attended community college, were under 35 years old when they last attended, and are overly represented by Black, Latino, Native American, and are mostly women (Causey et al., 2022).

However, nearly all higher education reforms have been designed with the traditional student pathway in mind and this narrow focus often results in strategies that hinder the progress of SCND. The grit narrative, in particular, is especially harmful for supporting the success of students who left higher education before receiving their degree. Grit's deficit-driven focus is on individual perseverance and tenacity without acknowledging institutional and environmental structures that place returning students against rigid institutional systems not designed for their existence, and undoubtedly not their successful transition back to college. Grit's focus on the individual having agency over structural barriers impacts returning students twice—when they cannot succeed in their first attempt and when they attempt to return to complete their degree. Advancing the importance of grit in the face of these long-standing traditional practices only sets up the potential to further disengage students from returning to and completing college.

In reflecting on institutional structures in postsecondary education, the concept of grit has become part of the nomenclature when assessing what spurs success, particularly for students of color, first-generation students, and low-income students. Applying the logic of grit to adult learners with SCND does them a disservice, however, as they face both external and internal structures in higher education that are at odds with their reentry. The deficit-minded perspective of grit can cause harm and form a stigma for a population already marginalized in a slow-changing college-going system. We propose that theories of grit are inadequate and inappropriate to define how returning students with SCND can be successful in returning to and completing college. We challenge the reader to think differently in how we measure and predict success for adult learners whose education may not be their first priority as they balance work and careers, family responsibilities, or institutional cultures that challenge college persistence.

Institutions must debunk the grit narrative, which pits marginalized students against one of the world's longest-standing bureaucratic systems and structures—higher education. To this end, institutions must understand who their students are and the students that their historic structures have excluded. The divergence of who higher education institutions seek to serve and those inadvertently excluded is not always represented by the data sets regularly examined; first-year student surveys are commonly used to lay the groundwork to prepare for each year's new cohort. Instead of relying on historical practices such as surveys, postsecondary institutions should consider if they are serving their mission and educating the students who seek to enroll.

Do colleges and universities reassess their institutional systems and processes to address administrative barriers? Do they acknowledge the experience and high-level skills working adults bring to the classroom? Are institutions re-thinking instructional andragogy and facilitating professional development alongside faculty to understand the priorities of working-adults and their motivation for returning to our institutions? How are institutions expanding their support toward the success of all students through an equity-minded approach to degree completion? These questions and more facilitate a deconstruction of and challenge to grit.

Rather than calling for student resilience in the face of a system not designed to serve them, higher education must call all-hands-on-deck to increase college completion rates via shifting values, creating cultures, and building structures with innovative thinking that centers returning students. Instead of demanding students push through outdated structures, colleges and universities must commit to re-engaging students with some college but no degree to help them earn their degrees.

Need for More College Graduates

The United States will face a shortage of college graduates to meet workforce demands, and there are several contributing factors. Decreasing childbirths, declining high school completions, the retirement of an aging workforce, and the worldwide pandemic have contributed to the gap in meeting labor market needs (Hetrick et al., 2021). We witnessed the increased challenges of those without a degree in the workforce facing higher unemployment issues than those with a college degree. This was exacerbated during the COVID-19 pandemic when employment rates differed tremendously and the recovery continues to be better for those with a college education, adding to the issues of equity and opportunity (Bohn & Lafortune, 2022). After decades of increasing postsecondary enrollment, the number of U.S. undergraduates began to decline in 2011 (de Brey et al., 2022), adding to the gravity of the issues facing higher education. Colleges and universities across the country have attempted reforms to not only increase the number of students coming through their doors but also ensure that they graduate in order to encourage more students to enroll. Leaning into student success with the focus of increasing college completion has even been tackled by city, state, and national higher education initiatives to improve access, admissions, persistence, and transfer rates, especially among first-generation, undergraduate, and low-income students. These efforts to tackle the need for a more educated workforce have led to the development of programs like College Promise.

At their core, College Promise programs have the goal to build and sustain a pipeline between K-12 systems and community colleges to fill the talent pipeline, ensuring an educated workforce for the future with a lens on low-income, high-need communities. The promise movement focus on building college-going cultures has resulted in 348 local and statewide College Promise programs across 47 states, increasing opportunities for access to college to begin at the community college. Such strategic initiatives, along with reframing the culture of postsecondary education, serve an evolving population of learners while transforming traditional structures of college preparedness, access, and persistence.

According to the 2020 report, *Some College and No Degree*, the number one reason that students left college was the need to work—the challenge of balancing school and work at the same time (17%), followed by financial hardship (12%), then other life events or personal problems (11%) (Strada Education Network, 2020). In our re-engagement efforts, we heard from a great number of students that they must work in order to afford the cost of living in California along with the challenge of balancing class and work schedules, leading many students to have to leave college. Students who face these challenges are also those whom higher education institutions were not designed to serve. These are students of color and adult learners. This is largely because of the age of students when they leave college and also because students of color are much more likely to leave college without a degree (California Competes, 2018). Colleges and universities struggle to graduate students with heavy obligations outside of school. And these challenges are not short-term issues that students can tackle and return to college; instead, these are challenges where just having grit alone falls short. Consequently, many of these students have not returned to college due to these challenges, which have remained unchanged (California Competes,

2018; Strada Education Network, 2020). Students who started college but left before being awarded a credential have been termed "Comebackers," "Stop-outs," "Stranded Students," or "Some College, No Degree."

Higher Education Agenda Centers Traditional College Students

Over the last decade, the national higher education agenda has undergone dramatic reform. We reflect on leadership at the federal, state, and city levels that have undertaken substantial policy change at the postsecondary level, investing in college completion initiatives across the country. In fact, President Obama's (2009) State of the Union Address focused on the need for more college graduates: "By 2020, America will once again have the highest proportion of college graduates in the world." Policy leaders continually call for increases in degree attainment, thereby incentivizing postsecondary leaders across the nation to formulate statewide goals and initiatives to increase completion rates. The evolving needs of the workforce, global competition, and need to support student persistence have directed attention to the necessity of postsecondary institutions to evolve and rethink educational models and transitioning to "becoming student-ready" by trying to meet the needs of all students (McNair et al., 2016). There seems to be a greater understanding that the campus role (and responsibility) is not solely to push students toward entrance onto college campuses, but through it to reach these completion goals.

College completion initiatives were born out of the demand for increasing graduation rates in postsecondary education to fulfill the needs of a growing competitive global economy. Researchers have long projected the country to be short of a college educated workforce to meet the demand (Carnevale, 2020; Carnevale et al., 2010). California was on the path to being 1.2 million degrees short of meeting the labor demands of the state (Johnson et al., 2015); the latest projections indicate the state will still fall short. This prediction has driven statewide initiatives including the California State University Graduation Initiative 2025, which builds off the previous student success initiatives. Postsecondary institutions were called to strengthen academic preparation programs, expand the use of data analytics and digital advising tools, and remove administrative barriers while addressing student engagement and well-being to increase graduation rates across its 23 university campuses. California Community Colleges similarly launched a Student Success Initiative that focused on supporting students who entered college not yet college ready through increased counseling, tutoring, and reforms to developmental education (Governor's Office, State of California, 2007).

Other states initiated similar degree completion initiatives to increase degree completion. Texas' "Build a Talent Strong Texas" expanded upon its degree completion goals to include goals specific to potential adult learners. They envision 60% of Texans 25–64 years old will receive a degree, certificate, or credential by 2030 with an expanded focus on work-based learning, short-term credential, or badges. Missouri's "15 to Finish" initiative encouraged full-time college students to take 15 credit units per semester to earn their bachelor's degrees in four years or associate's degree in two years. Students who take 15 units or more per semester will graduate earlier, be able to enter the workforce sooner, and contribute to the economy and the social mobility of their communities. Coalitions of postsecondary institutions came together to work toward the same goals. Organizations like Complete College America, Achieve the Dream, and University Innovation Alliance work with institutions to reform student success strategies by improving data collection and collaborating on research, in addition to fostering professional development for systemic changes to increase graduation rates and decrease equity gaps. They have served as a hub for research tools and data-driven decision making for higher education leaders to launch innovative strategies and interventions that are shared among communities of practice. Their research efforts have included using data analytics to inform proactive advising to students in need, completion grants for students close to completion, and credit for competency-based learning.

Well-intentioned student success efforts have reenergized higher education to be bold and innovative while engaging postsecondary leaders at rethinking systems that obstruct students from achieving their goal. The defining factor for assessing these completion goals has been four-year graduation rates with a firm focus on traditional pathways, often leaving out this population of students with some college, no degree. These college completion initiatives—created out of the need to improve graduation rates and eliminate equity gaps—have delved into wide multi-pronged strategies to improve institutional outcomes. While student success initiatives have become commonplace in postsecondary education to increase the number of college graduates, reengaging students with SCND is still making its way to the forefront of the breadth of institutional strategies and interventions. There is a vast opportunity to think about what it means to help a student finish what they started, even for those who veered off course in their college journey.

Some College, No Degree

The National Student Clearinghouse Research Center reports that 39 million students have some college, no degree. This population attended some type of postsecondary education but have yet to earn a degree or credential. Most are working full-time and challenged by balancing work, family, and school. They may have financial, academic, or health reasons that hinder completing their education. They may have not felt a sense of community or that they belonged on a campus structured for students with heavy out-of-school obligations. Some may have had opportunities moving forward in their places of employment and careers and no longer require a degree, making the benefit of finishing their credential seem less valuable.

A subset of Some College, No Degree is "Potential Completers." These are the students who completed at least two years of full-time academic progress, but have not graduated. Potential Completers are approximately 10% of the SCND nationally. According to the National Student Clearing-house (2019), they are more likely to re-enroll at the campus they first began their academic career and more likely to complete their degree in two years without stopping. As these students are closer to completion than others in the returning population, it is particularly imperative that we know who these students are as we prepare to support them.

Colleges are bringing light to the need to reinvest in these students who have left with some college, no degree. They have become an invisible student population in our student success conversations, expanding the focus of traditional outcomes beyond the four-year or six-year graduation rates. Yet, a number of institutions and even states are refocusing efforts on this population as they address the need to improve social mobility and college completion rates of historically underrepresented and underserved communities. The SCND are a critical population who is already a contributor to the economic vitality of our states. These efforts reveal how the conversation on grit—putting the onus of responsibility on an individual to be resilient to defeat systemic barriers—has failed to recognize how the interaction between a student's individual attributes and systemic barriers varies significantly. The ways in which structures are built nurture some populations and intentionally limit others. Ignoring this reality adds to the stigmas that these former students face for having fallen short of their collegiate aspirations, speaking volumes to what we narrowly define for student success—four-year graduation rates for first-time freshmen.

Higher Education's Limitations in Serving Those with Some College, No Degree

As colleges and universities witness declines in undergraduate enrollments, they will need to rethink their strategies to serve those with some college but no degree. They will need to start by considering why the student left and how to address those reasons to ensure that if the student returns, they do not face the same challenges or have strategies to navigate the institution. In our work with students who want to return to college after stopping out, we observe first-hand the layered and complex limitations of the policies and practices of higher education institutions for this population of students. These students are working full-time, are more reflective of the general adult learner population, and have much more extensive layers of responsibilities where school may not be their number one priority. They are heading back to college campuses with life experience, professional skills, and increased responsibilities. Many may be joining the ranks as a college student who has military service, who cares for children or elderly family members, or who balances professional careers that have little flexibility for returning to school.

The path back to college for a returning student is not without a host of twist and turns. They must navigate a path that was built with an onramp for the incoming high school or community college student, not for a non-traditional college student who has paused enrollment and may have taken a detour. Admissions, orientation, financial aid, and advisement structures have not institutionalized practices for these returning students. While the student is eager to return, they run into roadblocks of misaligned practices that are not intended for this student population. Students shared that when they wanted to return to the university, they had to resubmit their college application, repay college application fees, and do so eight months before the start of the academic year. They felt they had to re-compete for their seat at the university, adding to the feeling of no longer belonging at the university when they had stopped out. One prospective returning student shared with us:

> I shouldn't have to reapply like a new student—and I would have to reapply now for next fall—that is incredibly disconcerting. And I would have to go to new student orientation. I'm not a new student. I don't feel I have to go to the same process like a new student. We're returning! We already know the school. We should have the carpool lane, like the fast lane. We already know the school; we just want to get back in the lane.

The structures of most four-year U.S. institutions have not been created with the returning student in mind. The traditional path of the high school student to the four-year university or community college may have been common for conventional students. Nearly everything about the structure of colleges is shaped for the traditional student—from applying in the fall in the year before you want to matriculate, to student housing focusing on students without partners or children. Although some campuses may already have "adult-reentry," veterans, or similar centers for serving adult learners, a broader campus-wide effort requires building a returning student centric culture.

Because many students who might return to campus are carrying the responsibilities of managing careers, family, and taking courses to complete their degrees, they generally look to get in and complete their coursework required for their degree as efficiently as possible. Unlike the traditional 18- to 22-year-old first-year students, the deciding factor does not rest on the (bells and whistles) of new recreation centers, residential halls, or the reputation of athletics programs. In short, such students aim to complete the requirements for their degrees and graduate, and correlate what they are learning in the classroom to the skills required for today's workforce. In a study of California adults, 15% of those who planned to enroll in college in the next two years stated they preferred exclusively online courses and programs (California Competes, 2021). While online enrollments had been increasing before the pandemic, the pandemic likely led more prospective students to have the ability and interest to enroll in online courses, leading many to realize the benefits of taking courses remotely. This population of students are looking at—and evaluating—the ease of applying for transfer course credit, application of coursework to their career, flexibility of course offerings, and the quickest route possible to completing a degree that is convenient and affordable.

Policies and Practices that Put Adult Learners Behind

The process of returning can be even more challenging as the higher education system often has changed, in addition to it not being designed for students to exit before earning a degree. As a result, students who return are frequently navigating new admissions terrain. After deciding to return to complete their degree, students tend to face application processes designed for first-time freshmen or transfer students—none of which are right for them. Instead, these students sometimes reach out to the institution to understand what their process to return looks like and are faced with a plethora of forms, application fees, and multiple handoff points to return to campus. Many campuses ask these former students to reapply for admission, sending the message that they are no longer part of the community, and they must compete again for their seats. They are told the program requirements have changed, requiring additional courses, or not counting those already completed. They are held to a financial aid policy that has been structured for traditional college students, leaving them ineligible for some state or federal funding opportunities.

Not only are students with some college, no degree subjected to processes designed for the traditional college student, but they are also evaluated by metrics designed for that population, which undervalues what they bring to the classroom. Students with some college, no degree often return with years of work experience, military service, or skills. They may have already garnered skill sets and competencies outside the accredited postsecondary classroom. However, institutions struggle to comprehensively and coherently award credit for prior learning. These students may have to repeat college courses because their credits are not accepted for transfer, an obstacle also faced by some traditional college students (Simone, 2014) due to the lack of clear pathways and agreements to support credit transfer. And then these students, who now may have significant independent life experiences, question the value of classroom learning given their job training, professional development, or hands-on experience.

If You Need Another Reason to Care: Equity

Individuals with some college, no degree disproportionately come from underserved student populations. The students who are disproportionately less likely to persistent and complete overwhelmingly make up the population of those with some college, no degree. These are first-generation, low-income, and racially minoritized students. Serving those with some college, no degree will help close equity gaps for these populations.

What Needs to Be Implemented to Serve All Students

Higher education and policymakers need to step back and look at postsecondary institutions to ensure they are serving all students. Instead of placing traditional student success models on populations that don't fit, how can our policies, practices and reforms be more inclusive of returning students, rather than placing the impetus on already marginalized students facing tremendous structural barriers? Fortunately, the field of researchers and practitioners have begun identifying promising strategies to support access and success for those with some college, no degree (California Competes, 2018). The pandemic has brought attention to the need to revisit "stop-out" policies with some campuses extending the timeline, allowing students additional time given the challenges of college-going behavior during the pandemic. These strategies include shifts in campus culture and nurturing who the students are and what they bring with them, rather than asking them to conform to an outdated model of higher education.

An Inclusive Campus Culture that Values the Returning Student

For systems and structures to change, underlying cultures and values must also shift. By recognizing the value that those with some college, no degree bring, postsecondary institutions and systems must reform their cultures to not just be tolerant of these students but ensure they are truly wanted and belong. It is also imperative that the policies and practices of postsecondary institutions move from a deficit mindset that reduces the value of SCND student experiences. Cultivating an inclusive culture will drive the development of structures and practices that will enable success for returning students. For example, as institutions redesign websites, they will consider how returning students will experience the site. As faculty develop courses, they will consider what knowledge and skills students bring into the classroom and that these competencies may come from other postsecondary institutions, the workplace, or care responsibilities. In effect, shifts in culture and values will drive better practices and policies.

As we think about the institution of higher education—including access, admissions, orientation, enrollment, persistence, retention, and more—how are our systems being developed for the returning student? Postsecondary practices are structured for new students arriving directly from high school or community colleges and stepping onto campus for the first time with little to no knowledge of the college experience. Deadlines, timelines, policies, practices, etc. are set up for students headed on the traditional college-going path. There is little effort to account for returning students who may have amassed a wealth of professional skills and knowledge and would argue many of these attributes not acknowledged by the college or university.

Supporting Adult Learners Who Are Parents/Caregivers

A significant proportion of students with some college, no degree are parents or responsible for care of family members. Nationally, 25% of adults 25 and older with some college but no degree have children at home (Ruggles et al., 2022), and 49% of adult undergraduates have dependent children (NCES, n.d.). In fact, a survey by Strada Education Network (2020) stated that one of the main reasons students took college courses but did not complete their college degree was that they became pregnant or had children. This was also a major reason that the pandemic affected student parents following stay-at-home mandates and ensuring the educational needs of their children were prioritized before their own. Reengaging students with children or the responsibilities for family raised the need for student support services such as childcare, flexible schedules, student-parent communities, and subsidized childcare assistance (California Competes, 2023).

Evaluating the Landscape to Understand How Existing Policies and Practices Impact Returning Students

Understanding the campus landscape is important to identify practices that are effective in serving returning students. "An Adult Learner Toolkit for California Community Colleges" (SCAILE and SCCCC, 2021) guides campus leaders in a self-assessment on reviewing their support, along with academic policies and practices in serving adult-learners, the group to which

SCND students belong. Engaging campus stakeholders in rethinking institutional practices with a lens on the returning student is a positive first step to inform the shift in serving some college, no degree students.

Articulating the Skills and Experience Returning Students Bring to the College (Credit for Prior Learning)

Adult learners who return to college after having served in the military, engaged in professional certification, professional development, or military service have already developed college-level professional attributes and cognitive skills. Credit for prior learning acknowledges these experiences that returning students bring back to the college campus through course identifying, evaluating, and crediting these competencies. To clarify how postsecondary education structures focus on traditional 18-year-old recent high school graduates and fail to serve returning students, colleges almost universally have coherent and comprehensive policies to award credit for prior learning to traditional students. Advanced Placement and International Baccalaureate programs are institutionalized across postsecondary education and an opportunity to earn college credit. For high school students engaged in college-level learning outside the accredited college classroom, higher education created seamless pathways for them. Higher education must do the same for today's student—those with significant college-level learning stemming from work experience or other unaccredited educational and training systems.

Palomar College developed a credit of prior learning initiated by a campus-wide workgroup that included workforce development, credit for prior learning coordinator, technical curriculum reviewer, and an articulation officer who worked alongside faculty to identify appropriate evaluation methods for courses. Due to the large military presence on campus, they prioritized military service, training, and credentials as a starting point. They have developed a credit for prior learning website that provides a clear path toward articulation courses eligible for credit for prior learning.

Keen Attention to College Affordability and Financial Aid Structures

Financial aid is important in reengaging returning students. They are more likely to have outstanding debt from previous college enrollment and may be working. Financial challenges are generally one reason why they left college, and it may continue to be a reason why they don't come back. Specific funding opportunities, including returning student scholarships, completion grants, or debt forgiveness, are key services to engage returning students who may no longer be eligible for need-based grants due to accumulation of credits or expiration of their academic clock.

Students with outstanding debt are often stuck at a crossroads of returning to college—unable to register for classes due to financial holds (Karon et al., 2020), ineligible for financial aid until they do enroll, and subject to restrictive financial aid policy and deadlines set for traditional college-going cultures. Debt forgiveness initiatives have become a valuable resource for students with some college, no degree (Gatlin Jez, 2021). Such support is aligned with best practices in financial aid. For example, students who left City College of Chicago with a debt of $201 or more prior to July 1, 2020, are invited to participate in "Fresh Start," a debt relief program for returning students that includes them signing the "Fresh Start Commitment," attending financial empowerment coaching sessions, meeting with advising, submitting a Free Application for Federal Student Aid (FAFSA), and completing a credential. Students can participate in the program regardless of their last GPA, whether they have satisfactory academic progress (SAP) holds, or if they completed a degree elsewhere. This program is a model that rethinks financial aid, forgiving debt in exchange for new tuition and one that could remove a financial barrier for some college, no degree students.

Admissions Processes Designed for the Returning Student

Reforms in readmission and advising practice can ease the administrative burdens that institutions place on the student. Many postsecondary institutions have clear processes for first-time freshmen and transfer students to enroll. But for students outside these two traditional models, the path is less clear. The process for returning students includes resubmitting admissions applications, repaying application fees, waiting through the admissions process, and depending upon how long student has been disenrolled, resubmitting transcripts and awaiting review according to new program requirements. These steps toward returning are among the first administrative barriers returning students face. One student shared that when they attempted to return to the university, they "looked at the website to come back. It was scary. It's a maze and difficult to figure out where to come back. They eventually gave up." Before even deciding if returning is an option, students want to know what they need in order to graduate. They find themselves in a black hole of clarifying their path toward degree completion given they left the main road.

The need for institutions to require paper trails of change forms, petitions, checks and balances processes with administrative signoffs and committee reviews can send students on a game of hide-and-seek for readmission processes. This situation is slowly changing, though. California State University, Dominguez Hills examined its reentry process and found it to be unnecessarily cumbersome. To re-engage returning students back to campus, the university created a "re-entry form," waived application fees, shortened wait times, and streamlined the returning process using a concierge approach via a single point of contact. The elimination of an "application" went a long way in communicating to students that they belong, that they were welcomed, and that their disenrollment did not mean they were no longer part of the community. A curated recruitment plan with personalized high-touch phone calls and emails was completed. Upon receiving the personalized phone calls, one student shared: "It was a sign, because it had been in the back of my mind. I know I needed to complete this, but it was just complicated, and I work a lot. I didn't have time for all that paperwork." Students were provided wrap-around services by the college-based Student Success Centers, where advisors support their successful return to campus. Such practices are leading this highly diverse metropolitan university where 66% of the students are Pell-Grant Eligible, 79% are racially underrepresented, and 71% are the first of their family to graduate from college to creating a returning-student-centric culture of supporting student success for all students, including those who may have had to pause their path to a college degree.

Flexible and Predictable Course Scheduling in Various Modalities

Returning students come back to college balancing significant obligations and need as much flexibility and predictability as possible. Colleges and universities must allow students to apply and enroll more frequently. Having a single application window in the fall with matriculation the following fall works for traditional college students, but not for the returning student who seeks the shortest path to a credential. This student may only have a year left to complete, but would then need to wait a full year to even re-start classes, and even longer when accounting for the time between the decision to re-enroll and the application due date. Similarly, returning students are likely to be working and are more likely to have dependent children—scheduling obligations that they must juggle with their course schedule. When class offerings change every 4–5 months and with waitlists for high-demand courses, many returning students simply cannot adjust their work and childcare schedules to meet the frequently and unpredictable shifting schedules of courses. To meet this reality head-on, Shasta College in California created a program that sets the course schedule for the entire two-year program (California Competes, 2020). This program also allows for more frequent enrollment onramps and continually reassesses the needs of students to ensure the college is ready for the student, not the other way around.

Online courses and programs can also provide students greater flexibility, particularly asynchronous online courses that allow students to engage in course material as their demanding schedules allow. Students who no longer live in the vicinity of the institution where they had begun their college journey and must resume their studies at a different institution closer to home, moreover, may add to the number of courses needed on the road to graduation. As such, online degree programs have become a desired opportunity for many returning students with time and place limitations. From understanding these obstacles, the University of Utah developed "Return to the U," which provides a number of alternative routes for returning students. With a focus on adult-learners who stopped out, they have created a portfolio of options for University of Utah students who want to finish their degree. Online, hybrid program options are provided on the main campus or one of their many satellite centers and include flexible scheduling options with accelerated courses that are key for working professionals and students with limited schedules. For students who put their education on hold, flexible instruction options and strong support services are vital components for degree completion opportunities.

Systemwide Efforts Can Create Consistency for Returning Students

When returning students move around, re-enrolling at their original institution can be impossible. Campuses may not have the diversity of offerings for all students' needs. Statewide, and systemwide where applicable, policies may play into the barriers of reengaging SCND students. Lack of consistency in course numbering systems or articulation creates silos for supporting students to degree completion. Having statewide coordination to reengage returning students can make re-enrollment a reality and ease inefficiencies caused by administrative friction, the need for flexibility, and the loss of credits. Several states are leveraging their public higher education systems to do just this and are exemplars, as detailed next.

The Texas Higher Education Coordinating Board

The State of Texas reassessed their systemwide student success goals with intentionality in addressing non-traditional students increasing completion of credentials or degrees. Specifically, "Grad TX" is a statewide campaign to re-enroll students with 45 units and no Associate's Degree or 40 units and no Bachelor's degree. In partnership with campuses across the state, they focus on building connections and sharing promising practices that interrupt deficit-based grit discourse and the associated systems of exclusion surrounding traditional college-going practices in postsecondary education.

Colorado's One Million Degrees

Colorado is changing existing structures, further challenging the grit perspective by identifying those students who have left the community colleges. The One Million Degrees organization launched a two-year pilot, "Finish What You Started," which tackles the issue of low-income adult workers who have some college experience but no degree or certificate. The goal is to help them re-enroll and pursue a postsecondary credential in the state of Colorado. They have connected wrap-around supporting services along with career planning, student coaching, and connecting to community-based social services to increase credential completion in community colleges across Colorado.

Indiana's "You Can. Go Back."

Indiana launched the "You Can. Go Back." campaign to increase college-going rates across the state. They have a centralized, interactive website that connects prospective students according to their career interests and needs with a point of contact for respective programs that align with their preferences. Their high-touch outreach included direct mail, email, and phone calls to connect students to their website filled with resources. Their program has initiated flexible course offerings, provided financial grant incentives, and built a statewide commitment to degree completion for this population of students with some college, no degree.

Tennessee's Reconnects

Tennessee's Reconnects goal is to support more adults who return to college to gain new skills, advance in their workplace, or fulfill their personal goals of a college degree/credential. They are doing so by increasing graduation rates by offering free tuition to community or technical colleges to adults who do not have an associate's or bachelor's degree. Their Tennessee Reconnect Grant was engaged through legislation to provide last-dollar scholarships for eligible students to attend community college tuition-free.

Michigan's Reconnect

Michigan Reconnect is a key strategy to their "Sixty by 30" goal to increase the number of adults with a college degree or credential to 60% by 2030. The state has focused on identifying adults who are 25 years or older without a college degree to work alongside a Reconnect Navigator in connecting them back to their path toward a degree or certificate. The program pays in-district tuition for eligible students.

Recommendations

To disrupt current practices and systems in serving students with some college, no degree, it is imperative that we build a returning-student centric culture. That is to rethink practices and policies that were not built for the returning student in mind. We reflect on a number of those strategies and statewide initiatives and offer a summary of strategies in supporting reengagement of students with some college, no degree back to college:

- Streamlined re-enrollment process;
- Identify a point of contact with centralized information for all things Returning Students;
- High-touch recruitment campaign;
- Rethink student onboarding or orientation to look different from new students;
- Outreach to include admissions, financial aid, and advising support along the way;
- Create a sense of belonging, removing shame, welcoming students back;
- Train Advisors and Coaches in supporting Returning Students;
- Offer financial support in the means of debt forgiveness, completion grants, and scholarships;
- Review academic policy for Returning Students which may include Catalog Rights, Leave Policy, Academic Renewal, etc.;
- Increase clarity on the returning process online and in social media channels;
- Highlight flexibility with evening, hybrid, and weekend courses; and
- Clearly articulate skills taught, major map to industry, and higher earning averages.

These recommendations are a just a few examples of how institutions can meet critical needs in serving students and re-envision how they can be supported on our college campuses as we rethink student success for all students, including those who have left our university.

Grit Fails Students Facing Structural Barriers, Like Returning Students

Instead of calling for student resilience in the face of a system not designed to serve them, higher education must call all-hands-on-deck to increase college completion rates via shifting values, creating cultures, and building structures with innovative thinking that centers returning students. Instead of demanding students push through outdated structures, colleges and universities must commit to re-engaging students with some college but no degree to help them earn their degrees.

When students are provided wider access to the onramp to restart their college journey, the university increases its access to more students who are already challenged by balancing careers, personal responsibilities, and the challenges having been away from college. Postsecondary higher education must foster adult-learner centric practices if we are to use an equity-minded approach to support degree completion for all students, including those who have paused their college journey. Higher education must rethink its approach to supporting student success by acknowledging these compelling stories of students with some college, no degree in how our institutions can build a returning-student centric culture in welcoming them back to campus, provide the tools and services to meet their academic goals and objectives, and lead them to degree completion.

References

Bohn, S., & Lafortune, J. (2022, June 16). *In a tight labor market, does a college degree still matter for employment.* Public Policy Institute of California. https://www.ppic.org/blog/in-a-tight-labor-market-does-a-college-degree-still-matter-for-employment/

California Competes. (2018, October 18). *Back to college part one: California's imperative to re-engage adults.* https://californiacompetes.org/publications/back-to-college-part-one

California Competes. (2020). *From practice to policy: How institutions accelerate adult completion and fuel prosperity.* https://californiacompetes.org/publications/from-practice-to-policy-adults

California Competes. (2021). *Get ready: Introducing the millions of adults planning to enroll in college.* https://californiacompetes.org/publications/get-ready

California Competes. (2023). *A policy agenda for California student parents.* https://californiacompetes.org/publications/a-policy-agenda-for-california-student-parents

California's Future Higher Education. (2018, January). *California is facing a shortfall of college-educated workers.* Public Policy Institute of California. https://www.ppic.org/wp-content/uploads/r-118jjr.pdf

Carnevale, A. (2020, February 13). Ignore the hype. College is worth it. *Inside Higher Ed.* https://www.insidehighered.com/views/2020/02/13/why-one-should-ignore-reports-and-commentary-question-value-college-degree-opinion

Carnevale, A. P., Smith, N., & Strohl, J. (2010). *Help wanted: Projections of job and education requirements through 2018.* Lumina Foundation.

Causey, J., Kim, H., Ryu, M., Scheetz, A., & Shapiro, D. (2022, May). *Some college, no credential student outcomes, annual progress report – Academic year 2020/21.* National Student Clearinghouse Research Center.

Credé, M., Tynan, M. C., & Harms, P. D. (2017). Much ado about grit: A meta-analytic synthesis of the grit literature. *Journal of Personality and Social Psychology, 113*(3), 492–511. https://doi.org/10.1037/pspp0000102

de Brey, C., Zhang, A., & Duffy, S. (2022). *Digest of education statistics, 2020* (NCES 2022-009). National Center for Education Statistics, Institute of Education Sciences, U.S. Department of Education. https://nces.ed.gov/programs/digest/d21/tables/dt21_303.70.asp

Duckworth, A. (2013, May 9). *Grit: The power of passion and perseverance* [Video]. TED Conference. https://youtu.be/H14bBuluwB8

Gatlin Jez, S. (2021, June 25). Budget surplus can smooth the path to higher education. *Cal Matters.* https://calmatters.org/commentary/my-turn/2021/06/budget-surplus-can-smooth-the-path-to-higher-education/

Governor's Office, State of California. (2007). *Governor's budget 2007–08: Higher education CCC Student Success Initiative.* https://ebudget.ca.gov/2007-08-EN/Enacted/BudgetSummary/HED/26655620.html

Hanson, M. (2021, August 7). College enrollment & student demographic statistics. *Education Data Initiative.* https://educationdata.org/college-enrollment-statistics

Hetrick, R., Grieser, H., Sentz, R., Coffey, C., & Burrow, G. (2021). *The demographic drought.* EMSI. https://www.economicmodeling.com/wp-content/uploads/2022/02/Demographic-Drought-Bridging-the-Gap.pdf

Institute for Higher Education Policy (IHEP). (2011, September). Near completion: Framing the issue. *Institute for Higher Education Policy (IHEP).* https://files.eric.ed.gov/fulltext/ED539720.pdf

Johnson, H., Mejia, M. C., & Bohn, S. (October 2015). *Will California run out of college graduates?* Public Policy Institute of California. https://www.ppic.org/publication/will-california-run-out-of-college-graduates/

Karon, J., Ward, J. D., Hill, C. B., & Kurzweil, M. (2020). *Solving stranded credits: Assessing the scope and effects of transcript withholding on students, states, and institutions.* Ithaka S+R. https://doi.org/10.18665/sr.313978

Lumina Foundation. (n.d.). *A stronger nation: Learning beyond high school builds America's talent.* https://www.luminafoundation.org/stronger-nation

McNair, T. B., Albertine, S. L., Cooper, M. A., McDonald, N. L., & Major, T. (2016). *Becoming a student-ready college: A new culture of leadership for student success.* Jossey-Bass.

National Center for Education Statistics (NCES). (n.d.) *2015–16 national postsecondary student aid study, undergraduates.* Calculated from DataLab. https://nces.ed.gov/datalab/powerstats/table/vbbsnn

Obama, B. H. (2009). Remarks of President Barack Obama—As prepared for delivery; Address to Joint Session of Congress. http://www.whitehouse.gov/the_press_office/Remarks-of-President-Barack-Obama-Address-to-Joint-Session-of-Congress

Ruggles, S., Flood, S., Goeken, R., Schouweiler, M., & Sobek, M. (2022). *IPUMS USA: Version 12.0* [dataset]. IPUMS. https://www.ipums.org/projects/ipums-usa/d010.v12.0

Shasta College Attainment and Innovation Lab for Equity (SCAILE) and Success Center for California Community Colleges (SCCCC). (2021). *Improving equity and completion: An adult learner toolkit for California Community Colleges.* https://scmainweb.s3.us-west-1.amazonaws.com/files/resources/adult_learner_toolkit_may_2021.pdf

Simone, S. A. (2014). *Transferability of postsecondary credit following student transfer or coenrollment* (NCES 2014-0163). National Center for Education Statistics, Institute of Education Sciences, U.S. Department of Education. https://nces.ed.gov/pubsearch/pubsinfo.asp?pubid=2014163

Strada Education Network. (2020). *Some college and no degree.* Center for Education Consumer Insights. cci.stradaeducation.org/report/some-college-and-no-degree/.4

10

A COUNTERNARRATIVE TO GRIT THROUGH SCHOLARSHIP ON LATINX/A/O STUDENTS AND HSIs

A Systematic Review of the Literature

Kathleen Rzucidlo, Stacey R. Speller, Jorge Burmicky, and Robert T. Palmer

The experiences of Latinx/a/o students in higher education have received growing empirical attention by scholars and policymakers over recent decades (Bensimón et al., 2019; Garcia et al., 2017). Much of the literature on Latinx/a/student success has examined topics such as identity development (Perez, 2021), belonging (Huerta, 2022), and persistence (Flores & Park, 2015). Higher education scholars have focused on understanding structural barriers that inhibit Latinx/a/o students from achieving their educational goals, including but not limited to exclusionary institutional policies, racism, and the rising cost of higher education (Duran & Pérez, 2017; Hurtado et al., 2020; Ryu et al., 2021).

Many studies on Latinx/a/o students have taken place at Predominantly White Institutions (PWIs) (e.g., Gonzalez et al., 2018; Pérez, 2017). However, Hispanic-Serving Institutions (HSIs) have been at the forefront of advancing the educational outcomes of Latinx/a/o communities nationwide (Excelencia in Education, 2021). For example, HSIs make up approximately 17% of all institutions of higher education in the United States (HACU, 2021). Most importantly, HSIs enroll approximately two-thirds of all Latinx/a/o undergraduates (Excelencia in Education, 2022; HACU, 2021).

Given that HSIs serve as a main postsecondary gateway for Latinx/a/o students, it is critical to understand the experiences of this student population in this sector. For this chapter, we analyzed scholarship on Latinx/a/o student success at HSIs for the purpose of providing a counternarrative to grit. To accomplish this goal, we completed a systematic review of the literature while also exploring the concept of servingness (Garcia et al., 2019). To make our findings more relevant to practitioner audiences, we offer

DOI: 10.4324/9781003332497-13

implications for practice at the end of our chapter. Our analysis was guided by two central research questions:

1 What are current understandings of Latinx/a/o student success at HSIs?
2 In surveying the literature, how can we provide a counternarrative to grit?

Overview of Key Terms

Before we dive into our analysis, it is important to define key terms used throughout this chapter. We are aware that these terms have different meanings depending on the audience, and some are still evolving in terms of their definition(s). First, we used "Latinx/a/o" as a more inclusive term to refer to students of Latin American and Caribbean descent residing in the United States (Salinas, 2020). Second, derived from critical race theory (CRT), we used "counternarrative" to interrogate existing notions of grit through our investigation of literature about Latinx/a/o student success at HSIs and the concept of "servingness" (Blaisdell, 2021). In this chapter, our counternarrative seeks to acknowledge the different histories and experiences of oppression that Latinx/a/o people have encountered in educational contexts (Solórzano & Yosso, 2002) and how this may relate to achievement.

Third, grit has been defined as trait-level perseverance and the ability to sustain passion for long-term goals (Duckworth & Quinn, 2009). While literature about Latinx/a/o students is expanding, there is limited scholarship highlighting the nexus between Latinx/a/o student success and grit (Lopez & Horn, 2020). Rather than redefining grit, we have chosen to provide a counternarrative to the widely accepted definition from Duckworth and Quinn (2009) in relation to Latinx/a/o students by explicitly calling attention to structural factors that affect Latinx/a/o students in HSI contexts. We propose that campus offices, departments, and leaders must move forward and embrace the "S" in their HSI designation and serve students with supportive programming and initiatives to help them overcome barriers instead of hoping their students are resilient enough to persist and "grit" through difficult scenarios. Using this book chapter, we provide a counternarrative to grit with the goal of equipping higher education professionals with better tools to support Latinx/a/o students.

Fourth, the term "decolonize" has been used by many scholars in education (e.g., Garcia, 2018). We borrow from the context provided by Wilder (2013) to demonstrate that a call to decolonize HSIs is grounded in the history of colonization in the system of higher education. Such a system is politically and economically tied to the transatlantic slave trade and Indigenous genocide within the United States. Garcia and Okhidoi (2015) make the argument that the most effective way to study HSIs is through an organizational lens, particularly to encourage HSIs to "take social action in order to dismantle racist structures and discriminatory policies that continue to plague students of color in the postsecondary pipeline" (p. 93). In this chapter, we hope to make strides toward decolonizing these discriminatory ideologies and practices, such as grit, and introduce a counternarrative with more inclusive and supportive practices for Latinx/a/o students at HSIs and eHSIs.

Last, by building on the work of scholars who have studied HSIs, we use the concept of servingness as our conceptual framework which provides a counternarrative to grit. Garcia et al. (2017) developed a typology of HSIs organizational identities, which used organizational theory to place the onus on organizations rather than on individuals to understand how HSIs serve Latinx/a/o students. This narrative situates the HSI as the responsible entity to ensure an educational experience that provides curricular and co-curricular support for all Latinx/a/o student success, meeting them where they are and assisting them in order to help them achieve their goals in a true servingness-based approach. In what follows, we explain how we used servingness as our conceptual framework.

Conceptual Framework

We define "servingness" using Garcia et al.'s (2019) multidimensional approach to conceptualize what it means to refrain from simply enrolling Latinx/a/o students to actually serving their academic needs. Servingness addresses the educational needs of Latinx/a/o students through culturally and racially affirming policies, practices, and pedagogies (Garcia et al., 2019). Garcia et al. developed indicators and structures of serving Latinx/a/o students, which are organized into four major themes: (a) outcomes, (b) experiences, (c) internal organizational dimensions, and (d) external influences. The authors consider "servingness" a term that is intentional and directed toward an institution's organizational identity, enrolling a minimum of 25% Latinx/a/o, producing an equitable number of outcomes for Latinx students, and enacting a culture that enhances the educational and racial/ethnic experience of Latinx students (Garcia et al., 2017). Therefore, race and ethnicity should be considered a part of servingness, and yet research demonstrates that HSI funding streams miss their opportunities to reveal racial inequalities in student outcomes and experiences, hindering servingness for racially minoritized groups (Bensimon, 2012).

Instead of placing the onus on Latinx/a/o students who "lack" grit (Rodríguez et al., 2018), in this chapter we shift the grit narrative toward educational systems, particularly the ways in which schools (e.g., K-12, community colleges, bachelor's degree-granting institutions) fall short of meeting the needs of Latinx/a/o communities. In turn, using servingness as a counternarrative to grit, we examined how Latinx/a/o students overcome barriers imposed by educational systems that were not historically designed for them in mind (Alemán, 2009; Pérez, 2017). We also used this opportunity to highlight the strengths that Latinx/a/o students and communities bring to postsecondary education, which are often overlooked (Yosso, 2005).

Given the robust body of work that Garcia et al. (2019) and Garcia et al. (2017) have undertaken to conceptualize the meaning of servingness at HSIs, we used this concept to examine literature on HSIs and Latinx/a/o student success. Further, we used servingness to provide a counternarrative to the traditional concept and notions of grit as it pertains to Latinx/a/o students at HSIs.

Methodology

We followed Burmicky and McClure's (2021) matrix approach to conduct our systematic review of the literature. Burmicky and McClure drew from Neuman and Gough's (2020) framework for conducting literature reviews, which involves several stages. The first stage involved identifying the research questions, which we centered around examining the literature on Latinx/a/o students at HSIs to provide a counternarrative to grit. Second, we identified servingness as our conceptual framework to help us conduct our analysis. Third, we developed selection criteria which helped us narrow down our search to include the following sources: peer-reviewed articles, scholarly books, and book chapters (Burmicky & McClure, 2021).

For our first search, the inclusion terms were as follows: Hispanic-Serving Institutions, Hispanic, and students. This search yielded 245 results. For our second search, the inclusion terms were as follows: Hispanic-Serving Institution, Latino, and students. This search yielded 23 results. We compared both lists generated by the separate searches to check that there were no overlapping or repeated pieces. To make sure we did not miss any pieces, we engaged in forward or snowball searching (i.e., who has cited the piece) (Ortagus et al., 2020) and backward searching (examining the reference cited) (Duran, 2019). We relied on Google Scholar for the forward or snowfall searching. In total, after screening the results based on the aims and scope of our research questions, we narrowed down the results to 107 pieces of literature.

Once we identified the pieces that we wanted to review based on the selection criteria above, we developed a matrix method to synthesize the literature more efficiently (Goldman & Schmalz, 2004). This strategy allowed us to compare, contrast, and merge disparate themes into one coherent whole (Neuman & Gough, 2020).

Findings

We discuss our findings in three broad categories: providing a counternarrative to grit, understanding the meaning of servingness, and cultivating a culture of care.

Providing a Counternarrative to Grit

Our review of the literature led us to identify that grit has been associated with student persistence, especially among first-semester Latinx/a/o students (Bailey, 2021). However, Puente and Ramirez (2021) underscored that programs must depart from viewing first-generation, low-income, and/ or students of color as not being successful due to lacking ability to succeed and instead move toward an understanding of the historically accumulated impact of race and racism on the lives of students of color. Furthermore, according to Tewell (2020), grit and other deficit perspectives are fundamentally about how to maintain broken systems, without requiring significant changes or sacrifices on the part of privileged classes. A more productive focus may be to think about how programs and institutions can best serve students.

In discussing grit, Duckworth (2016) highlights the importance of passion and perseverance. The examples of grit that Duckworth described in her book are people who had someone in their life, usually parents, who expressed continual support of their interests. As Schreiner (2017) described, the privilege of violin lessons and the ability to buy musical instruments go further than just childhood activities and hobbies; they translate later in life to college success and completion rates. Similarly, Schreiner's point of view provides an opportunity to understand (a) the love and support Latinx/a/o students also receive from their parents as a distinct form of their parents' knowledge of systems and structures, and (b) how these systems and structures expand or constrain the economic privileges parents confer to their children.

The comparatively lower college admission, retention, and graduation rates among Latinx/a/o students can be attributed to several structural factors, including but not limited to institutional racism, poverty, and inequitable access to quality K-12 education (Lardier et al., 2020). In this section, we provide a counternarrative to grit, as informed by our survey of the literature on Latino/a/x students at HSIs. To contextualize this finding, we begin with a quote by Albert Einstein: "Everybody is a genius, but if you judge a fish by its ability to climb a tree, it will live its whole life believing that it is stupid" (Kelly, 2004, p. 80). We use this quote to acknowledge the far-reaching structural factors that influence an individual's ability and perceptions to succeed outside of their own effort or grit, especially racially minoritized students in postsecondary education (Solórzano & Yosso, 2002).

Grit is often referred to as an integral determinant of success, having the tenacious pursuit of a dominant superordinate goal despite setbacks (Duckworth & Gross, 2014). Although many characteristics make someone successful, Duckworth et al. (2007) argued that grit is most present among prominent leaders across every profession and field. Grit is selected above charisma, emotional intelligence, and self-confidence as it pertains to measuring an individual's likelihood to be successful. Thus, before providing a counternarrative, we must first understand the scholarly background of grit, specifically in the context of students of color.

Research has documented that there are disparities between upper-income white students and first-generation, working-class, students of color in terms of educational outcomes. These disparities are mostly as a result of having to catch up with the "broken system," which drastically favors economically privileged. For example, Tewell (2020) asserted that "grit is an overly simplified answer to entrenched problems, requiring students to adapt to a broken system and failing to engage with the core causes of educational disparities" (p. 147). Referring back to Albert Einstein's quote, the ideology of grit would judge fish on how well they can climb trees and label them as "needing to be grittier." As a result, it is imperative to look at Latinx/a/o student success through a holistic lens that includes other metrics of success outside of graduation rates, retention rates, and test scores (Garcia et al., 2017, 2019). According to a report of the National Center for Education Statistics authored by Kena et al. (2015), a high-income student with an SAT score in the bottom quartile has a greater chance of completing college (30%) than a low-income student with an SAT score in the top quartile of the nation (26%). Individual grittiness cannot fix a system that maintains successful practices for some and dehumanizing practices for others.

A deficit ideology frames student challenges and failures as the result of their own limitations, attitudes, behaviors, mindsets, and other characteristics (Gorski, 2016; Valencia, 1997). Many scholars have begun to also interrogate the ideology of grit. For example, Gorski (2016) asserted that a grit ideology is even more dangerous than the deficit ideology on which it was founded. He noted that those with a deficit ideology ignore the structural barriers for success and attribute failure to the mindsets of the individual person or student. In contrast, those who believe in a grit ideology are well-aware of and even acknowledge structural barriers; however, rather than working to remove the barriers, they focus on cultivating the grit of the individual student in order for them to be successful rather than supported (Gorski, 2016).

Overwhelmingly, much of the literature brought up the tension that exists between definitions of success through traditional metrics and understanding the systemic barriers that historically marginalized populations face. As Almeida et al. (2021) highlighted, traditional definitions of grit diminish the role of institutional actors within a student's success. Vargas et al. (2019) highlighted that racial inequality is widespread in higher education—it affects our students and it influences their experiences throughout their time at our institutions. Scholars and practitioners must begin the work to decolonize the ideology of grit as well as other ideologies that leave our students of color to fend for themselves in higher education.

In discussing the discourse about Title V funding and its impact on Latinx/a/o student success, Aguilar-Smith (2021) argued that the race-evasive pursuit of grant seeking capitalizes on Latinx/a/o students by effectively ghosting the "H" in HSIs and gravely distorting the "S" in HSIs from *serving* to *$erving*. In her article, Aguilar-Smith described the tension that HSI presidents face for using Title V funds to "serve all students," even though racial equity gaps are often most magnified among Latinx/a/o students. Garcia (2018) called on scholars and practitioners to consider the concept of servingness through a lens of decolonization. We challenge scholars and practitioners to consider grit through a lens of decolonization to adequately support Latinx/a/o students. To build our counternarrative to grit, we provide implications for practice by cultivating a culture of care framed by Garcia's framework of servingness.

Understanding/Conceptualizing Servingness

Although HSIs have been federally recognized since 1992 and have rapidly increased in numbers for the last three decades, the concept of *servingness* at HSIs is relatively new. As highlighted in our conceptual framework, Garcia et al. (2019) synthesized the literature and provided a multidimensional conceptual framework for understanding "servingness" in HSIs. Their work developed indicators and structures of serving Latinx/a/o students, which are organized into four major themes: (a) outcomes, (b) experiences, (c) internal organizational dimensions, and (d) external influences.

Several articles explored and detailed such indicators and structures at specific HSIs and emerging HSIs, also known as eHSIs.[1] We analyzed how scholars framed servingness and provided promising practices of institutional efforts that signal commitments toward becoming HSIs. For example,

Torres and Zerquera (2012) identified successful HSIs as environments that focus on student success through the following: improving student services to support Latinx/a/o students; developing curriculum that better aligns with the Latinx/a/o student interests; having leaders who are proactive in developing a commitment to Latinx/a/o student success; partnering with their surrounding communities (which usually have a large Latinx/a/o population), including high schools and other postsecondary institutions; and embracing diversity while enhancing the Latinx/a/o campus climate.

We also found scholarship that described programs that have been implemented at HSIs and eHSIs that directly align with servingness. We share a quote from a study by Brooks et al. (2012), which examined a teacher education program at an HSI:

> Teachers of color not only share the cultural backgrounds of their students, but also: (a) hold students of color to a higher academic standard that they are then more likely to obtain, (b) serve as cultural and linguistic translators for these students, (c) act as advocates for students who are silenced or invisible in school settings, and (d) intervene when racism and discrimination alienate or isolate students of color.
>
> *(p. 351)*

Similarly, Garcia et al. (2017) revealed the invaluable support and advocacy that cultural connections create when faculty and staff connect with Latinx/a/o students via language. While both articles discussed representation and the hiring of Latinx/a/o faculty as a means to serve the Latinx/a/o student population, Brooks et al. asserted the critical importance of having teachers of all backgrounds that affirm students' ethnic, linguistic, and socio-economic identities. Brooks et al. and Garcia et al. gave tangible examples for how to serve Latinx/a/o students, which included providing community-based experiences, culturally responsive pedagogy, and continuous professional development. These methods of serving Latinx/a/o students can begin to bridge the gap and provide support by meeting the students where they are at and not requiring students to simply have grit and push through spaces where they may feel neither supported nor accepted.

In addition, we found relevant pieces that spoke directly to faculty roles in supporting students. For example, Ching (2022) offered insight into Polkinghorne's (2004) concept of "background knowledge." Ching described "background knowledge" as color-conscious faculty who have the ability to understand how policies and practices disproportionately disadvantage Latinx/a/o students. Ching's work also examined how faculty can change their practices to better serve these students. Specifically, Ching argued that faculty can better serve Latinx/a/o students by critically examining the role that they play in fostering student achievement, learning, development, and sense of belonging.

Cultivating a Culture of Care

Previous research has shown that Latinx/a/o students, including those attending HSIs, are often still confronted with feelings of insecurity or lack of sense of belonging, which undermine their morale and academic success (Cuellar & Johnson-Ahorlu, 2016; Maestas et al., 2007; Sanchez, 2019). This is because although HSIs are meant to serve Latinx/a/o students, they often ascribe to white, Eurocentric norms, especially when it comes to organizational policies and practices (Urrieta, 2009). Enrolling in an HSI is not enough to combat feelings of isolation and lack of sense of belonging. Thus, several researchers have urged scholars and practitioners at HSIs to elevate their Latinx/a/o-serving culture by increasing their campuses' ability to foster sense of belonging, cultural connections, identifications on campus, and self-authorship (Cuellar, 2014; Guardia & Evans, 2008; Maestas et al., 2007; Sebanc et al., 2009; Urrieta, 2009). Most of the literature emphasized the value of creating caring campus cultures where Latinx/a/o students feel seen, valued, and culturally validated (Rendón, 1994), which is a way these efforts can disrupt the grit narrative by providing support and building connections for Latinx/a/o students. The challenge is that many of these efforts often fall on the shoulders of racially minoritized faculty and staff who are already feeling burnt out and overworked by their current responsibilities (Solis & Durán, 2022).

Several works we reviewed discussed the importance of promoting a caring culture on campus toward Latinx/a/o student success. For example, some literature discussed a culture of care by employing widely used student outcomes and development theories such as sense of belonging (e.g., Buskirk-Cohen & Plants, 2019; Comeaux et al., 2021; Cruz et al., 2021; Maestas et al., 2007; Zumbrunn et al., 2014). For example, Comeaux et al. (2021) underscored that HSIs are under greater scrutiny for having low student graduation rates, including others by traditional metrics of success set by profit-driven college rankings and measuring tools that center whiteness and affluence (e.g., foundations, grants). Even though many HSIs enroll a large percentage of working-class, first-generation college students (Excelencia in Education, 2022), few metrics recognize the value of HSIs in providing broad access to postsecondary education. Given this context, much of the scholarship on this topic used asset-based framing further disrupting grit by interrogating or placing the onus on systems rather than individuals (Garriott et al., 2019).

Previous research has examples of ways to implement a counternarrative to grit theory. Comeaux et al. (2021) urged HSI practitioners to take the time to understand the racial climate of their campus, especially from the perspective of racially minoritized students who have not historically been well-served by their colleges. Understanding the campus racial climate can lead to implementation of more suitable racially and culturally affirming policies and practices. Vela et al. (2019) explored Latinx/a/o students' vocational outcome expectations. In their study, the authors found that Latinx/a/o college students have more positive vocational outcome expectations when they perceive higher levels of meaning in life, as well as having strong family bonds. As such, Vela and colleagues recommended for practitioners to develop programs, policies, and practices that have stronger adherence to Latinx/a/o values, as well as more acknowledgement of students' family members (2019). Some of these programs, policies, and practices could be culturally sustaining and responsive curricular and co-curricular activities—including but not limited to ethnic studies and peer support programs. Other activities may include structured trainings that foster (a) racial and cultural awareness and (b) meaningful cross-racial exchanges that challenge students to think beyond their own thoughts, lived experiences, and world views (Comeaux et al., 2021). In essence, when Latinx/a/o students feel cared for, valued, validated, and represented through institutional policies, practices, and norms, they are able to thrive during their college experience, and achieve better educational outcomes.

Implications for Research and Practice

Servingness is multidimensional (Garcia et al., 2019) and both Latinx/a/o students and HSIs are heterogenous groups. The literature does not support the concept of servingness as one-size-fits-all. Namely, HSIs are diverse organizations that include two-year, four-year, private, public, liberal arts, vocational, religiously affiliated, or secular institutions. Moreover, Latinx/a/os are a "heterogeneous group varying by country of origin, socioeconomic background, generational status, language preference, immigration status, academic preparation" (Garcia & Okhidoi, 2015, p. 346). Therefore, a counternarrative to grit calls for a multidimensional approach to policy, scholarship, and practice, as detailed by Garcia et al. (2019).

Furthermore, Title V grant decision-makers, Latinx/a/o policy advocacy groups—namely Hispanic Association of Colleges and Universities (HACU) and Excelencia in Education—and HSI/eHSI campus presidents and administrators must have a diversified knowledge and perspective on both HSI/eHSI and Latinx/a/o identities to lead and implement transformative organizational structures. Educational leaders, specifically HSI practitioners working with Title V funding, must be intentional in discovering systems and mechanisms that can directly serve the diverse Latinx/a/o students at their unique postsecondary institutions.

A counternarrative to grit requires scholars, practitioners, and policymakers to avoid one-size-fits-all approaches and to center the histories and experiences of Latinx/a/o students while considering interlocking systems of oppression (e.g., racism, white supremacy) (Solórzano & Yosso, 2002). Also, it is important to be intentional about research and praxis informing one another as an effort to enact true servingness at our institutions.

The findings for this chapter suggest that when HSIs and eHSIs have racial/ethnic conscious faculty, they create a presence of culturally relevant curricula and programs that can empower and liberate the Latinx/a/o student population which elevates the concept of servingness. For example, Garcia and Okhidoi (2015) highlighted the use of a Chicana/o Studies Department and Educational Opportunity Program (EOP) as structures within an HSI that provide culturally relevant curricula and programs to Latinx/a/o students. The authors had three primary recommendations regarding how institutions could better serve Latinx/a/o students through curricula: (a) Institutions should make ethnic studies courses a part of the general education requirements for graduation; (b) Ethnic studies can be institutionalized by making it a department with appropriate resources; and (c) Universities and colleges must encourage other departments on campus to offer courses that address racial/ethnic content within their programs (Garcia & Okhidoi, 2015). HSIs that make culturally relevant curriculum a part of the overall campus goals for learning ultimately shift the campus culture and provide a platform for ethnic studies programs to be used as models, as well as for faculty to become experts on how to effectively teach Latinx/a/o students (Garcia & Okhidoi, 2015).

Decolonize Grit to Remove Barriers

The call to decolonize has many different approaches, and scholars are grappling with this term and what it could mean within the field of education. While Tuck and Yang (2012) defined this term as a literal call for the return of Indigenous land and life, we adopt this as "a term that recognizes the 'colonial matrix of power' that is grounded in historical coloniality and operates in four realms of modernity, including economic, political, civic, and the epistemological realms" (Cervantes & Saldaña, 2015, p. 133). As cited by Marin (2019), HSIs were not created as a result of a "particular organizational agenda" (Ballysingh et al., 2017, p. 13) or "to serve a given population" (p. 13) as Historically Black Colleges and Universities were created to do, for example. Rather, existing institutions obtained HSI designations based on enrollment numbers of Latinx students. As a result, "the majority of HSIs do not overtly express a mission focused on serving Latinx students" (p. 13) but, instead, remain centered on the mission that preceded their HSI designation. Through our exploration of the literature, we learned that many scholars have suggested that many HSIs are not in fact "Hispanic-serving" because they tend to operate like traditionally white institutions rather than addressing the educational and systemic challenges that Latinx/a/o communities face (Marin, 2019).

Although HSIs demonstrate success in opening the doors to Latino/a/x students, these same institutions have been noted as lacking guidance on how to assess and improve their ability to serve their Latino/a/x students (Franco & Hernández, 2018). Instead of working to reconcile white guilt and complicity, leaders of HSIs must move forward with a transformative path to creating systems that serve their Latino/a/x student population. By providing a counter narrative of grit, practitioners and scholars can begin to address the many barriers our students face on campus including, but not limited to, housing and food insecurity, lack of access to support services, and unjust school policies that can stand in the way of their success and persistence (Gorski, 2016).

Although our immediate literature review did not spend much time addressing the individual student needs, Almeida et al. (2021) emphasized the need to shift away from grit and toward a model of social capital which acknowledges the role of resources on campus, not the individual being responsible for shaping student success. By decolonizing the concept of grit and identifying the university's role in addressing student-based needs instead of the student's need to be resilient, we can address the university's role to provide support measures to increase retention, persistence, and overall success rates for Latino/a/x students within higher education. These supports could come in the form of student programs (e.g., food pantries, culturally competent advising sessions, additional funding, and scholarship opportunities) and social spaces (e.g., commuter lounges, designated study spaces, cultural student organizations) with the intent to facilitate social capital that would benefit Latino/a/x students at HSIs, which in turn would encourage their persistence through higher education and lead them to accomplishing their long-term goals (Almeida et al., 2021).

Bringing a Culture of Care to Campus Life

Last, our exploration of the literature underscored the importance of creating caring cultures for Latinx/a/o students at HSIs. Our analysis led us to understand that faculty and practitioners at HSIs should not assume that Latinx/a/o student needs are being met without being intentional about making sure that students feel seen, valued, and culturally validated. To conclude our chapter, we present several questions for HSI practitioners and administrators to ponder:

- What are the ways in which my department's practices create a culture of care for Latinx/a/o students? Can I give specific examples?
- What are the ways in which my department's curriculum and pedagogical approach center the needs of Latinx/a/o students? Can I give specific examples?
- How am I partnering with practitioners on campus to develop a culture of care? Am I forming strong partnerships across campus that allow us to create much needed systemic change?
- In creating a culture of care, how am I trying to interrupt systems of power, such as inequitable institutional policies, whiteness, and the adherence to traditional success metrics? In the same vein, how am I fostering a culture of care that acknowledges the precedent of colonial structures and projects in postsecondary education?
- In serving Latinx/a/o students holistically, how do I prioritize their intersecting identities, including but not limited to adult learners, caregivers, and part-time students? How am I making sure that these identities and lived experiences are represented in the classroom and our campus life? Rather than focusing on students' grit, how am I making sure that students are valued for who they are and for what they bring to our campus? Does my campus culture encourage this type of authenticity?

As scholar-practitioners committed to the success of marginalized student populations, we hope that these questions, along with the findings from our work, equip higher education leaders with a counternarrative to grit that better promotes Latinx/a/o student success.

Note

1 "Excelencia developed the emerging HSI category—institutions with undergraduate FTE Hispanic enrollment of 15–24.9%—to track the growth of potential HSIs."

References

Aguilar-Smith, S. (2021). Seeking to serve or $erve? Hispanic-serving institutions' race-evasive pursuit of racialized funding. *AERA Open*. https://doi.org/10.1177/23328584211057097

Alemán, E. Jr. (2009). LatCrit educational leadership and advocacy: Struggling over whiteness as property in Texas school finance. *Equity & Excellence in Education*, *42*(2), 183–201. https://doi.org/10.1080/10665680902744246

Almeida, D. J., Byrne, A. M., Smith, R. M., & Ruiz, S. (2021). How relevant is grit? The importance of social capital in first-generation college students' academic success. *Journal of College Student Retention: Research, Theory & Practice, 23*(3), 539–559. https://doi.org/10.1177/1521025119854

Bailey, J. L. (2021). *Grit as a predictor of retention for first-year Latino students at a Hispanic-serving institution* [Unpublished doctoral dissertation]. Seton Hall University.

Ballysingh, T. A., Zerquera, D. D., Turner, C. S., & Sáenz, V. B. (2017). Answering the call: Hispanic-serving institutions as leaders in the quest for access, excellence, and equity in American higher education. *Association of Mexican American Educators Journal Special Issue, 11*(3), 6–28. https://doi.org/10.24974/amae.11.3.359

Bensimon, E. M. (2012). The equity scorecard: Theory of change. In E. M. Bensimon & L. Malcom (Eds.), *Confronting equity issues on campus: Implementing the equity scorecard in theory and practice* (pp. 17–44). Stylus Publishing.

Bensimón, E. M., Dowd, A. C., Stanton-Salazar, R., & Dávila, B. A. (2019). The role of institutional agents in providing institutional support to Latinx students in STEM. *Review of Higher Education, 42*(4), 1689–1721. https://doi.org/10.1353/rhe.2019.0080

Blaisdell, B. (2021). Counternarrative as strategy: Embedding critical race theory to develop an antiracist school identity. *International Journal of Qualitative Studies in Education.* https://doi.org/10.1080/09518398.2021.1942299

Brooks, M., West-Olatunji, C., Blackmon, A., Froelich, K., De La Torre, W., Montano, T., & Smith, R. (2012). Minority-serving institutions and their contribution to advancing multicultural teacher education pedagogy. *Education, 133*(2), 349–360.

Burmicky, J., & McClure, K. R. (2021). Presidential leadership at broad access institutions: Analyzing literature for current applications and future research. In G. Crisp, C. Orphan, & K. R. McClure (Eds.), *Unlocking opportunity through broadly accessible institutions* (pp. 163–178). Routledge.

Buskirk-Cohen, A. A., & Plants, A. (2019). Caring about success: students' perceptions of professors' caring matters more than grit. *International Journal of Teaching and Learning in Higher Education, 31*(1), 108–114.

Cervantes, M. A., & Saldaña, L. P. (2015). Hip hop and nueva canción as decolonial pedagogies of epistemic justice. *Decolonization: Indigeneity Education Society, 4*(1).

Ching, C. D. (2022). Supporting Latinx students in Hispanic-serving institutions: An exploration of faculty perceptions and actions. *Journal of Latinos and Education, 21*(1), 39–58. https://doi.org/10.1080/15348431.2019.1612398

Comeaux, E., Grummert, S. E., & Cruz, N. A. (2021). Strategies of resistance among racially minoritized students at a Hispanic-serving institution: A critical race theory perspective. *The Journal of Higher Education, 92*(3), 465–498. https://doi.org/10.1080/00221546.2020.1851569

Cruz, R. G., Lecocke, M., Martines, I., & Lurie, A. (2021). Peer coaching program development: A framework of first-year Latina/o student persistence pursuing STEM pathways at a Hispanic serving institution. *Journal of Hispanic Higher Education, 20*(4), 365–384. https://doi.org/10.1177/1538192719867096

Cuellar, M. (2014). The impact of Hispanic-serving institutions (HSIs), emerging HSIs, and non-HSIs on Latina/o academic self-concept. *The Review of Higher Education, 37*(4), 499–530. https://doi.org/10.1353/rhe.2014.0032

Cuellar, M., & Johnson-Ahorlu, R. N. (2016). Examining the complexity of the campus racial climate at a Hispanic-serving community college. *Community College Review, 44*(2), 135–152. https://doi.org/10.1177/0091552116632584

Duckworth, A., & Gross, J. J. (2014). Self-control and grit: Related but separable determinants of success. *Current Directions in Psychological Science, 23*(5), 319–325. https://doi.org/10.1177/0963721414541462

Duckworth, A. L. (2016). *Grit: The power of passion and perseverance.* Scribner/Simon & Schuster.

Duckworth, A. L., Peterson, C., Matthews, M. D., & Kelly, D. R. (2007). Grit: Perseverance and passion for long-term goals. *Journal of Personality and Social Psychology, 92*(6), 1087–1101. https://doi.org/10.1037/0022-3514.92.6.1087

Duckworth, A. L., & Quinn, P. D. (2009). Development and validation of the short grit scale (Grit-S). *Journal of Personality Assessment, 91*(2), 166–174. https://doi.org/10.1080/00223890802634290

Duran, A. (2019). Queer and of color: A systematic literature review on queer students of color in higher education scholarship. *Journal of Diversity in Higher Education, 12*(4), 390–400. https://doi.org/10.1037/dhe0000084

Duran, A., & Pérez, D. II. (2017). Queering la familia: A phenomenological study reconceptualizing familial capital for queer Latino men. *Journal of College Student Development, 58*(8), 1149–1165. https://doi.org/10.1353/csd.2017.0091

Excelencia in Education. (2021). *Emerging Hispanic-serving institutions (eHSIs): 2020–21.* Excelencia in Education.

Excelencia in Education. (2022). *Hispanic-serving institutions (HSIs): 2020–21.* Excelencia in Education.

Flores, S. M., & Park, T. J. (2015). The effect of enrolling in a minority-serving institution for Black and Hispanic students in Texas. *Research in Higher Education, 56*(3), 247–278. https://doi.org/10.1007/s11162-014-9342-y

Franco, M. A., & Hernández, S. (2018). Assessing the capacity of Hispanic serving institutions to serve Latinx students: Moving beyond compositional diversity. *New Directions for Institutional Research, 2018*(177), 57–71. https://doi.org/10.1002/ir.20256

Garcia, G. A. (2018). Decolonizing Hispanic-serving institutions: A framework for organizing. *Journal of Hispanic Higher Education, 17*(2), 132–147. https://doi.org/10.1177/1538192717734289

Garcia, G. A., Huerta, A. H., Ramirez, J. J., & Patrón, O. E. (2017). Contexts that matter to the leadership development of Latino male college students: A mixed methods perspective. *Journal of College Student Development, 58*(1), 1–18. https://doi.org/10.1353/csd.2017.0000

Garcia, G. A., Núñez, A.-M., & Sansone, V. A. (2019). Toward a multidimensional conceptual framework for understanding "servingness" in Hispanic-serving institutions: A synthesis of the research. *Review of Educational Research, 89*(5), 745–784. https://doi.org/10.3102/0034654319864591

Garcia, G. A., & Okhidoi, O. (2015). Culturally relevant practices that "serve" students at a Hispanic serving institution. *Innovative Higher Education, 40*(4), 345–357. https://doi.org/10.1007/s10755-015-9318-7

Garriott, P. O., Navarro, R. L., Flores, L. Y., Lee, H.-S., Carrero Pinedo, A., Slivensky, D., Muñoz, M., Atilano, R., Lin, C.-L., Gonzalez, R., Luna, L., & Lee, B. H.

(2019). Surviving and thriving: Voices of Latina/o engineering students at a Hispanic serving institution. *Journal of Counseling Psychology*, 66(4), 437–448. https://doi.org/10.1037/cou0000351

Goldman, K. D., & Schmalz, K. J. (2004). The matrix method of literature reviews. *Health Promotion Practice*, 5(1), 5–7. https://doi.org/10.1177/1524839903258885

Gonzalez, C., Graber, J., Galvez, D., & Locke, L. A. (2018). "They say they value diversity, but I don't see it": Academic and social experiences of first generation Latinx students at a predominately white Midwest institution. In J. Hoffman, P. Blessinger, & M. Makhanya (Eds.), *Perspectives on diverse student identities in higher education: International perspectives on equity and inclusion* (pp. 61–74). Emerald Publishing Limited.

Gorski, P. C. (2016). Poverty and the ideological imperative: A call to unhook from deficit and grit ideology and to strive for structural ideology in teacher education. *Journal of Education for Teaching*, 42(4), 378–386. https://doi.org/10.1080/02607476.2016.1215546

Guardia, J. R., & Evans, N. J. (2008). Factors influencing the ethnic identity development of Latino fraternity members at a Hispanic-serving institution. *Journal of College Student Development*, 49(3), 163–181. https://doi.org/10.1353/csd.0.0011

Hispanic Association of Colleges and Universities (HACU). (2021, April 6). Hispanic serving institutions across the nation total 569. https://www.hacu.net/NewsBot.asp?MODE=VIEW&ID=3322

Huerta, A. H. (2022). Exploring undergraduate students' emotional vulnerability in men of color programs. *Journal of College Student Development*, 63(1), 49–66.

Hurtado, S., Ramos, H. V., Perez, E., & Lopez-Salgado, X. (2020). Latinx student assets, college readiness, and access: Are we making progress? *Education Sciences*, 10(4), 100. https://doi.org/10.3390/educsci10040100

Kelly, M. (2004). *The rhythm of life: Living every day with passion ad purpose.* Fireside.

Kena, G., Musu-Gillette, L., Robinson, J., Smith, W., Nelson, V., Robles-Villalba, V., Soo, W., Ballard, D., Wang, X., Rathbun, A., & Zhang, J. (2015). *The condition of education 2015.* National Center for Education Statistics, U.S. Department of Education.

Lardier, D. T. Jr., Lee, C.-Y. S., Rodas, J. M., Garcia-Reid, P., & Reid, R. J. (2020). The effect of perceived college-related stress on depression, life satisfaction, and school satisfaction: The coping strategies of Hispanic college students from a Hispanic serving institution. *Education and Urban Society*, 52(8), 1204–1222. https://doi.org/10.1177/0013124519896845

Lopez, J. D., & Horn, J. M. (2020). Grit and retention among first year Hispanic college students at a Hispanic serving institution. *Hispanic Journal of Behavioral Sciences*, 42(2), 264–270. https://doi.org/10.1177/0739986320910153

Maestas, R., Vaquera, G. S., & Zehr, L. M. (2007). Factors impacting sense of belonging at a Hispanic-serving institution. *Journal of Hispanic Higher Education*, 6(3), 237–256. https://doi.org/10.1177/1538192707302801

Marin, P. (2019). Is "business as usual" enough to be Hispanic-serving? Becoming a Hispanic-serving research institution. *Journal of Hispanic Higher Education*, 18(2), 165–181. https://doi.org/10.1177/1538192719832250

Neuman, M., & Gough, D. (2020). Systematic reviews in educational research: Methodology, perspectives and application. In O. Zawacki-Richter, M. Kerres, S.

Bedenlier, M. Bond, & K. Buntins (Eds.), *Systematic reviews in educational research* (pp. 3–22). Springer.

Ortagus, J. C., Kelchen, R., Rosinger, K., & Voorhees, N. (2020). Performance-based funding in American higher education: A systematic synthesis of the intended and unintended consequences. *Educational Evaluation and Policy Analysis, 42*(4), 520–550. https://doi.org/10.3102/0162373720953128

Pérez, D. II. (2017). In pursuit of success: Latino male college students exercising academic determination and community cultural wealth. *Journal of College Student Development, 58*(2), 123–140. https://doi.org/10.1353/csd.2017.0011

Perez, N. (2021). Nested contexts of reception: Latinx identity development across a new immigrant community. *Ethnic and Racial Studies, 44*(11), 1995–2015. https://doi.org/10.1080/01419870.2020.1807036

Polkinghorne, D. E. (2004). *Practice and the human sciences: The case for a judgment-based practice of care.* SUNY Press.

Puente, M., & Ramirez, B. R. (2021). Relearning self, recentering comunidad, and reidentifying within academia: A culturally relevant approach to summer bridge programs for incoming Latinx undergraduate students. *About Campus, 25*(6), 23–28.

Rendón, L. I. (1994). Validating culturally diverse students: Toward a new model of learning and student development. *Innovative Higher Education, 19*(1), 33–51. https://doi.org/10.1007/BF01191156

Rodríguez, C., Martinez, M. A., & Valle, F. (Eds.). (2018). *Latino educational leadership: Serving Latino communities and preparing Latinx leaders across the P-20 pipeline.* IAP.

Ryu, W., Burmicky, J., Sáenz, V. B., & Ponjuán, L. (2021). Exploring educational and workforce data trends on Latino boys and men: Implications for research and practice. In E. G. Murillo, D. Delgado Bernal, S. Morales, L. Urrieta, E. Ruiz Bybee, J. Sánchez Muñoz, V. B. Sáenz, D. Villanueva, & M. Machado-Casas (Eds.), *Handbook on Latinos in education: Theory, research, and practice* (2nd ed.; pp. 237–248). Routledge.

Salinas, C. (2020). The complexity of the "x" in Latinx: How Latinx/a/o students relate to, identify with, and understand the term Latinx. *Journal of Hispanic Higher Education, 19*(2), 149–168. https://doi.org/10.1177/1538192719900382

Sanchez, M. E. (2019). Perceptions of campus climate and experiences of racial micro-aggressions for Latinos at Hispanic-serving institutions. *Journal of Hispanic Higher Education, 18*(3), 240–253. https://doi.org/10.1177/1538192717739351

Schreiner, L. A. (2017). The privilege of grit. *About Campus, 22*(5), 11–20. https://doi.org/10.1002/abc.21303

Sebanc, A. M., Hernandez, M. D., & Alvarado, M. (2009). Understanding, connection, and identification: Friendship features of bilingual Spanish–English speaking undergraduates. *Journal of Adolescent Research, 24*(2), 194–217. https://doi.org/10.1177/0743558408329953

Solis, B., & Durán, R. P. (2022). Latinx community college students' transition to a 4-year public research-intensive university. *Journal of Hispanic Higher Education, 21*(1), 49–66. https://doi.org/10.1177/1538192719899628

Solórzano, D. G., & Yosso, T. J. (2002). Critical race methodology: Counter-storytelling as an analytical framework for education research. *Qualitative Inquiry, 8*(2), 23–44. https://doi.org/10.1177/107780040200800103

Tewell, E. (2020). The problem with grit: Dismantling deficit thinking in library instruction. *Libraries and the Academy*, *20*(1), 137–159. https://doi.org/10.1353/pla.2020.0007

Torres, V., & Zerquera, D. (2012). Hispanic-serving institutions: Patterns, predictions, and implications for informing policy discussions. *Journal of Hispanic Higher Education*, *11*(3), 259–278. https://doi.org/10.1177/1538192712441371

Tuck, E., & Yang, K. W. (2012). Decolonization is not a metaphor. *Decolonization: Indigeneity, Education, & Society*, *1*(1), 1–40. https://doi.org/10.25058/20112742.n38.04

Urrieta, L. (2009). *Working from within: Chicana and Chicano activist educators in whitestream schools*. University of Arizona Press.

Valencia, R. (1997). *The evolution of deficit thinking: Educational thought and practice*. Falmer Press.

Vargas, N., Villa-Palomino, J., & Davis, E. (2019). Latinx faculty representation and resource allocation at Hispanic service institutions. *Race Ethnicity and Education*, *23*(1), 39–54. https://doi.org/10.1080/13613324.2019.1679749

Vela, J. C., Lerma, E., Whittenberg, J. F., Hinojosa, Y., & Rodriguez, K. (2019). The role of positive psychology, cultural, and family factors in Latina/o college students' vocational outcome expectations. *Journal of Employment Counseling*, *56*(4), 164–179. https://doi.org/10.1002/joec.12131

Wilder, C. S. (2013). *Ebony and ivy: Race, slavery, and the troubled history of America's universities*. Bloomsbury Press.

Yosso, T. (2005). Whose culture has capital? A critical race theory discussion of community cultural wealth. *Race Ethnicity and Education*, *8*(1), 69–91. https://doi.org/10.1080/1361332052000341006

Zumbrunn, S., McKim, C., Buhs, E., & Hawley, L. R. (2014). Support, belonging, motivation, and engagement in the college classroom: A mixed method study. *Instructional Science*, *42*(5), 661–684. https://doi.org/10.1007/s11251-014-9310-0

11

HOLO I KA ʻAUWAI, FLOWING WITH THE POWER OF THE STREAM

Empowerment-Based Evaluation and Research

Anna M. Ortiz and Maenette K. P. Benham

Duckworth et al.'s (2007) concept of grit, as it is discussed in this book, is an individual construct: a person has grit. Some have more grit than others, which then also implies that some have no grit at all. Because grit is an individual, internal construct, a person is called to develop grit to counter structural, systemic barriers that may impede success as defined in educational settings. The construct relies on individuals to change, rather than on structures and institutions to change. The individualist approach challenges the norms of many collectivist communities: communities of color, Indigenous, underserved, and youth-focused communities that encourage empowerment through ancestry, community, and connection to a collective future as foundational to student success.

Our work as participant evaluators in many community-based projects has demonstrated that when youth are encouraged to connect with their sources of knowledge, they also find purpose, strength, critical understanding, and confidence to not only be individually successful but to prioritize how their achievements and agency can make inroads to community transformation and change. This is important since these communities, families, and students experience the same structural inequities that prevent college students from being equitably equipped to be successful in predominantly and historically white institutional environments.

Communities without social, economic, and political capital where many of our college students are raised are ones—much like African American communities (as described by Ladson-Billings, 2015)—that already have the components of grit (perseverance, resilience, optimism, confidence, creativity) simply by surviving. We agree with Gonzales (2016) when she challenged the

DOI: 10.4324/9781003332497-14

claim by Duckworth et al. (2007) that grit enables people to respond to adversity with resilience and optimism through working harder and sustaining the ability to maintain focused passions over time to attain goals, thus "staying the course in the face of barriers" (Gonzales, 2016, p. 115). When faced with structural racism and socioeconomic inequities, communities and projects we describe in this chapter show that they more than stay the course.

The original intent in this chapter was to explore the ways in which we have used evaluation (and research in general) as a way to build capacity in communities where they are empowered to imagine and create their own futures and to give their members what they need to enact their own vision of success. However, in the process of gathering our artifacts (reports, books, articles, memories), we reflected on what these projects and communities have to offer in the argument against grit, which has been made so eloquently by our colleagues in this book. We have come to the conclusion that we can offer a perspective on (a) "if not grit, then what?" and (b) how to create the *what* in our institutions of higher education so that students experience a more seamless transition. In their pursuit of excellent higher education experiences and outcomes, we argue that students can access and value the perspectives they have learned in their homes, families, and communities.

Thus, in this chapter we ground what we describe and propose in our experience as evaluators in community-based and higher education grant-funded projects. The overall purpose of evaluation is to improve programs either while they are in process (formative) or when complete to inform future programs (summative). These purposes are indeed valid and we have used both in our projects. However, a deeper consideration of *formative* evaluation where discoveries are ongoing sources for experience-grounded change is at the heart of participant evaluation, particularly in community settings. Experience-grounded change represents a form of community partnerships that is different from how we typically operationalize community partnerships in higher education. As we make evident in the chapter, our roles in these projects were to (a) help communities identify their strengths and challenges, and (b) develop their capacity to conduct their own assessment of their programs and services according to goals that they set, and (c) set new goals based on what they learn. Our aim is to help readers, especially those who find themselves in similar evaluation and leadership roles, to use approaches and methods that not only (or even) examine individual achievement and action, but also examine how communities are moved forward, changed, and improved.

In over 30 years of work, we have found that specific research methods encourage students to deconstruct societal forces that have been designed to exclude them from Western definitions of success. It is important to note that such methods allow students to discover their own (and their communities') levers of success. Gonzales (2016) supports the use of Critical Qualitative

Inquiry (CQI) because it counters "grit research that favors control over context, numbers over nuance, and objectivity over justice" (p. 118). We suggest that CQI can also transform the individuals involved and brings greater volition and agency to the community that remains; community transformation can enable future generations to benefit from the liberatory nature of projects that are often funded for relatively short durations. Evaluation and research that is critical, transformative, and truly *participatory* blurs the lines between research and evaluation and program implementation in ways that empower communities and youth (pre-college and college students) to deconstruct societal forces that impact them in order to create change that affects the individual through community and group development.

Utilization of research and evaluation (and by extension assessment) methods that build community *and* show that programs and people make progress as a result of external and internal investments is critical, as educational interventions that are designed to serve under-resourced communities, especially Indigenous communities, are grant-funded. They have been woefully underfunded because of the same systemic and institutional structures that ask individuals to develop grit. Thus, communities can become highly dependent on federal, state, and private funding through time-bound programs to support both community development as well as social and educational services. Further, educational interventions often require program evaluation and ongoing assessment to maintain and secure additional funding.

Program evaluation of funded programs is often compliance-based rather than empowerment-based and this is problematic for many reasons; in contrast, empowerment-based evaluation builds capacity and focuses on the needs, history, societal positions, and futures of people and their communities. Compliance-based evaluation focuses on objectives and the ability of programs to meet them. This evaluation would typically involve external evaluators who take a functional approach toward their work, examining program activities and evaluating their effectiveness in achieving goals stated in initial proposals. Deconstructing the complex and hurried nature of requests for proposals and support for writing those proposals is beyond the scope of this chapter, but suffice to say that garnering the community engagement necessary to set up the program for empowerment-based evaluation is a rare occurrence. While some funders continue to require robust program evaluation, others are actually de-emphasizing the importance of this function in the overall grant, resulting in decreased resources to fund robust evaluation, such as some federally funded programs that now limit the amount that can be spent on evaluation activities. Finally, it can be difficult to find experienced and culturally competent evaluators, which results in the kind of evaluation that subtly (or not so subtly) reinforces individualist approaches like grit and unknowingly (or intentionally) reinforces assimilation to predominantly white definitions of success.

An Indigenous Worldview critical qualitative inquiry, which undergirds our approach to participant evaluation, draws from a range of data (e.g., numeric, life, and ancestral stories; natural and earth movements). It employs multiple gathering strategies, like authentic participant observation, digital storytelling, Q-sort methodology, asset mapping, and pláticas. What is key is that the process of these methods value generativity, which derives meaning from shared ancestral and contemporary knowledge in its many storied texts. For example, in Benham's three volumes that comprise *In Our Mother's Voice*, each of the three participating groups of scholars participated in a process that drew from their particular worldviews—from the quantitative to the qualitative—which they expressed through story. The generative process of story-sharing challenged the voices of teachers, students, scholars, and administrators to weave their stories of nā pua, nā lei, and nā mamo (past-present-future) into a "critical movement that opens a gracious space to live-into the *Contemporary is Native* truth" (Ah Nee-Benham, 2008, p. 11).

It is through this generative and collective story-making process that the sharing of ancestral and contemporary knowledge is studied and appreciated, and displays diverse ways that Indigenous Knowledge tangles with and makes sense of capacious questions. An Indigenous Worldview critical qualitative inquiry approach is similar to the one we take in writing this chapter. In 2002, we contributed to a chapter confronting racism and ageism in the academy where we entered into a dialogue, weaving a story, offering and building on one another's perspectives around a shared phenomenon (Cooper et al., 2002). Later, Norris et al. (2012) would create duoethnography as a form of narrative to where researchers/writers give meaning to a "common phenomena as it was experienced throughout their lives" (Given, 2012).

In this chapter, we first present three important concepts that provide alternatives to grit. Then we describe attributes that are valued by Western perspectives, but leave Indigenous, urban, and rural communities marginalized by societal structures leaving them with great need, but also great talent, knowledge, and capacity. We start with the *Epistemology of Place*, where historical, genealogical, and geographical aspects of where we and our ancestors have lived and flourished is prioritized. *Intergenerational Engagement* provides a context where youth, college students, and elders learn from each other, respecting the knowledge that each bring to community success. *Collaboration over Competition* is a natural value for empowerment-based, capacity building approaches and calls to reject zero-sum approaches that prevent meeting the needs of all in favor of selecting specific segments as beneficiaries of funding and programs. We take examples from the numerous projects we have been involved with throughout the years. One such early project was *In Our Mother's Voices*, where Benham first worked with Tribal College and University presidents, and in the second phase brought mid-career, emerging scholars and students into the project. *Sustaining the Soul That Serves* took us from the Children's Defense Fund Freedom Schools in the urban setting to the rural Native American communities in Arizona and the Pueblos of Cochiti, including Laguna, Acoma, Jemez, and Zia.

Statements of positionality are tricky as we—Indigenous scholars—come to our work with a satchel of both unifying and contrary stories. For Benham, she appreciates the honesty of Critical Race Theory as a tool to examine education. As Freire (1973) writes: "To surmount the situation of oppression, people must first critically recognize its causes, so that through transforming action they can create a new situation, one which makes possible the pursuit of a fuller humanity" (p. 29). This idea of understanding the origin action/ideology that drives oppression is essential to social justice. Hence, Benham's Kānaka worldview begins with searching for an understanding of the roots that tie people to their places and practices, and the many paths that these ways of being in the world have traveled toward a place of hope and power. For Ortiz, Indigeneity is a part of her experience as a *Mestiza* person. The connection to roots and place and the experience of being displaced when convenient, *used* when needed and managing tension when traversing multiple (often competing) worldviews feeds into a critical consciousness that frames an approach to education and research characteristic of critical inquiry. A part of that is the unconditional commitment to conducting research and evaluation *for good*. This is accomplished by honoring the experiences of communities and people, centering their reality and epistemology, and working with them to develop capacity for community empowerment through telling their own stories in impactful ways.

Although we both claim social identities marginalized historically and contemporarily in U. S. society, we share the challenge of building credibility as outsiders within these communities and how our work as participant evaluators and project co-lead (Benham in *In My Mother's Voice*) helped communities to identify their own strengths and plan for futures they defined. We paired again the Kellogg Leadership for Social Change (KLCC) projects where the study/evaluation team used a variety of research methods throughout the project for participants to tell their own stories. Many of these methods have been documented in the volume *Reframing Community Partnerships in Education* (Guajardo et al., 2016), which reports on the Community Learning Exchange programs that evolved from the KLCC project. We describe *photovoice, asset mapping, and plática* methods used by Miguel and Francisco Guajardo in their work at the border in Edcouch, Texas; and the Q-sort method used by Matthew Militello and Christopher Janson. We share experiences as participant evaluators in several federally funded projects at University of Hawai'i campuses focused on increasing the success of Native Hawaiians in post-secondary education. Throughout the chapter, what is clear is that evaluation and research in these communities is largely a process of collecting stories in context: historically positioned stories that live within relationships and how—when context and history are understood—they strengthen those relationships toward community growth.

Although few of our examples are located within traditional institutions of higher education, the lessons learned are certainly applicable within them. Further, they demonstrate that communities, their organizations, and schools are places that higher education can *learn from*, disrupting the normative hierarchy of knowledge production. In each section, we give examples of how the same approaches can be used within colleges and universities to help students draw upon the strengths of their group histories, genealogies, and communities to succeed in higher education. Theoretically, this chapter is related to alternative concepts of student success such as community cultural wealth (Yosso, 2005), an emancipatory approach to research (Pasque et al., 2012), and the pedagogical perspective that Freire (1973) advanced that calls for communities to liberate themselves through dialogic methods of their creation that best represent their way forward.

Concepts for Empowerment and Capacity Building

The Historical Context of the Community and Relationships Across Communities: The Epistemology of Place

An essential construct of community-based, culturally enlightened evaluation is a thoughtful understanding of the multilayered contexts that position people and their actions. This intentionality we call *epistemology of place*. Nainoa Thompson, Native Hawaiian Pwo navigator and president of the Polynesian Voyaging Society (PVS), tells the story of graduating from high school with half-a-semester of Hawaiian History, which led to his floundering and frustration of being directionless. He felt as though he had no roots.

On the PVS website, Thompson's introduction begins with his journey to ground himself, particularly with his kumu/teachers:

> Among many other important mentors, Yoshio Kawano took him at an early age to tide pools to explore the mysteries of the inshore ocean; Herb Kāne introduced him to the stars his ancestors used to navigate great ocean distances; and Pwo navigator Mau Piailug taught him to see the natural signs he would use to guide Hōkūle'a, a replica of an ancient Polynesian voyaging canoe, throughout Polynesia. Nainoa's father taught him the universal values of voyaging—of having a vision of islands rising from the sea, of self-discipline, preparation, courage, risk-taking and the

spirit of aloha that would bind a crew on arduous journeys. On long voyages, under a dome of stars and surrounded by the vast empty ocean, Nainoa came to appreciate the Hawaiian concept of "mālama"—care taking. Astronaut Lacy Veach, who observed the Hawaiian Islands from space, helped Nainoa understand "mālama" from a planetary perspective. "The best place to think about the fate of our planet is right here in our islands," Veach told Nainoa. "If we can create a model for well-being here in Hawaiʻi we can make a contribution to the entire world."

(Polynesian Voyaging Society, 2023)

Nainoa's story teaches us to embrace "place" as your kumu/teacher and open yourself to the abundance of all that nourishes and at the same time commit to mālama, care for all the elements that sustain life.

In 1997, we began our return to the source of knowing through the initiative we titled, In Our Mother's Voice (IOMV) (Ah Nee-Benham & Cooper, 2000). We gathered at Sol y Sombra Ranch in Santa Fe, New Mexico. As carriers of knowledge and voice, 14 Indigenous scholars and kumu travelled from Australia, Tasmania, Aotearoa, Hawaiʻi, Alaska, Canada, and across Indian Country (North America) and gathered to share and explore the complexities of what "place" teaches and its importance in both our formal/school institutions and informal/familial and community settings. We could not have predicted the sacred, natural events that would inspire and move us. Indeed, we were all gently reminded of what has sustained Indigenous peoples for centuries—the sacredness of the stories that place shares. Our kumu included Indigenous scholars committed to preserving and growing the native language and culture of the Maori, Okanagan, Oneida, Native Hawaiians, Nyungar, Blackfeet, Alaska Natives, Cochiti Pueblo, and other Australian Aboriginal peoples. Commitment to Indigenous Sovereignty, Native leadership and policy, and the institutionalization of education and curriculum to sustain Indigenous languages and knowledge characterized overarching goals of the work.

These storytellers participated in three consecutive facilitated sessions: (a) Planning: Sharing Individual Visions for Native Education; (b) Nourishing: Generating a Collective Vision for Native Education; and (c) Harvesting: Defining a Collective Vision and Action Steps. The sharing circles invited each participant to describe their vision for their community's educational system. They each participated, sharing their nations/tribes origin story as well as the history of contact and impact of settlers. Weaved through their stories were songs, dances, poetry, and art. We wept together for our losses and we learned each other's songs and dances in appreciation for mother earth. The sustained vigil to honor every element of our stories resulted in a cogent and elegant vision for Indigenous education we entitled, "Go to the Source." This was reminiscent of our climb to the ancient Kiva of the Cochiti people.

At the core of this vision is a healthy, self-empowered, Indigenous grounded learner. Learning and teaching policies and practices needed to be grounded on four principles, all equally key to successful Indigenous students, families, and communities:

- Critical development of the intellect which like strong cordage weaves both/and Native-ancestral ways of seeing and doing with contemporary ways of seeing and doing.
- Intentional and sustained promotion for health and well-being of our mind, body, spirit, and mālama honua/caring for every element of mother earth.
- Revitalization and normalization of our Native languages, cultural practices and protocols, and art.
- Strengthened connection to the kumu/the source, the spiritual wisdom of our ancestors that are manifested in the abundance of our mother earth.

Darrell Kipp passionately spoke to this model that honored the epistemology of place:

> We cannot dismiss our history of extermination and the removal of our people … Assimilation through the Indian boarding schools was a large part of this history in which schools were used to acculturate and socialize new values and another way of seeing the world. Today we see the effects of capitalization. … The selling of the Native! Through all of this we see ourselves, our young people and our old people, struggling with the negotiation between the old and the new. So, what occurs in our educational settings is extremely important! Teaching our youth how to maintain the essence and the meaning of their heritage through language and cultural practices is important. And, teaching our youth how to negotiate between the traditional and the contemporary is important. Our model is important because it exemplifies a process, a natural process that acknowledges the importance of building relationships within our communities, with our environment, and with other cultures. So, education connects students to "living" in their physical, spiritual and native environments. This is important!
>
> *(Ah Nee-Benham & Cooper, 2000, pp. 19–20)*

This quotation holds key elements in understanding how, historically, value systems like grit have been used to separate Indigenous people from their sources of connection, strength, and knowledge. Indian boarding schools were created by a public and government that thought *they* knew what was best for the future of Indian people, forcing assimilation to dominant values by forced removal of their young people. That loss of language, culture, connection to place, and to family members has caused a number of mis-characterizations of issues that are now improperly considered as representations of dysfunctional Indigenous communities (e.g., see Lajimodiere, 2019; Littlemoon & Ridgway, 2009). Through revitalizing communities, language, and culture, as well as reinforcing the connection of youth to place, ancestors, and elders, we create a *natural process* that eschews the need for interventions to make folks "grittier" (Ladson-Billings, 2015).

Intergenerational Engagement

The key principle of intergenerational engagement is grounded in the sophisticated Native Hawaiian worldview of *kuaʻana-kaikaina* (the older and the younger sibling). It begins in a reciprocal process of teaching and learning between a teacher and student that generates new knowledge and action. This active passing of ancestral knowledge from one generation to the next provides a clarity of *kuleana* (responsibility to all) that supports new voices to address current problems, *E lawe i ke aʻo a ʻmālama, a e ʻoi mau ka naʻauao*, or to take the knowledge of our ancestral lineage and use it in new ways. This principle of clarity and coherence is consistent throughout our work and was demonstrated in every community that participated in the KLCC initiative.

KLCC marked a shift from Kellogg's focus on individual leadership development—a hallmark of previous Kellogg leadership programs—to actively engaging citizens in community issues and change. The vision was to develop a group of diverse community leaders that would work across differences, e.g., geographical, racial, cultural, age, class, or faith, by mobilizing collective action to improve local conditions and the quality of life in their communities. There were a total of 11 community participants, six of whom focused on the theme of Valuing and Building Youth-Adult Partnership to Advance Just Communities. The Llano Grande Center located in Edcouch, Texas, became the beacon for intergenerational engagement. Their strong footing in both the public high school and the local community led to successful college pathways for their predominantly Mexican American students. By adding a social advocacy curriculum that brought together youth and adults, or *kuaʻana-kaikaina*, to address problems in their community, these participants illustrated the power and purpose of this synergistic partnership.

The story of this partnership is one of the collaborative works between youth and adults for the purpose of addressing an issue that could not be addressed effectively by adult leaders alone. The school superintendent understood the limitations of the adult leaders, so enlisted youth leaders (which included students in the high school and recent graduates) to head an effort to pass a $21 million bond issue to build new schools in a South Texas community. This strategic response grew out of the skill sets that youth had actively developed alongside their adult mentors and partners. Together they learned the histories of their communities and their quilted and storied cultural nuances. Additionally, they studied the economic and political tensions overtime and their implications for their public school system—and in turn how that impacted student success. Armed with this knowledge of place, they developed a media strategy and a community forum strategy that would provide much needed information and facilitated opportunities for community members to discuss the points of view. In this close-knit collaboration, they learned and strengthened their skills in research, interviewing, video production, public speaking, and group facili-tation. Ultimately, the bond was passed.

Among all that we have learned about collective leadership, advocacy, and community change, what is essential is that particularly meaningful relation-ships between youths and adults—in which both people mentor each other and learn from each other—bring to light the assets and resiliency of people and community Ah Nee-Benham (2010). The action of civic engagement is a critical practice that students of all ages practice in community, in partici-pation with others. This collective action is necessary to cultivate vibrant and just communities and is an essential process that sustains the promise of democracy. In Phase II of KLCC, there were similar successes. In Caretta, West Virginia, Big Creek People in Action involved youth, community, and businesses to develop place-based service projects. The Michigan Boys & Girls Club of Benton Harbor involved students, teachers, and community members to expand leadership learning opportunities. The Lummi CEDAR Project (Washington State) brought youth and elders together to learn Lummi culture and language as they worked to rebuild families and com-munity. In Denver, Colorado, Mi Casa Resource Center for Women, Inc., youths, and adults became allies to improve education. ROCA, a multicul-tural youth and adult-led organization in Chelsea, Massachusetts, created more pathways for community youth to participate in community leadership development programs to steward programs that addressed many of their social and economic problems.

Intergenerational engagement in these community development initia-tives offers several counters to the use of grit to promote student success. Interventions to grow grit in students are inherently top down, expert to learner, knowing to the unknowing, adult to child. Paternalism, often a con-sequence of whiteness, undergirds the call to increase grit and is founda-tional in programs developed to make this happen. Seldom do higher education leaders, administrators, program leaders, or faculty consider that they have something to learn from their students and that with the exchange of learning, something more powerful becomes possible, such as institutional transformation. Likewise, we seldom encourage students facing difficulty to actually look to their family members or elders in their communities as sources of knowledge and resources for support, instead treating them as if their life in higher education is independent from home and community (Tachine, 2017, 2022; Tachine et al., 2016).

Through the Lens of Story-Making: Collaboration Over Competition

Story-making requires the collection and analysis of a body of data that captures the oral, visual, sound/music, documents and records, numeric, historical, art forms and more of a people, place, their legacy and present activity. Then weaving these diverse sets of data in a way that presents the work and the DNA of a community of people. The value of story-making to Indigenous peoples is vital for within the moʻōlelo (story) resides their life force. Engaging this process as the key approach to evaluation was essential to the W. K. Kellogg Foundation's Native American Higher Education Initiative (NAHEI, 1994–2000). NAHEI came at a critical moment of development for Tribal Colleges and Universities (TCUs). Since the establishment of the first tribal college, Navajo Community College, in 1968, tribal colleges multiplied across Indian country with increased students, programs, and graduate programs. Yet, they were sorely underfunded, which hindered their ability to have parity with mainstream institutions. After 30 years of work to distinguish themselves as self-determined institutions that supported almost every aspect of their community's life, they were designated as land-grant institutions in 1994. NAHEI was developed to support their expanding role to strengthen the communities they serve (see Benham & Stein, 2003). There are three key elements to story-making that emerged from the moʻolelo that speaks to the importance of collective leadership: (a) "All of us or none of us!"; (b) This is story-making and "We" need to tell the story; and (c) From the "I" to the Public "Eye" to the "WE."

NAHEI took a departure from the traditional approach to philanthropic funding that is often prescriptive, top-down, assimilating, and exclusive. In recounting the initiative's origin, Dr. Henrietta Mann (Mann, 2003) recounted that the W. K. Kellogg Foundation had invited tribal college presidents to their Battle Creek headquarters in 1992. They presented the NAHEI initiative that would, in brief, invite TCUs to submit proposals for funding through traditional request for proposal (RFP) process. Proposals would be reviewed and awards to several TCU institutions would be made. The tribal college presidents listened respectfully and then asked the Kellogg Foundation representatives to leave the room so that they could discuss the offer. After their discussion, the Kellogg Foundation employees were invited back into the room at which time, Dr. Mann writes, "Dr. Lionel Bordeaux, President of Sinte Gleska University, articulated the basic ground rule for the W. K. Kellogg Foundation initiative by stating, "It is all of us, or none of us." This position was culturally congruent with the concept of inclusiveness that has characterized the TCU movement" (xix). The decision of the tribal college presidents to insist that they were prioritizing Indigenous ways of knowing and doing represented a move toward a collective community effort. This also signaled that this initiative would be different, one where they determined what was best for the colleges, their students, and the communities they served. One that decentered the white man's way of knowing and doing.

This was the first time in the history of W. K. Kellogg Foundation funding that they were asked to step away from the norm of competitive funding and to work with this complex community of 30+ TCUs to define a transformational initiative that would uplift the whole TCU movement. In 1994, the Kellogg Foundation initiated a 7-year, $30 million dollar initiative that included three sets of participants. The first were all the TCUs and three federal entities (Haskell Indian Nations University, Southwestern Indian Polytechnic Institute, and the Institute of American Indian Arts). The second included the American Indian College Fund, the National Institute for Native Leadership in Higher Education, and the AIHEC (American Indian Higher Education Consortium) Student Congress. The third included mainstream institutions of higher education with programs that met the needs of Native students. An initiative that began with the idea of funding a handful of institutions was developed through a participative process that included Kellogg Foundation program directors and TCU leaders to strengthen an ecosystem of Indigenous Higher Education Institutions.

NAHEI introduced networking gatherings that were held on tribal lands, hence, reaffirming the importance of Indigenous place, people, and culture. Consequently, the approach to evaluation was one that sought to draw out ancestral stories that presented TCU leaders with culturally grounded and informed tools to address the challenges of generational trauma through pathways of healing. This was presented through the process called "elder reflections" that were intentionally included in every gathering. The elders opened the day and closed the day. They reminded all participants that the success of one institution is tightly linked to the power of inclusivity generated by all: "It is all of us, or none of us."

Although proponents of grit have not claimed that there is a limited amount of grit in the world, the individualistic nature of how they advocate developing grit in people certainly neglects the power of collaboration and covertly reinforces values related to competition over scarce resources. This story of the Tribal Colleges and Universities' refusal to participate in a program that would have had individual institutions competing for funds did two things. First, it called for a foundation, grounded in tradition but open to learning, to change its way of thinking about transformation—from benefitting a few, to creating a venue for large-scale transformation of an entire segment of higher education. Second, the case also demonstrates how resource-strapped, historically neglected institutions develop a collective voice for change. A parallel movement in higher education is seen in pockets where student-initiated recruitment and retention programs succeed because those who are "being served" take control over their own programs (Maldonado et al., 2005). Imagine that if, instead of establishing student success initiatives and developing grit through them, colleges and universities funded ethnic student organizations, ethnic studies programs and departments or multicultural centers to design their own student success initiatives and encouraged collaboration through more flexible administrative structures, rather than relying on these entities solely for cultural programming. Like the TCUs in the NAHEI project, entire segments of an institution would collectively address culturally grounded and informed student success initiatives.

Research and Evaluation Methods for Empowerment and Capacity Building

When we were in our doctoral programs, qualitative research did not enjoy widespread acceptance as it does today. We promise this is not a story of walking miles in the snow to get to our qual methods class! There was a strong tension between maintaining objectivity as much as possible by "managing our subjectivity" and by trying not to "go native" by engaging with the people and communities we were studying. However, we also learned about reciprocity, a concept that requires the researcher to consider that we are guests in our sites and that we may have opportunities, even responsibilities to contribute. Authentic participation evaluation calls on the evaluator or researcher to "help out" even if it might change the course of events. We have always taken the responsibility seriously, which is why it is difficult in the stories we recount in this chapter to remember if we were evaluators, facilitators, or even project leads.

My (Ortiz) first evaluation project was as a half-time graduate assistantship as an internal evaluator for a cross-cultural mediation program. I worked closely (at times sharing an office) with program staff where we jointly developed evaluation tools and where findings and insights from participant observation were regularly shared with program implementers. The team worked together to implement the program in an iterative way, as a less formal formative evaluation process. This resulted in greater capacity building. In later evaluation projects, particularly in the U. S. Department of Education grant that provided the original funding for Native Hawaiian Student Services at the University of Hawai'i at Mānoa, I worked closely with the data analyst as she developed data systems needed to monitor the progress of Native Hawaiian students. This was key to better understanding their students and to building their capacity to secure future grants and, more importantly, to provide data necessary for institutionalization of program components. Similarly, in the KLCC projects described earlier in the chapter, it was important that part of our work as evaluators was to work with communities to develop their data collection, management, and reporting capacity so that their programs and services would be sustained once our work with them ended.

These examples reflect intergenerational work and collaboration. We needed to shift the framework for external evaluation from objective observer, bound to the measurement and study of program activities meeting program goals, to learning more about the community and its members so that we find our usefulness based on their expressed needs. They also required humility, something that is often missing in evaluation work, reminding us that we enter environments knowing nothing about their lived experiences no matter how much we know about higher education, research, and evaluation. In many projects we would have been "sunk" without respectful humility. When we worked as evaluators on Sustaining the Soul that Serves, a Fetzer Foundation funded project to work with community service groups to prioritize self- and community-care for their members, we traveled to Window Rock, Arizona, the capital of the Navajo Nation near the state's border with New Mexico. Here, we were honored with visiting the home of a participant's grandmother, a respected elder in the community. She lived in a home without electricity or indoor plumbing and had a dirt floor. It was clear that this community did not need help developing something like grit—they already had it.

This is the connection to grit that we make in telling this story. When educational institutions try to help people develop grit, it so often comes from a place of pity and blame. Rhetoric often includes, "If only those people could help themselves, if only they could work harder, etc. they wouldn't be in the situation they are now." The "we can help them" reeks of a colonial mindset, paternalism, and white supremacy. The consequence is actually the opposite as programs, interventions, and messages focused on grit often incite shame in those they attempt to help. In this part of the chapter, we remember lessons learned in authentic participation evaluation and share methods that were used to help build capacity in the projects previously discussed, drawing largely on the consolidated work of Guajardo et al. (2016), who were also involved in many of the projects.

Asset Mapping

Asset mapping is closely associated with the concept of community cultural wealth and aligns with the argument we make about the importance of tapping into students' source of knowledge. Used extensively in various studies and projects centered in community (see Kramer et al., 2014; Luo et al., 2022), asset mapping is a more focused social network analysis, which has been used extensively to explore relationships, connections, and resources, etc., in any variety of settings. In evaluation, social network analysis is used to map how participants might use program resources in their community or as another way to understand impact. This method was used extensively in the NAHEI project to help participants to map relationships because with Native people relationships are paramount. Asset mapping can be used with students to identity sources of strength, knowledge, talent, etc., in their families, communities, friendship groups or even their own experiences. Francisco Guajardo et al. (2016) described how this was used to "rehabilitate the self-esteem" of his community by partnering with high school students to walk "the streets of their hometown going door to door to take stock of the assets extant within homes and neighborhoods" (p. 57). Through the analysis of the maps, among the conclusions that students drew was that proficiency in Spanish was viewed as valuable as proficiency in English.

In a higher education setting, moreover, asset mapping may have similar effects as a programmatic strategy in place of those that may be suggested by grit-based interventions. Tara Yosso's (2005) model of community cultural wealth can be a starter to helping students to identify assets in their lives that are normally ignored by traditional education as sources of strength. In their example of finding that Spanish was as valuable as English, Guajardo's students exemplify Linguistic Capital, a part of Yosso's model. The other Capitals—Aspirational, Familial, Social, Navigational and Resistant—also hold potential for the rehabilitation of students' self-esteem and allow them to identify actual sources of help in their educational journey and help in challenging systemic forms of oppression while doing so.

Q-Sort Methodology

Militello and Janson have used Q-Sort Methodology in several research studies that are community-based and in studies that have a more direct application in education, such as in counseling settings (Militello et al., 2013; Militello & Janson, 2014). They have also used Q-Sort Methodology in evaluation activities "in historically marginalized communities where there is a reluctance to engage in traditional evaluative processes" (Guajardo et al., 2016, p. 90); they refer to this methodology as InQuiry. The method gathers information about attitudes and values by offering statements that participants *sort* or analyze to offer perspectives on the topic. They posit that this works well in marginalized communities, in part when the evaluators or researchers work in concert with participants to author the statements. The collaborative approach results in statements that better capture the nuances and complexities of the phenomena in the community. The sort can be as simple as asking participants to rank order the importance of the statements or to identify those which most represent their experience and those that are outside of it.

Application to programs and interventions that promote student success can follow the same process. For example, if the topic under investigation is a classroom, and whether there may be climates that foster or detract from student success, program staff can work with a small group of students to develop statements that represent the range of experiences with this topic. In a group setting, all students in the program can engage in the sort. A set of instructions might ask them to select those that they have experienced, those they wish they had experienced, those that contribute to their success, and those that do not. Debriefing in small groups can both help students to discover that they do not have isolated experiences and allow for the possibility that they can construct common expectations for instructors, curriculum, and pedagogy that can be of use to faculty development initiatives. Furthermore, debriefing also allows students to understand how the behavior of others impact their success, not necessarily their own capacity.

Digital Storytelling

There have been several applications of digital storytelling in research and evaluation, sometimes under different names such as photovoice (Branch Douglas, 1998; Guajardo et al., 2016; Militello & Guajardo, 2013; Wang & Burris, 1997). The essence of digital storytelling is in having participants capture a phenomena through video and pictures that they then compile or analyze through a story of what the phenomena means to them. Guajardo et al. (2016) used this method in a number of the Community Learning Exchange and in the KLCC project. They describe a DigiHunt where participants engage in a scavenger hunt for examples that demonstrate their meaning-making around a central question. Teams are used to further the analytic capacity of the exercise in portraying a collective understanding of the question in their locations (a community, a school, a college or university). Teams collect visual representations that are then compiled into a story of the location's response to the question. The outcome of this data collection is similar to that of asset mapping in that participants find resources or barriers and then strategize to optimize the resources through strategies to overcome the barriers.

In higher education, an intervention like this can be used in team-building sessions for programs, classes, or student organizations. Like asset mapping, students can uncover people and resources that they can use to be successful, and they can also gain a better understanding of how structural forces (racism, exclusion, administrative barriers) may set them up for failure. This enables students to locate difficulties they face in succeeding rather than their own externally identified deficits. This deconstruction provides an avenue for a deeper understanding of those forces and a more authentic appraisal of their strengths, assets, and resources available to them. All these examples are more favorable than the call to work harder and focus more, and draw upon internal, individualistic motivation to succeed, which are all things that grit interventions reinforce.

Pláticas

Like other methods described here, *Pláticas*, a method grounded in Chicana feminist epistemology (see Morales et al., 2023), allows for storytelling from the participant perspective with the benefit of telling the story with others to develop shared meaning-making. This method offers a level of simplicity in terms of the actual process; it can be as simple as a group sitting in a circle responding to a "grand" question posed by the researcher or evaluator, enabling them to dialogue, asking their own questions of one another seeking clarification and commonality along the way. Pláticas are being used in research featuring the experiences of Latinos/as/x as they represent a way of storytelling that is culturally grounded. This is demonstrated by Guajardo and Guajardo (2013) when they share how Pláticas were a daily occurrence in their family's home, offering an opportunity to share the day, lessons learned, and connections to family, its history, neighbors and community.

Pláticas make for fruitful class assignments that encourage students to deeply explore their histories, sources of strength and connection, and those connections to their futures. The method can also be used in programs and interventions to develop community on campus. Counseling and multicultural centers can offer regular Pláticas for groups of students to support student success. They counter conventional ways of instilling grit in that they are community-oriented and rely on students identifying their own sources of strength and to come to understand that much of what they need to gain the components of grit (perseverance, resilience, optimism, confidence, and creativity) are within them, their friendship groups, families, and communities.

Conclusion

We have attempted to provide concrete alternatives to grit that are grounded in the communities, cultures, and families of students, particularly ones who come from collectivist cultures. It is no coincidence that our examples are grounded in Indigenous communities as those have been ones that have been stripped of their ways of being as a result of a history of settler colonialism (Patel, 2019; Smith et al., 2019) they have experienced since the white man came to these lands. Knowledge and sources of strength are found in place, in ancestors, families, and communities; our job in higher education is to help students learn about these and embrace them as ways to move them forward in the world. The story of Nainoa's father teaching him about the "the universal values of voyaging" that bind the crew on a voyage—self-discipline, preparation, courage, risk-taking, and the spirit of aloha—reinforce that grit is not the way. By relying on the teaching of kumu and the guidance of the stars, ocean, and land, the collaborative nature of voyaging produces values akin to those grit outcomes, but ones that are so much more connected to the people *we* are. The evaluation and research methods that we presented not only gather data but also help to empower students and communities. They all are about storytelling, drawing strength and knowledge from connecting the way *we* are to those who have come before us, for within the mo'ōlelo resides life force.

By focusing on the assets of communities, families, place, ancestry, and history when working with students, we take them out of the transactional space of traditional higher education institutions and away from paternalistic interventions and expectations such as grit, and allow for volition, agency, and empowerment, which goes much further to prepare students for the future. Through these alternatives to grit, it is much easier to imagine a future where, taking the lead from our students, we collectively truly transform communities and how we live in them.

References

Ah Nee-Benham, M. K. P. (Ed.). (2008). *Indigenous educational models for contemporary practice: In our mother's voice, Volume II.* Lawrence Erlbaum Associates.

Ah Nee-Benham, M. K. P. (Ed.). (2010). *Collective leadership for community change.* Lawrence Erlbaum Associates.

Ah Nee-Benham, M. K. P., & Cooper, J. (2000, Spring). *Indigenous educational models for contemporary practice: In our mother's voice.* Lawrence Erlbaum Associates.

Benham, M. K. A., & Stein, W. J. (Eds.). (2003). *The renaissance of American Indian higher education: Capturing the dream.* Routledge.

Branch Douglas, K. (1998). Impressions: African American first-year students' perceptions of a predominantly white university. *The Journal of Negro Education, 67*(4), 416–431. https://doi.org/10.2307/2668141

Cooper, J. E., Ortiz, A. M., Benham, M. K. P., & Woods Scherr, M. (2002). Finding a home in the academy: Confronting racism and ageism. In J. E. Cooper & D. D. Stevens (Eds.), *Tenure in the scared grove: Issue and strategies for women and minority faculty.* SUNY Press.

Duckworth, A. L., Peterson, C., Matthews, M. D., & Kelly, D. R. (2007). Grit: Perseverance and passion for long term goals. *Journal of Personality and Social Psychology, 92*(6), 1087–1101. https://doi.org/10.1037/0022-3514.92.6.1087

Freire, P. (1973). *Pedagogy of the oppressed.* The Seabury Press.

Given, L. M. (2012). Duoethnography. In L. M. Given (Ed.), *The SAGE encyclopedia of qualitative research.* SAGE. https://doi.org/10.4135/9781412963909

Gonzales, L. D. (2016). Revising the grounds for the study of grit: Critical qualitative inquiry in post-secondary education organizational research. In P. A. Pasque & V. M. Lechuga (Eds.), *Qualitative inquiry in higher education organization and policy research* (pp. 113–128). Routledge.

Guajardo, F., & Guajardo, M. (2013). The power of plática. *Reflections: A Journal of Public Rhetoric, Civic Writing, and Service Learning, 13*(1) (Fall 2013), 159–164.

Guajardo, M. A., Guajardo, F., Janson, C. & Militello, M. (2016). *Reframing community partnerships in education: Uniting the power of place and wisdom of the people.* Routledge.

Kramer, S., Amos, T. Lazarus, S., & Seedat, M. (2014). The philosophical assumptions and challenges of asset mapping approaches to community engagement. *The Journal of Psychology in Africa, 22*(4), 537–544. https://doi.org/10.1080/14330237.2012.10820565

Ladson-Billings, G. (2015, April 22). Now I Need to Have Grit. Black and Smart Word Press. https://blackandsmart.wordpress.com/2015/04/22/now-i-need-to-have-grit/

Lajimodiere, D. K. (2019). *Stringing rosaries: The history of unforgiveable, and the healing of Northern Plains American Indian boarding school survivors.* North Dakota State University Press.

Littlemoon, W., & Ridgway, J. (2009). *They call me uncivilized: The memoir of an everyday Lakota man from Wounded Knee.* iUniverse.

Luo, Y., Ruggiano, N., Bolt, D., Witt, J., Anderson, M., Gray, J., & Jiang, Z. (2022). Community asset mapping in public health: A review of applications and approaches. *Social Work in Public Health, 38*(3), 171–181. https://doi.org/10.1080/19371918.2022.2114568

Maldonado, D. E. Z., Rhoads, R., & Buenavista, T. L. (2005). The student-initiated retention project: Theoretical contributions and the role of self-empowerment. *American Educational Research Journal, 42*(4), 605–638. https://www.jstor.org/stable/3699474

Mann, H. (2003). Prologue elder reflections. In M. K. P. Ah Nee-Benham & W. Stein (Eds.), *The renaissance of American Indian higher education: Capturing the dream* (xvii–xxix). Lawrence Erlbaum Associates.

Militello, M., Bass, L., Jackson, K. T., & Wang, Y. (2013). How data are used and misused in schools: Perceptions from teachers and principals. *Education Sciences, 3*(2), 98–120. https://doi.org/10.3390/educsci3020098

Militello, M., & Guajardo, F. (2013). Virtually speaking: How digital storytelling can facilitate organizational learning. *Journal of Community Positive Practices, 13*(2), 81–91.

Militello, M., & Janson, C. (2014). The urban school reform opera: The obstructions to transforming school counseling practices. *Education and Urban Society, 46*(7), 743–772. https://doi.org/10.1177/0013124512468007

Morales, S., Flores, A. I., Gaxiola Serrano, T. J., & Delgado Bernal, D. (2023). Feminist pláticas as methodological disruption: Drawing upon embodied knowledge, vulnerability, healing and resistance. *International Journal of Qualitative Studies in Education.* https://doi.org/10.1080/09518398.2023.2181441

Norris, J., Sawyer, R. D., & Lund, D. (2012). *Duoethnography: Dialogic methods for social, health and educational research.* Routledge.

Pasque, P., Carducci, R., Kuntz, A., & Gildersleeve, R. (2012). *Qualitative inquiry for equity in higher education: Methodological innovations, implications, and interventions.* Jossey-Bass.

Patel, L. (2019). Fugitive practices: Learning in a settler colony. *Educational Studies, 55*(3), 253–261. https://doi.org/10.1080/00131946.2019.1605368

Polynesian Voyaging Society. (2023). Crew profile: Nainoa Thompson. https://www.hokulea.com/crewmember/nainoa-thompson/

Smith, L. T., Tuck, E., & Yang, K. W. (Eds.). (2019). *Indigenous and decolonizing studies in education.* Routledge.

Tachine, A. R. (2017). Home away from home: Native American students' sense of belonging during their first year in college. *The Journal of Higher Education, 88*(5), 785–807. https://doi.org/10.1080/00221546.2016.1257322

Tachine, A. R. (2022). *Native presence and sovereignty in college.* Teachers College Press.

Tachine, A. R., Bird, E. Y., & Cabrera, N. L. (2016). Sharing circles: An Indigenous methodological approach for researching with groups of Indigenous peoples. *International Review of Qualitative Research, 9*(3), 277–295. https://doi.org/10.1525/irqr.2016.9.3.277

Wang, C., & Burris, M. A. (1997). Photovoice: Concept, methodology, and use for participatory needs assessment. *Health Education & Behavior, 24*(3), 369–387. https://doi.org/10.1177/109019819702400309

Yosso, T. (2005). Whose culture has capital? A critical race theory discussion of community cultural wealth. *Race Ethnicity and Education, 8*(1), 69–91. https://doi.org/10.1080/1361332052000341006

12

CENTERING THE STUDENT IN UNDERGRADUATE RESEARCH AS A RETENTION STRATEGY

Rocío Mendoza, Elyzza M. Aparicio, Deborah Faye Carter, and Angela M. Locks

At the height of the racial reckoning in September of 2020,[1] the four of us participated on a virtual panel titled, "Racial Equity in Undergraduate Research" as part of a "Scholar Strike" (Butler & Gannon, 2020) series hosted at one of our home institutions. We shared our personal and professional experiences in undergraduate research as former undergraduate participants, and now as scholars studying undergraduate research, and practitioners leading undergraduate research programs. Given our extensive experiences, we discussed the benefits of undergraduate research as a higher education practice and its utility as an area of scholarship. Incorporating our critical lenses and racialized/gendered experiences as Black women and Chicana/Latinas, we also observed how undergraduate research experiences, because they are part of our (too often) extractive higher education systems, can reproduce harm to students of color involved.

The panel was a generative discussion of the promises and caveats of undergraduate research experiences (UREs) and practices. This chapter is an extension of that conversation, aiming to examine the contexts and facets of UREs and shed light on how commonly held beliefs and practices may perpetuate harmful notions of grit to the detriment of students of color. We also offer ways to reimagine UREs as a retention strategy and broaden ways to intentionally support minoritized students. We begin with conceptualizing grit as it relates to undergraduate research, followed by a discussion of undergraduate research, including definitions, and key practices. We then highlight limitations of undergraduate research as it is currently defined in mainstream programs and offer more inclusive, equity-minded approaches and practices to challenge how grit is embedded in this practice.

DOI: 10.4324/9781003332497-15

Undergraduate Research Experiences (UREs) Overdue for a Critical Analysis

For years, scholars in education have examined how the concept of grit (Duckworth et al., 2007) underlines the ideologies, pedagogical practices and policies aimed at addressing inequities and disparities for minoritized students in K-12 (Gorski, 2016; Love, 2019). Similarly, we argue that well-intentioned "best practices" in higher education may also fall prey to perpetuating deficit notions of minoritized students when their racialized, gendered, and socioeconomic realities are not considered, which can ultimately, reinforce harmful ideas of "academic success" (Hatfield et al., 2022). UREs, which are often described and categorized as "high-impact practices," are an example of a double-edge sword; while UREs may hold potential for their multi-faceted elements to support student achievement (such as connection to faculty research mentoring, exposure to research skills, and preparation to graduate school), oftentimes the core assumptions behind such programs are less examined.

We recognize that studies abound (to which we have also contributed) documenting the powerful impact that UREs can have, especially for minoritized students across multiple dimensions (Carter et al., 2013, 2019; Locks & Gregerman, 2008; Oseguera et al., 2019, 2022). As we take a critical perspective to highlight systemic structures of power and privilege, we note how some of the overarching complexities and challenges of undergraduate research opportunities may in fact help to reinforce grit; from gaining access to research, to promoting individualism and a meritocratic belief in academia.

Higher education institutions have a long history of exclusion and can often be sites of harm and violence for students of color (Hurtado et al., 2003; Wilder, 2013). Further, the ideologies of hyper individualism, competitiveness, and disciplinary cultures, particularly in STEM fields (Carter et al., 2019; Mau et al., 2020; Morton et al., 2019) can make UREs particularly susceptible to reproducing harm. We argue that examining UREs and the ideologies that undergird this practice are a moral commitment to reimagining how these practices can be sites of persistence and possibility for students. As we explore alternative approaches and practices in UREs, we also draw upon conceptual and theoretical frameworks that can help to inform and guide these practices, including justice equity (Gorski, 2016; Osei-Kofi et al., 2010) and ethic of care (Noddings, 1992). We begin the next section by defining and mapping out the many iterations of UREs in practice.

Varying Forms of UREs

Broadly defined, undergraduate research experiences are academic experiences that involve one or more undergraduate students who conduct(s) research with the support and typically with the supervision of a faculty

TABLE 12.1 Common Undergraduate Research Practices May Include Any of the Following

Engage students in research practices including the ability to argue from evidence

Aim to generate novel information with an emphasis on discovery and innovation or to determine whether recent preliminary results can be replicated

Focus on significant, relevant problems of interest to STEM researchers and, in some cases, a broader community (e.g., civic engagement)

Emphasize and expect collaboration and teamwork

Involve iterative refinement of experimental design, experimental questions, or data obtained

Allow students to master specific research techniques

Help students engage in reflection about the problems being investigated and the work being undertaken to address those problems

Require communication of results, either through publication or presentations in various STEM venues

Are structured and guided by a mentor, with students assuming increasing ownership of some aspects of the project over time

member. For this chapter, we consider undergraduate research experiences as consisting of any of the characteristics in Table 12.1, as defined by the National Academies of Sciences, Engineering and Medicine (NASEM, 2017, pp. 34–35).

We acknowledge that these characteristics defined in Table 12.1 focus on those who were pursuing STEM, but we believe many of these elements, such as "expect collaboration and teamwork" and "structured and guided by a mentor..." also occur in UREs in other fields and disciplines. In addition to what the NASEM report considers important features of UREs, the report notes that not every URE will have all these characteristics, and some non-URE experiences have some of these characteristics as well.

UREs take many different forms on campuses, which can oftentimes make it difficult to define, much less examine (Beckman & Hensel, 2009). For example, there are independent forms of undergraduate research, where a faculty member recruits a student (or several) to support them in their research or lab work (apprenticeship-style). There are also structured, wrap-around programs that connect students to faculty mentors and research opportunities and offer academic, social and financial support; and, there are UREs that are part of research requirements such as a senior thesis, capstone project, internship, consortium and project-based experiences, and community-based research programs (Lopatto, 2010; NASEM, 2017). Lastly, there are course-based research opportunities (Auchincloss et al., 2017), where students learn about the fundamentals of research and can carry out their own study as part of a course. The broad aims for many UREs are to strengthen the pipeline to graduate school and train future researchers and faculty. At their best, UREs are also about training future thinkers and producers of knowledge who seek to improve the conditions of their communities through research, and in producing college graduates who are literate in key disciplinary concepts and methods (McGee & Bentley, 2017).

We acknowledge that these different forms of UREs yield different outcomes for students, especially considering the duration of time a student spends engaged in a URE and the unique disciplinary cultures in specific fields such as in STEM. However, we believe the goals and scope of UREs are common enough to discuss the challenges and possibilities if they can improve the inclusivity and experiences for students of color.

Critiques of Grit and in Undergraduate Research Practice

Duckworth et al. (2007) assert that grit, a combination of sustained passion and perseverance for long-term goals, is what leads to the success of high achieving individuals. While this idea has permeated many guiding frameworks and practices in education, scholars have also called for a more critical and nuanced understanding of Duckworth's concept of grit (see Credé et al., 2017; Kirchgasler, 2018; Ris, 2015). For example, Kirchgasler (2018) applies a sociocultural and historical analysis to the origins of Duckworth's concept of grit and argues that it is entrenched in ideas of rugged individualism, and exceptionalism. Chapter 2 of this book delves more deeply into the background of this concept. What is notable is that these historical foundations do not only apply to grit, but to other philosophies of teaching and educational outcomes as well (Ris, 2015). What has been diminished in the focus on addressing individual student behavior is how educational institutions are/can be structured to support student success.

Access to Research Opportunities

An important consideration of access to educational opportunities in higher education is how students know about undergraduate research experiences. It is unclear how students go about making decisions about their initial participation in a research opportunity in the context of broader structural factors. For example, given that many students work at least part time and need jobs to help them pay for college expenses, students may not be able to engage in such opportunities given their time and budget constraints. According to NCES (2022), 74% of college students work part time and 40% students work full-time to support themselves and their families. For many, working at least one part-time job is necessary to support their studies, which may limit the kinds of students who can engage in this opportunity. Many may feel that they cannot meet their coursework and work demands *and* pursue research in a sustainable manner. While many institutions offer structured programs that provide financial support for students, these programs are often smaller in scope and can only support a small number of students a year, likely a remnant of when such programs were largely white and male.

Another factor affecting access to UREs is that most students participate in a research opportunity later in their college career—as juniors and seniors. According to Buffalari et al. (2020), 25–40% of students participate in undergraduate research (UR) in their senior year, which far outweighs the 5% of students who report participating in UR their first year. However, studies have also shown that earlier engagement in research can provide critical access and other academic benefits for students (Hathaway et al., 2002; Hurtado et al., 2008; Nagda et al., 1998).

Constraints on student time is one factor limiting access to research opportunities. Students who are interested and aware of undergraduate research may be dissuaded from doing so due to negative experiences in racialized institutional environments. Rodríguez Amaya et al. (2018) explored the undergraduate research perceptions and experiences of Latinx students in STEM attending a Hispanic Serving Institution (HSI) and found that despite students reporting having an awareness of research activities at their institution, they were not actually participating in research. There may be multiple reasons why this is the case. In particular fields, there is a broader conception about research as an activity that only "scientists" engage in, rather than an academic opportunity that students, regardless of career aspirations can pursue (Rodríguez Amaya et al., 2018). Battling these preconceptions also involves changing faculty behavior as well; Harper (2009) explains that higher education institutions often expect "minority undergraduates to comfortably initiate interactions with faculty, seek out engagement opportunities with the same ease as their white peers, and visit campus offices staffed by people who lack cultural competence..." (p. 43), which can often place the responsibility on the student to seek out such opportunities and support systems. When students do seek out such opportunities, Milkman et al. (2015) found that students who emailed faculty expressing an interest in joining their research projects, encountered racial and gender biases from faculty. It is important that institutions and departments are mindful of how to encourage faculty and staff to be more supportive of student interest and to foster research interest as early.

Disciplinary Differences

Academic disciplines have distinct values, assumptions, and beliefs that shape their culture, including what knowledge is valid and whose voices matter (Becher, 1981). For example, Carter et al. (2019) highlight the ways racism is deeply embedded in development of sciences as academic disciplines, including people of color being the subjects of research, versus being the *researchers* by tracing the history in STEM fields. This history contributes to how disciplines identify those with potential talent, and what knowledge they value as furthering the discipline. The apprenticeship model has been a decades-long tradition for training new scientists (Hunter et al., 2007). Underlying this assumption is that there is a one-directional relationship, where the faculty is the sage and has important knowledge to pass on to the trainee. This is closely connected to positivist views of research and the research process, which supports grit.

Faculty Roles and Interactions

Faculty mentoring is considered the cornerstone of undergraduate research and an important component of students' academic development, which seems to be a key part of encouraging first-generation and/or low-income students to pursue graduate school (Piatt et al., 2019). Faculty can have significant effects on students' academic outcomes; some faculty, particularly those in well-resourced fields and disciplines, may have opportunities to affect many students per year. There are often little to no formal training opportunities for faculty in research supervision and mentoring; faculty learn how to mentor and supervise based on their own experiences and socialization to the discipline (Cawyer et al., 2002). Thus, even well-intentioned faculty may inadvertently gatekeep minoritized students and reinforce harmful views of "successful students" based on racially exclusive disciplinary norms (Morton et al., 2019). Faculty who are committed to the grit mindset, that individual effort is most important to academic achievement without regard to structural and environmental factors, may be reinforcing harmful perceptions of their disciplines as unwelcoming and exclusive.

Faculty who adhere to conceptualizations of grit may recognize the needs of their students, but the responsibility for solving these issues rest with the individual student. Gorski (2016), explains, "adherents to grit ideology recognize the structural barriers" (p. 382), but that individuals are tasked with overcoming those barriers. Instead of considering how to address structural barriers that affect student outcomes and help broad populations of students, a solution from a grit perspective is to identify students who are not achieving well and encourage them to meet objectives. However, researchers have yet to identify ways to increase grit in students; so often students are left to their own resources as they attempt to be successful. In STEM, minoritized students who do not engage in whiteness, patriarchy, and heteronormativity in expected ways may find themselves excluded from prized opportunities to engage with faculty outside of the classroom.

Reimagining Undergraduate Research Experiences as a Retention Strategy

We have examined the major components of UREs and described the ways that grit can often be embedded in the major elements of these practices. In the next parts of this chapter, we focus on faculty and staff roles as well as exemplar programs that help to challenge notions of grit in higher education. Below, we describe how faculty and staff can be integral to undergraduate research experiences in ways that challenge a grit ideology and serve as retention strategies for students of color.

Program Priorities Defining Success and Outcomes

To reiterate, undergraduate research programs play an important role in creating pathways to graduate school and the research enterprise more broadly. Programs are oftentimes bound by externally placed target goals such as producing high numbers of graduate school admissions among its participants (e.g., McNair, NIH BUILD, etc.). Without intentionally developing programming that challenge and define success outcomes more broadly, programs may inadvertently create an environment that continues to reinforce narrow notions of success markers in academia, such as presenting at conferences and publishing in peer-reviewed journals. This, however, requires effective administrative leadership and staff management skills, which as practitioners, we have observed that faculty do not typically have the formal training or background. The program leadership is an important aspect to consider, as the overarching goals and objectives of many of these programs continue to define how we think about success in higher education.

Most program directors' intent may be to help uncover the "hidden curriculum" of academia and graduate school while focusing on narrow markers of success; this runs the risk of reinforcing a belief in a meritocracy without communicating the ways in which institutional and societal structures can play a part in achieving one's goals. Individual efforts are important, but students will need to be prepared to face barriers that may affect their intended trajectories.

Faculty and URE Relationship

Earlier we described ways in which faculty may be a barrier to students interested in STEM majors and careers. We also want to highlight ways in which faculty can be key benefits of an undergraduate research experience. Lopatto (2003), for example, describes how students benefit from working with faculty in undergraduate research, including gaining in-depth knowledge and research skills in a content area, and working to troubleshoot problems, and strengthen their communication skills.

Acquiring these academic skills and working with faculty can also help students with developing a sense of confidence in doing research (Hathaway et al., 2002). Broadly, the literature about faculty involvement in UREs can be conceptualized in two different categories: (a) faculty mindset and their perceptions of students and (b) faculty training and how they engage in successful supervision of students.

Faculty mindset regarding students' potential for achievement affects how they evaluate students and which students they want to supervise. If faculty are committed to reducing disparities in STEM for example, they need to approach their supervision and pedagogy work with justice in mind (Gorski, 2016). Gorski believes that to best supervise and support students, one must first shift their ideological orientation to a justice oriented one, in which they have a "fundamental understanding" (p. 379), of the structural barriers and economic conditions that low-income, first-generation, and/or students of color face. Similarly, McGee and Stovall (2015) reflect that "it is important to remember that racial inequities are structured to restrict Black students' academic opportunities and continue to devalue their intellect" (p. 511). Considering that higher education institutions have been historically structured to maintain racial/ethnic group disparities, faculty need to be oriented toward justice to meaningfully address these structures and create more long-term change.

The way we understand problems relates to how we understand how to solve those problems (Gorski, 2016). If faculty subscribe to deficit ideologies that students fail to achieve because of cultural deficits or failure of character, this may lead to faculty believing that students are not trying hard enough, or that they are simply not "cut out" for an URE opportunity. It is common for faculty in STEM to think students are not working hard enough in classes and is the cause for not being successful in their STEM majors (Canning et al., 2019; Steele & Aronson, 1995). A framing for "justice orientation," or to be "equity literate" (Gorski, 2016, p. 379) would mean that faculty have a structural ideology of inequality and understand the systemic barriers that may hinder students' participation and progress in their URE. Faculty who have structural (justice) conceptualizations of inequality are more likely to reflect on their supervision and pedagogy, try to be as transparent as possible, and work with others on campus to remove systemic barriers that affect students' academic success.

As previously discussed here and in other chapters of this book, research shows that barriers to students majoring in STEM can be the culture of STEM disciplines and classes themselves (McGee & Stovall, 2015). Students of color often experience negative racial climates in STEM fields as well as in their interactions with faculty and peers who believe they will not be successful in the courses. Another major barrier for first-generation, low-income, and students of color pursuing STEM is academic preparation in high school. Students who attend less resourced high schools and have less access to AP courses tend to not be as successful pursuing STEM degrees as other students. For example, Indigenous nursing students found that "cultural, financial, and academic support" (Stoffel & Cain, 2018, p. 129) were important factors for their academic success. Students' biggest barriers to achievement in STEM and other disciplines is not a lack of grit, but rather the campus/classroom environment, college preparation, and perhaps the faculty members' choices of classroom pedagogies. Faculty need to be aware of the limits of "grit" and how they themselves can structure undergraduate research experiences to demystify disciplinary knowledge to help students apply what they know.

In addition to faculty mindset, faculty training and support for successful mentoring and supervision must also be considered. Rosas Alquicira et al. (2022) assert that faculty mentors' research agenda and productivity benefits from engagement in UREs, and faculty can "stay up-to-date with discipline content and technology, as well as develop professional networks that enhance faculty and student opportunities" (p. 64). From this vantage point, UREs can be spaces that can enhance collaboration and result in mutually beneficial supports. While faculty often benefit from supervising undergraduate students, mentoring/supervising students of color does not come without significant stress on faculty members. For example, Schwartz (2012) discusses the "personal toll" on faculty who become mentors to underrepresented students of color and/or first-generation students. Faculty tend to do mentoring for underrepresented populations of students because they believe the students need guides into the disciplinary cultures of STEM disciplines. In under-resourced higher education institutions, faculty try to do their best mentoring students, while also being concerned that "students are not getting high quality research training due to the condition" of research equipment and labs. In Schwartz's study, some faculty mentors felt that their purpose was to help guide students until they could transfer into a better resourced institution. However, Schwartz also noted that faculty members who believed institutions did not invest in quality laboratory and research facilities, and who did not have long-term plans for broadening undergraduate research experiences to more students, tended not to want to supervise undergraduate students themselves. Despite doing the best they can, faculty are often limited by institutional resources, including professional development focused on equity they have available to support their students. This can also greatly vary by those who have institutional support and access to external funding and lab/research equipment (DeAngelo et al., 2016).

Faculty, program directors, and administrators may wonder if "hand holding" in the form of support and services is helpful to students (may make students less gritty), but there is more evidence that first-generation and/or students of color do not have equal access to information and may need additional support to achieve and experience equitable outcomes. There are also pedagogical implications for supporting the work of faculty who mentor or seek to support UREs, particularly when aiming for a more "justice-oriented"- centered URE practice. Having undergraduate research programs that have wrap-around services (advising, financial aid counselor, basic needs assistance, connections to supportive staff and programs around campus) are key to helping link students with other areas of the college and university and can better address the structural barriers so many often face through their college journeys.

Student-Centered Staff

Staff in Student or Academic Affairs offices are key to the development and sustainability of UREs. They are an under-researched part of UREs, but these individuals help with the creation and run the day-to-day operations in undergraduate research programs, provide support to students involved in UREs, assist in making connections and referrals, and are enabled to know the students so they can better support them and their college experiences. While many times the onus of seeking key staff members falls on the student, the reverse tends to be the approach for staff who are part of undergraduate research programs, as it is the staff who are in close contact with students from the very beginning of their time in UREs program.

Many staff, as part of their roles and responsibilities, are high-touch and proactive with students, making sure that support is consistent throughout a student's experience. Staff are also cultural agents, and sometimes a buffer between faculty and students, that play a critical role in assisting students as they navigate college (Museus & Quaye, 2009). Staff sometimes are charged with structuring support programming to promote academic success by providing students with information about time management skills, workshops on research skills, and study habits (Mayhew et al., 2016). Often, staff members may be the first point of contact to provide information to students about undergraduate research experiences. They are individuals who are involved in outreach activities such as tabling at events and going to high schools to raise awareness about URE opportunities, as well as helping to pursue grants to expand UREs for increased access. Staff are key in disseminating information on their campus and local communities about programmatic opportunities available to students while at the same time encouraging them to participate in such experiences as undergraduate research.

Peer Advising: Helping with Retaining Students

Many UREs also feature peer advisors, who can help alleviate some of the burden on faculty supervisors/mentors enabling them to enhance the ways in which they serve students. Students likely benefit from interacting with trained peers, whose experiences more closely resemble their own (Lopatto, 2010; Newton & Ender, 2010). This is especially important because early in college, students may be intimidated when asking faculty for assistance and faculty may not know all the services available to students, especially on larger campuses. Undergraduate research can be a new experience for students and generate numerous questions that involve different skills and areas of the campus. Having a peer advisor who has experience with UR and is knowledgeable about the campus can help students gain more insight and support. For example, peer advisors offer first-hand insight into how they managed their UR experiences, and different ways they networked and participated in activities such as publishing, conferences, and obtaining funding. In addition to helping students navigate the campus, scholars have also found that their persistence rates were significantly impacted by the type and quality of interactions they had with their peers (Lane, 2020; Yomtov et al., 2017). Peer advising is often structured as supplementary to core offerings (Carlstrom & Miller, 2013; Locks & Gregerman, 2008). Given its significant positive effects on student outcomes, it may be that institutions need to increase the implementation of peer support programs. Having students paired with a peer advisor can be an intentional part of an institution's goals and recruitment and retention of students (Crisp & Cruz, 2009; Yomtov et al., 2017).

Exemplar Programs

There are several URE programs that we consider as notable for their structure and the educational outcomes they produce. Importantly, the approaches of these programs aimed to support students of color, particularly in STEM fields, serve as exemplars for students of color engaged in the undergraduate research enterprise. These programs were specifically developed to address the structural challenges and barriers minoritized students face in accessing research opportunities, navigating college and beyond. They also center on developing academic skills necessary for research, community building and family inclusion, and have a deep investment and commitment to the students' health and well-being.

The programs described below include undergraduate research as a core part of its programs and are utilized to help train students and support their educational goals and achievements. They have multiple components including peer supports and study groups, advising, tutoring, mentoring, and summer research opportunities and internships. In addition, the programs offer varying levels of financial aid in the forms of stipends or hourly pay, and some support for travel. The culminating activity also includes a research symposium, where students present the projects they have been working on (often in the form of poster presentations) and invite faculty sponsors, family, and friends to the event. By being intentional in their aims and scope, the following programs provide a space for students to show up as their authentic selves. We discuss unique features of each program in the subsequent sections.

Extended Pipeline Approach: Mellon Mays Undergraduate Fellowship (MMUF)

The Mellon Mays Undergraduate Fellowships Program (MMUF, 2023), funded by the Mellon Foundation was started in 1988 with eight private postsecondary institutions in the U.S. The Mellon Mays Undergraduate Fellowships Program was specifically chartered to "...remedy the serious shortage of faculty of color in higher education" (MMUF, 2023) and offers different levels of support throughout a students' undergraduate and graduate school journeys. In its 34 years, MMUF has grown to include 48 institutions, including two consortia comprised of minority servicing institutions, Historically Black Colleges and Universities (HBCUs) and Hispanic-Serving Institutions (HSIs). MMUF recently reached a significant milestone of 1,000 program participants who have earned PhDs. The long-term impact of the MMUF as a producer of at least two generations of doctorates underscores its critical role in diversifying the faculty and researcher ranks. Nearly 200 MMUF alumni hold tenured faculty positions.

MMUF programs typically identify rising juniors in their second year of college, although a few programs select incoming transfer students. In addition to direct financial support, the Mellon Foundation supports a number of regional conferences where students have an opportunity to present their scholarship alongside their regional peers. MMUF also supports alumni after baccalaureate degree completion and post-graduate school. Alumni can avail themselves of a gap year program, designed to allow students to bolster their research skills and knowledge and prepare materials for graduate school. As enrolled graduate students, MMUF fellows continue to have access to financial support, program symposia and networking opportunities with other fellows.

Comprehensive Engagement Model-Meyerhoff Scholars Program

The Meyerhoff Scholars Program also began in 1988 at the Baltimore County campus of the University of Maryland to provide African American males an undergraduate research experience. The program was designed specifically for those interested in earning a doctoral degree in engineering, science, or math.

The program began with a cohort of 19 students and began admitting women to the program in 1990.

There is evidence that the holistic nature of the Meyerhoff Scholars Program is particularly helpful in producing better rates of persistence and higher GPAs. For example, participants report a higher sense of belonging attributed to students being in community with others who share their identities and an interest in science (Maton et al., 2012). Moreover, Meyerhoff scholars have higher GPAs, graduation rates and graduation school acceptance rates (Maton et al., 2000).

There have been recent efforts to replicate the program at other institutions. The Howard Hughes Medical Institute (HHMI) has supported the replication of the program at Penn State and North Carolina State; the program is also being replicated at the University of California Berkeley and UC San Diego campuses (Sto. Domingo et al., 2019).

Federally Funded Model: The Ronald E. McNair Postbaccalaureate Achievement Program

The Ronald E. McNair Postbaccalaureate Achievement Program is one of eight Federal (TRIO) Programs that are aimed at supporting students from marginalized backgrounds. The McNair Program was established in 1986 and is the only TRIO program whose goal is to increase the number of underrepresented students who earn Ph.Ds. Similar to MMUF and Meyerhoff, McNair programs include a number of resources and activities to assist students in "...securing admission to and financial assistance for enrollment in graduate programs" (Ronald E. McNair Postbaccalaureate Achievement Program, 2021). Additionally, the McNair Programs may also offer other programs and services like counseling, mentoring, opportunities to attend civic and cultural events and other activities of enrichment. Further, the Department of Education mandates that all McNair campus cohorts must have at least two-thirds low-income participants and/or potential first-generation college students, with the remaining cohort members belonging to underrepresented groups in graduate education. In this way, McNair programs specifically target first-generation, low-income, and/or students of color, with hopes that the program elements will help them persist and go on to graduate school.

Retention Program Model-Undergraduate Research Opportunity Program (UROP)

There are initiatives, programs, and centralized offices across the 23 campuses in the California State University system that offer URE opportunities. Currently, there is one campus that offers a URE whose focus is on serving first- and second-year students. A one-year program, the Undergraduate Research

Opportunity Program (UROP) at CSU Long Beach, is unique in that it focuses on engaging students in research and the creative process with faculty at earlier timepoints in their educational pathway.

As participants enter the program, they are paired with a peer advisor who previously participated in UROP. In this peer mentorship model, peer advisors can draw from their own experiences in UROP, how they handled multiple responsibilities including being a student and research assistant, and they overall provide insight and guidance. Alumni of the program also play a key role for current UROP students as they are invited speakers to share insights that include working in the field or industry and attending graduate school. The program began with 25 students in 2013 and currently serves 130 students. UROP is based on the University of Michigan's model which began in 1988 to increase retention and improve academic performance of underrepresented students of color (Nagda et al., 1998).

Key Components to Reimagining Undergraduate Research Experiences as a Retention Strategy

The above exemplar programs have key components that provide peer, staff, and faculty support to students to help remove the barriers they may face in navigating through college. Among these components are selecting justice-oriented faculty for involvement in their program, student-centered staff, and wrap-around approaches to meeting student needs. We highlighted the ways that faculty research mentors can adopt a justice orientation to their mentoring that displays a critical understanding of the racialized barriers students can face in their disciplines. Additionally, student-centered staff that understand student needs is essential in effectively developing and directing programs. Finally, we featured URE programs that aim to have broader equity goals of supporting students at various points in their academic journey and diversifying the professoriate and beyond.

While these programs have a different orientation than cultivating grit, they motivate and empower students toward their academic goals and social well-being. They were designed as an explicit recognition of the structural barriers that students face, and as interventions to address these barriers. We argue that URE programs demonstrate an ethic of care because they address barriers by providing the multi-level support students need.

Ethic of Care in URE Practices

Noddings (1992) states that care should be at the heart of the educational system, which can come from the institution, or more specifically, from administrators, staff, and faculty. Ethic of care also emphasizes "…the tie between relationship and responsibility" (Gilligan, 1993, p. 173), and thus the need and importance that ethic of care looks different for every individual given their unique situation and needs. In describing the mentoring of Black and Latino male high school students, Watson et al. (2016) further refined ethic of care to *culturally relevant care*, drawing from critical and social justice frameworks to describe a "...process in which one's humanity is affirmed by building community, trust, warm demanding, and integrating the cultures and experiences of community members" (p. 986). We draw from these frameworks of ethic of care to describe the important role this plays in URE practices, where intentionality and a proactive approach can take place.

Directors, administration, faculty, and peer advisors in undergraduate research experiences and programs can create programing based on an ethic of care. For example, when a student requires attention, especially when there is limited knowledge and awareness, we have to be mindful of enacting "proactive" philosophies (Museus, 2021) to connect the student and their families to resources more efficiently and effectively. By having a deeper knowledge and understanding of students participating in UREs, we can generate more meaningful experiences, share resources, and connect them with others in the campus community. An ethic of care also requires staff, faculty, and others to consider how students' needs are being met and what we can do to improve student experiences, which differs from focusing on how students can become grittier. Furthermore, an ethic of care also positively changes our environment as we learn to connect the ethics of care to our natural world and environment (Held, 2006).

Principles of Practice: Racially Inclusive Practices in Undergraduate Research

We have identified three principles of practice in administering undergraduate research programs that are important to the ethic of care for students: (a) consistency, (b) transparency, and (c) intentionality by faculty, staff, administrators, and the university community in UREs. First, being consistent with students during their time in college is critical for students' decision-making agency because it empowers them in making informed choices while also strengthening their ability in self-directing their choices during their time in college. Programs also should be administered with consistency, hold all mentors to the same expectations, and hold all students to the same expectations as well. Deadlines for applications should align with deadlines for other programs and work in concert with the college or university academic calendars. There also should be multiple points in time for students to participate in the program.

A second principle of practice is transparency. Communication about undergraduate research experiences should be predictable and routine—perhaps housed on a general section of an institution's website that is easily discovered. College staff and faculty are a key part of higher education institutions who share (and reproduce) the culture and espoused values of said institutions (Weidman, 1989). They also play an important role in creating transparency and sharing key information. For example, many times, students do not know what UREs are and cannot make decisions about something that is unknown to them. Helping use academic departments and other offices around campus to communicate the value of opportunities offered will be helpful in broadening the impact of the programs.

Undergraduate research is dependent on faculty engagement and mentorship; many undergraduate research programs are led by faculty themselves. It is important to provide faculty with professional development opportunities to help them engage by reflecting and modifying their pedagogy to be more supportive of first-generation and/or students of color. Developing literacies around equity-mindedness and racial inclusion, centered on justice, remain key in helping faculty make a positive impact on students' interest and persistence in many academic fields. Faculty must acknowledge explicitly the historical legacies of exclusion and ongoing present challenges that students of color in higher education face, particularly in STEM fields and disciplines (Carter et al., 2019). Staff and faculty need to internalize moral commitments to address and disrupt historical barriers so that UREs can be more inclusive and produce positive academic outcomes.

Intentionality in UREs also includes acknowledging that our programs are not one size fits all; rather, program directors need to be intentional about recognizing the unique needs of students as they arrive in college and adjust to students' needs as they continue toward graduation. In this way, staff, faculty, and administrators are guided by an ethic of care (Noddings, 1992), culturally relevant care (Watson et al., 2016), and justice orientation (Gorski, 2016) to support students and value their individual identities, contexts, and experiences.

UREs are also places of co-creation with students, staff, and faculty. When students are placed in a position to take responsibility for their academics and educational pathway, they become active participants in the process of learning (Bovill et al., 2015). UREs are an area where students can be co-creators as they engage in research, give insight regarding a research project, share their insights in a team dynamic and are encouraged to voice their opinions and make unique contributions. Co-creation can take a variety of forms and across disciplines. Students and staff or students and faculty can collaborate to: (re)design the content of courses for research, learning and teaching; undertake disciplinary research; and design assessments such as essay questions or choose between different assessment methods.

Despite having a long history of exclusion, institutions of higher education are places to serve all students who attend. UREs can offer key ways by which students' educational pathways can be shaped. Through transparency, consistency, and intentionality, staff and faculty can develop program elements to serve students' needs and positively affect well-being and achievement.

Summary

We argue that the interlocking of systemic barriers such as racism, sexism, and poverty that students face in their academic journeys is seldom acknowledged as a foundational context in the discussion of grit, which only addresses individual passion and perseverance for long-term goals. Consequently, most practices and definitions of successful outcomes in UREs can emulate the logics of grit. As we described in this chapter, consistency, transparency, and intentionality through an ethic of care, culturally relevant care and a justice orientation can offer a foundation for campuses and their personnel to disrupt the institutionalized racism that excludes students of color from the undergraduate enterprise. This chapter offered specific and concrete examples of what this can look like in UREs. We end this chapter with the following reflection questions for those working in UREs and other high-impact practices who wish to challenge and examine the underlying logics of grit in their practices:

- How do we define success in this URE/program? How might these definitions disrupt notions of whiteness and meritocracy?
- How can we expand definitions of success to acknowledge the well-being and care of our students?
- How can faculty be fully engaged partners in developing definitions, conceptualizations, and equity mindedness in UREs?
- What might consistency, transparency, and intentionality look like in our everyday URE practices?

Note

1 The U.S. saw a record number of Black Lives Matter protestors denouncing the murder of George Floyd and others at the hands of police violence. "The scale, demands and impact of these protests rattled the contemporary guardians of the racial status quo" (Ray, 2022, xxiv).

References

Auchincloss, L. C., Laursen, S. L., Branchaw, J. L., Eagan, K., Graham, M., Hanauer, D. I., Larwi, G., McLinn, C. M., Pelaez, N., Rowland, S., Towns, M., Trautmann, N. M., Varma-Nelson, P., Weston, T. J., & Dolan, E. L. (2017, October 13). Assessment of course-based undergraduate research experiences: A meeting report. *The American Society for Cell Biology.* https://doi.org/10.1187/cbe.14-01-0004

Becher, T. (1981). Towards a definition of disciplinary cultures. *Studies in Higher Education, 6*(2), 109–122. https://doi.org/10.1080/03075078112331379362

Beckman, M., & Hensel, N. (2009). Making explicit the implicit: Defining undergraduate research. *CUR Quarterly, 29*(4), 40–44.

Bovill, C., Jordan, L., & Watters, N. (2015). Transnational approaches to teaching and learning in higher education: Challenges and possible guiding principles. *Teaching in Higher Education, 20*(1), 12–23.

Buffalari, D., Fernandes, J. J., Chase, L., Lom, B., McMurray, M. S., Morrison, M. E., & Stavnezer, A. J. (2020). Integrating research into the undergraduate curriculum: 1. Early research experiences and training. *Journal of Undergraduate Neuroscience Education, 19*(1), A52–A63.

Butler, A., & Gannon, K. (2020, September 2). Scholar strike. *Academe Blog: The Blog of Academe Magazine.* https://academeblog.org/2020/09/02/scholar-strike/

Canning, E. A., Muenks, K., Green, D. J., & Murphy, M. C. (2019). STEM faculty who believe ability is fixed have larger racial achievement gaps and inspire less student motivation in their classes. *Science Advances, 5*(2), eaau4734.

Carlstrom, A. H., & Miller, M. A. (Eds.). (2013). *2011 NACADA national survey of academic advising* (Monograph No. 25). National Academic Advising Association. https://nacada.ksu.edu/Resources/Clearinghouse/View-Articles/2011-NACADA-National-Survey.aspx

Carter, D. F., Locks, A. M., & Winkle-Wagner, R. (2013). From when and where I enter: Theoretical and empirical considerations of minority students' transition to college. *Higher Education: Handbook of Theory and Research, 28*, 93–149. https://doi.org/10.1007/978-94-007-5836-0_3

Carter, D. F., Razo Dueñas, J. E., & Mendoza, R. (2019). Critical examination of the role of STEM in propagating and maintaining race and gender disparities. *Higher Education: Handbook of Theory and Research, 34*, 39–97. https://doi.org/10.1007/978-3-030-03457-3_2

Cawyer, C. S., Simonds, C., & Davis, S. (2002). Mentoring to facilitate socialization: The case of the new faculty member. *International Journal of Qualitative Studies in Education, 15*(2), 225–242. https://doi.org/10.1080/09518390110111938

Credé, M., Tynan, M. C., & Harms, P. D. (2017). Much ado about grit: A meta-analytic synthesis of the grit literature. *Journal of Personality and Social Psychology, 113*(3), 492–511. https://doi.org/10.1037/pspp0000102

Crisp, G., & Cruz, I. (2009). Mentoring college students: A critical review of the literature between 1990 and 2007. *Research in Higher Education, 50*, 525–545.

DeAngelo, L., Mason, J., & Winters, D. (2016). Faculty engagement in mentoring undergraduate students: How institutional environments regulate and promote extra-role behavior. *Innovative Higher Education, 41*, 317–332.

Duckworth, A. L., Peterson, C., Matthews, M. D., & Kelly, D. R. (2007). Grit: Perseverance and passion for long-term goals. *Journal of Personality and Social Psychology, 92*(6), 1087–1101. https://doi.org/10.1037/0022-3514.92.6.1087

Gilligan, C. (1993). *In a different voice: Psychological theory and women's development*. Harvard University Press.

Gorski, P. C. (2016). *Reaching and teaching students in poverty: Strategies for erasing the opportunity gap*. Teachers College Press.

Harper, S. R. (2009). Race-conscious student and the equitable distribution of enriching educational experiences. *Liberal Education, 95*(4), 38–45. http://www.aacu.org/publications-research/periodicals/race-conscious-student-engagement-practices-and-equitable

Hatfield, N., Brown, N., & Topaz, C. M. (2022). Do introductory courses disproportionately drive minoritized students out of STEM pathways? *PNAS Nexus, 1*(4), 167. https://doi.org/10.1093/pnasnexus/pgac167

Hathaway, R. S., Nagda, B. A., & Gregerman, S. R. (2002). The relationship of undergraduate research participation to graduate and professional education pursuit: An empirical study. *Journal of College Student Development, 43*(5), 614–631.

Held, V. (2006). *The ethics of care: Personal, political, and global*. Oxford University Press.

Hunter, A.-B., Laursen, S. L., & Seymour, E. (2007). Becoming a scientist: The role of undergraduate research in students' cognitive, personal, and professional development. *Science Education, 91*(1), 36–74. https://doi.org/10.1002/sce.20173

Hurtado, S., Dey, E. L., Gurin, P. Y., & Gurin, G. (2003). College environments, diversity, and student learning. In J.C. Smart (Ed.), *Higher education: Handbook of theory and research* (Vol. 18, pp. 145–189). Springer.

Hurtado, S., Eagan, M. K., Cabrera, N. L., Lin, M. H., Park, J., & Lopez, M. (2008). Training future scientists: Predicting first-year minority student participation in health science research. *Research in Higher Education, 49*(2), 126–152. https://doi.org/10.1007/s11162-007-9068-1

Kirchgasler, C. (2018). True grit? Making a scientific object and pedagogical tool. *American Educational Research Journal, 55*(4), 693–720.

Lane, S. R. (2020). Addressing the stressful first year in college: Could peer mentoring be a critical strategy? *Journal of College Student Retention: Research, Theory & Practice, 22*(3), 481–496. https://doi.org/10.1177/1521025118773319

Locks, A. M., & Gregerman, S. R. (2008). Undergraduate research as an institutional retention strategy: The University of Michigan model. In R. Taraban & R. L. Blanton (Eds.), *Creating effective undergraduate research programs in science: The transformation from student to scientist* (pp. 11–32). Teachers College Press.

Lopatto, D. (2003). The essential features of undergraduate research. *Council on Undergraduate Research Quarterly, 23*(3), 139–142.

Lopatto, D. (2010). Undergraduate research as a high-impact student experience. *Peer Review, 12*(2), 27–31.

Love, B. L. (2019). *We want to do more than survive: Abolitionist teaching and the pursuit of educational freedom*. Beacon Press.

Maton, K. I., Hrabowski III, F. A., & Schmitt, C. L. (2000). African American college students excelling in the sciences: College and postcollege outcomes in the Meyerhoff Scholars Program. *Journal of Research in Science Teaching: The Official Journal of the National Association for Research in Science Teaching, 37*(7), 629–654. https://doi.org/10.1002/1098-2736(200009)37:7<629::AID-TEA2>3.0.CO;2-8

Maton, K. I., Pollard, S. A., McDougall Weise, T. V., & Hrabowski, F. A. (2012). Meyerhoff Scholars Program: A strengths-based, institution-wide approach to increasing diversity in science, technology, engineering, and mathematics. *The*

Mount Sinai Journal of Medicine: A Journal of Translation and Personalized Medicine, *79*, 610–623. https://doi.org/10.1002/msj.21341

Mau, W. C., Chen, S. J., Li, J., & Johnson, E. (2020). Gender difference in STEM career aspiration and social-cognitive factors in collectivist and individualist cultures. *Administrative Issues Journal: Connecting Education, Practice, and Research*, *10*(1), 30–45. https://doi.org/10.5929/2020.10.1.3

Mayhew, M. J., Rockenbach, A. N., Bowman, N. A., Seifert, T. A., & Wolniak, G. C. (2016). *How college affects students: 21st century evidence that higher education works* (Vol. 1). John Wiley & Sons.

McGee, E., & Bentley, L. (2017). The equity ethic: Black and Latinx college students reengineering their STEM careers toward justice. *American Journal of Education*, *124*(1), 1–36. https://doi.org/10.1086/693954

McGee, E. O., & Stovall, D. (2015). Reimagining critical race theory in education: Mental health, healing, and the pathway to liberatory praxis. *Educational Theory*, *65*(5), 491–511.

Milkman, K. L., Akinola, M., & Chugh, D. (2015). What happens before? A field experiment exploring how pay and representation differentially shape bias on the pathway into organizations. *Journal of Applied Psychology*, *100*(6), 1678–1712. https://doi.org/10.1037/apl0000022

Morton, T. R., Gee, D. S., & Woodson, A. N. (2019). Being vs. becoming: Transcending STEM identity development through Afropessimism, moving toward a Black X consciousness in STEM. *The Journal of Negro Education*, *88*(3), 327–342.

Museus, S. D. (2021). Revisiting the role of academic advising in equitably serving diverse college students. *The Journal of the National Academic Advising Association*, *41*(1), 26–32.

Museus, S. D., & Quaye, S. J. (2009). Toward an intercultural perspective of racial and ethnic minority college student persistence. *The Review of Higher Education*, *33*(1), 67–94.

Nagda, B. A., Gregerman, S. R., Jonides, J., von Hippel, W., & Lerner, J. S. (1998). Undergraduate student-faculty research partnerships affect student retention. *The Review of Higher Education*, *22*(1), 55–72. https://doi.org/10.7709/jnegroeducation.88.3.0327

National Academies of Sciences, Engineering, and Medicine (NASEM). 2017. *Undergraduate research experiences for STEM students: Successes, challenges, and opportunities.* The National Academies Press. https://doi.org/10.17226/24622.

National Center for Education Statistics. (2022). College Student Employment. Condition of Education. U.S. Department of Education, Institute of Education Sciences. https://nces.ed.gov/programs/coe/indicator/ssa

Newton, F. B., & Ender, S. C. (2010). *Students helping students: A guide for peer educators on college campuses.* John Wiley & Sons.

Noddings, N. (1992). In defense of caring. *The Journal of Clinical Ethics*, *3*(1), 15–18. https://doi.org/10.7709/jnegroeducation.88.3.0327

Oseguera, L., Park, H. J., De Los Rios, M. J., Aparicio, E. M., & Johnson, R. (2019). Examining the role of scientific identity in Black student retention in a STEM scholar program. *Journal of Negro Education*, *88*(3), 229–248.

Oseguera, L., Rios, J. D. L., Park, H. J., Aparicio, E. M., & Rao, S. (2022). Understanding who stays in a STEM scholar program for underrepresented students: High-achieving scholars and short-term program retention. *Journal of College*

Student Retention: Research, Theory & Practice, 24(3), 773–809. https://doi.org/10.1177/1521025120950693

Osei-Kofi, N., Shahjahan, R. A., & Patton, L. D. (2010). Centering social justice in the study of higher education: The challenges and possibilities for institutional change. *Equity & Excellence in Education, 43*(3), 326–340. https://doi.org/10.1080/10665684.2010.483639

Piatt, E., Merolla, D., Pringle, E., & Serpe, R. T. (2019). The role of science identity salience in graduate school enrollment for first-generation, low-income, underrepresented students. *The Journal of Negro Education, 88*(3), 269–280. https://www.jstor.org/stable/10.7709/jnegroeducation.88.3.0269

Ray, V. (2022). *On critical race theory: Why it matters & why you should care.* Random House.

Ris, E. W. (2015). Grit: A short history of a useful concept. *Journal of Educational Controversy, 10*(1), article 3.

Rodríguez Amaya, L., Betancourt, T., Collins, K. H., Hinojosa, O., & Corona, C. (2018). Undergraduate research experiences: Mentoring, awareness, and perceptions—A case study at a Hispanic-serving institution. *International Journal of STEM Education, 5*(1), 1–13.

Ronald E. McNair Postbaccalaureate Achievement Program. (2021–2022). https://www2.ed.gov/programs/triomcnair/index.html

Rosas Alquicira, E. F., Guertin, L., Tvelia, S., Berquist, P. J., & Cole, M. W. (2022). Undergraduate research at community colleges: A pathway to achieve student, faculty, and institutional success. *New Directions for Community Colleges, 2022*(199), 63–75. https://doi.org/10.1002/cc.20524

Schwartz, J. (2012). Faculty as undergraduate research mentors for students of color: Taking into account the costs. *Science Education, 96*(3), 527–542.

Steele, C. M., & Aronson, J. (1995). Stereotype threat and the intellectual test performance of African Americans. *Journal of Personality and Social Psychology, 69*(5), 797.

Sto. Domingo, M. R., Sharp, S., Freeman, A., Freeman Jr, T., Harmon, K., Wiggs, M., & Summers, M. F. (2019). Replicating Meyerhoff for inclusive excellence in STEM. *Science, 364*(6438), 335–337. https://doi.org/10.1126/science.aar5540

Stoffel, J. M., & Cain, J. (2018). Review of grit and resilience literature within health professions education. *American Journal of Pharmaceutical Education, 82*(2), 6150. https://doi.org/10.5688/ajpe6150

The Mellon Mays Undergraduate Fellowship. (2023). *About history.* https://www.mmuf.org/about/history

Watson, W., Sealey-Ruiz, Y., & Jackson, I. (2016). Daring to care: The role of culturally relevant care in mentoring Black and Latino male high school students. *Race Ethnicity and Education, 19*(5), 980–1002. https://doi.org/10.1080/13613324.2014.911169

Weidman, J. (1989). Undergraduate socialization: A conceptual approach. *Higher Education: Handbook of Theory and Research, 5*(2), 289–322.

Wilder, C. S. (2013). *Ebony and ivy: Race, slavery, and the troubled history of America's universities.* Bloomsbury Publishing USA.

Yomtov, D., Plunkett, S. W., Efrat, R., & Marin, A. G. (2017). Can peer mentors improve first-year experiences of university students? *Journal of College Student Retention: Research, Theory & Practice, 19*(1), 25–44. https://doi.org/10.1177/1521025115611398

13

CONCLUSION

The Problem with Grit is White Supremacy

Rocío Mendoza, Deborah Faye Carter, and Angela M. Locks

Tyrone Howard, in a keynote speech during a Juneteenth symposium at California State University, offered the following words of critique about grit:

> How dare you, Professor Duckworth, tell me that poor folks don't have grit! ... So to me this whole grit argument is veiled racism. Let's just say our systems are fine, our systems are perfect, but they just don't try hard enough. They don't want it bad enough, they just don't seem to be motivated enough. We've got to challenge that whole way of thinking.
>
> *(Howard, 2022)*

While Duckworth's conceptualization of grit has been enormously popular with the general public and has inspired the interest of parents, leaders of K-12 schools, and practitioners in higher education, at the same time, some scholars in the educational research community and in psychology have remained more skeptical about grit and whether the concept captures something meaningful about educational achievement processes.

In discussing the connections between white supremacy and grit, we refer to Solórzano's definition of white supremacy from Chapter 3: "the assigning of values to real or imagined differences to justify the perceived inherent superiority of whites over African Americans and other People of Color and warrants the right and power of whites to dominance." Conceptually, grit is linked to white supremacy in at least two ways: (a) the historical origin of the concept comes from nineteenth-century eugenicist scholars and the U. S. cultural tenet of rugged individualism; and (b) descriptions of gritty

DOI: 10.4324/9781003332497-16

personality attributes share ideals of the white middle class. It is worth repeating Howard's (2022) words above: "We've got to challenge that whole way of thinking." By challenging it, we synthesize the contributing authors' claims about the limitations of grit as a concept and focus on future directions of educational achievement research. In the final section of the chapter, we consider a future in higher education that is more equitable and the ways scholars, practitioners, and others can move toward justice.

Eugenics, the Frontier, and Grit

The two quotes below are emblematic of deep contradictions embedded in grit as theoretical concept.

> [grit] is a reference to the Western, you know, starring John Wayne, which is about a little 13-year-old girl who sort of does this really gritty, amazing thing... It's a very, I think, American idea in some ways, you know, really pursuing something against all odds.
> —*Angela Duckworth, [Montagne, 2014]*

> Cowboys have remained, in the hearts of most Americans, an evocative representation of American values: love of freedom, fairness, individualism, toughness, enterprise, forward-looking attitude, and whiteness.
> —*(Yellow Bird, 2004)*

While grit may have emerged as a buzzword in education intervention circles in the last decade, the historical origins of the word run much deeper. Popular uses of the word *grit* evoke the frontier west, toughness, mental fortitude; but the frontier in North America was a site for centuries-long processes of genocide, oppression, violence, and exploitation. The cowboys are always the heroes of the story, but who were cowboys persevering against? Grit as a concept and idea has historical roots in political sentiments and popular culture. A person having grit is one who displayed a "rugged individualism" and survived harsh rural conditions in "desolate" and "open" lands. In tracing grit's historical origins, Carter, Razo Dueñas, and Mendoza in Chapter 2 demonstrate the connections between rugged individualism and Westward expansion to settler colonialism.

Tied to grit's roots in settler colonialism are the links grit has to eugenics. Acevedo in Chapter 6 and Carter, Razo Dueñas, and Mendoza in Chapter 2 discuss the historical roots of the intelligence movement, from which research on grit emerged. Duckworth (with and without co-authors) repeatedly cites the late-nineteenth century publications of Francis Galton, widely known for his eugenics beliefs and scientific racism. Galton was interested in aspects of human personality, but he was also a eugenicist who believed that personality was mostly innate, genetic, and differed by racial group. Duckworth et al. (2007) discussed Galton's work on examining high achievers and how this framed their conceptualization of grit:

> More than 100 years prior to our work on grit, Galton (1892) collected biographical information on eminent judges, statesmen, scientists, poets, musicians, painters, wrestlers, and others. Ability alone, he concluded, did not bring about success in any field. Rather, he believed high achievers to be triply blessed by "ability combined with zeal and with capacity for hard [labor]."
>
> *(p. 33)*

Sound familiar? Duckworth et al. (2007) trace the concept of grit, their research design in exploring grit, and interpretation of results to a person who was deeply invested in the concept of racial inferiority. Similarly, Acevedo argues in Chapter 6, "Choosing to base a concept on a racist foundation continues to reinforce white supremacy in contemporary times and ignores the contexts that Latina/o/x students likely have to navigate when maintaining a commitment to their goal." Given that Duckworth and co-authors believe that aspects of grit are innate, it is difficult to reconcile how the problematic foundations of the concept might be useful for us today as we understand the achievements of the broad diversity of people in the United States.

Character Education as Tools of Exclusion

In addition to the troubling origins of grit, there are more contemporary ideas of personality and achievement that remain exclusionary and oppressive. Grit is the latest in a series of similar concepts ("character education," "resilience") designed to stratify children based on who best performs white, middle-class behaviors in the classroom. In higher education, these preferred behaviors align quite closely with racial and socioeconomic status hierarchies. Ris (2015), who has been cited by several chapter authors, argues that the current narrative around grit is similar to the 1960s conversations around the "culture of poverty" (p. 10). Instead of addressing systemic issues that create inequality, though, we are asking students to "buck up" and persevere. We are asking students to be "gritty," assuming that students can persist in the face of tremendous challenges; however, following this logic also means that "the way to help poor people is to make sure their lives remain difficult" (Ris, 2015, p. 11). Along with our colleagues in this volume, we are concerned with how continuing to use grit as a concept and framework harms students of color navigating higher education. In Chapter 5, Mac, Venturanza, Trinh, and Yi describe how grit both renders Asian American students invisible and hypervisible at the same time: "… we must recognize that grit is a racialized construct that maintains and advances the current system of inequities." This is not to say that advocates of grit do not acknowledge structural barriers; but if a solution to inequities is to focus on individual students "having more grit," such policies reinforce racialized structural barriers and perpetuate meritocracy ideology and deficit thinking. It is important to emphasize, as Waterman in Chapter 4 has, that our students and communities *already* have the grit, resilience, and "cultural integrity and self-preservation" to persist.

Academic Achievement

The expressed purpose of grit is to explain why some people are more successful than others but the contributing authors of this volume have described different theoretical and empirical approaches to how we conceptualize achievement. In Chapter 8, Fregoso highlights that Black and Latine/x men's successful transfer to and persistence in baccalaureate-granting institutions seems to be more affected by financial assistance than individual motivation. Similarly, Sanders and Jez in Chapter 9 broaden ideas of academic achievement and retention by focusing their attention on college students with some college, no degree. Sanders and Jez challenge notions of a traditional timelines to degree, especially considering that some students face life circumstances that include being "independent without stable housing, [or] caring for children or an elderly family member." In Chapter 4, Waterman's critique of grit shares Sanders and Jez's observations of some students being on a different attainment schedule. Waterman critiques the Western concept of time in academia as linear; in comparison, some students' lives include community and familial relationships, in addition to the pursuit of higher education degrees. It does not make the attainment of a degree at any age less valuable. Ortiz and Ah Nee-Benham in Chapter 11 also deepen our ideas of academic achievement in their discussion of assessment and research with Indigenous and other communities of color. The authors critique the ways that compliance-based evaluation often is framed by narratives of grit that favor individual persistence and effort.

Discussions of educational achievement, particularly for students of color, need to include discussions of systemic racism. Solórzano's Chapter 3 includes one of the most succinct depictions of systemic racism we have seen, connecting de facto and de jure systemic exclusion to educational systems and white supremacy and its "material conditions." Solórzano builds on this argument by (a) emphasizing the importance of everyday structural racism, (b) making note that such racism is at once, interpersonal, institutional, and internalized, and (c) suggesting that such racism, given its comprehensive pervasiveness, is the key to understanding why students complete their degrees or are pushed out of the academy.

Institutional Contexts and Support

Across multiple settings and practices, contributors also focused on how higher education institutions, and scholars/practitioners who work in them, can support student achievement and educational attainment. Specifically, Mahoney's findings in Chapter 7 underscore the need for institutional resources in the form of faculty capable of engaging African American students and holistic STEM-focused programs; Mahoney also implies that there should be sufficient numbers of African Americans enrolled on any given campus for students to form "genuine networks of social support." Additionally, Mendoza, Aparicio, Carter, and Locks in Chapter 12 highlight how grit can be particularly pernicious in the values and outcomes embedded in undergraduate research. Rzucidlo, Speller, Burmicky, and Palmer in Chapter 10 conclude their analyses of servingness of HSIs as a counternarrative to grit with important and practical questions about a culture of care and curricular and pedagogical approaches for Latinx/a/o students in HSI contexts, all focused on disrupting systems of power that create, rather than remove barriers for students.

Implications

Together, the chapters in this volume provide several implications for higher education research and practice. First, it is important to treat all students as academically capable; their goals need to be affirmed and they are each deserving of academic opportunities to support their needs and increase their skills. Faculty, staff, and administrators need to be trained to support all students across racial/ethnic groups, socioeconomic statuses, gender identities, sexual orientations, veteran status, disabilities, and more. The environments in which students learn have significant impact on the educational outcomes students are able to achieve.

Part of treating students as academically capable is also focusing on how campuses can better support them. How can administrators, staff, and faculty marshal resources more effectively and make sure they are distributed to the people who need them? In the case of this book, undergraduate research programs (Chapter 12) are one model of how academic support programs (with additional wraparound services) can help students develop knowledge and skills, while also positively affecting their persistence. In addition, Sanders and Jez discuss a population for which there is rarely scholarly attention: some college, no degree. What can campuses do to help those – who once attended college and then left – complete their baccalaureate degrees?

Several of the chapters remind us that the approach of focusing on students' assets and strengths, instead of their deficits, is a key way forward toward improving college access and success. As researchers, highlighting ways in which students problem solve, seek to meet their needs, *echándole ganas* in culturally rooted ways, and aspire to achieve is important work that can help identify where our institutions fall short. As contributors highlight, our communities already have the language and methods to draw on strengths and resilience in the face of adversity, echoed in Jayakumar et al. (2013).

We encourage the use of critical theories in conceptualizations of student achievement processes: Ortiz and Ah Nee-Benham discuss evaluation and research methods to better describe the nuances of collectivist cultures, including ways of knowing (Kramer et al., 2012), and pláticas (Morales et al., 2023) for creating sustainable change and empowerment. These methods and practices can more accurately portray the aspirations, goals, contexts, and needs of students of color and other marginalized groups. Together the chapters remind us of the importance of higher education partnerships with communities to encourage access to college and success after enrolling (Person et al., 2021).

A second implication is being critical of "trends and fads" promoted in the area of educational interventions and reforms. As we stated in the introduction, what is new is never new. It is helpful to understand the origins of newly popular terms and concepts that gain a stronghold in education reform circles. Who is funding the initiatives? What are some of the underlying assumptions of the "promising best practices"? So much of the history of policies and interventions to reduce inequality perpetuate deficit thinking and uphold white supremacy. To understand if proposed new interventions may address core issues, we must determine whether the intervention addresses structural barriers to attainment or focuses solely on student behaviors. How does the proposed reform conceptualize academic success? Is there flexibility in the reform or intervention to be adaptable to the wide-ranging needs of the broad populations that a campus may serve?

Third, there are implications for higher education practice that come from this book. Student affairs and academic affairs professionals, given their direct interaction with students, are in key roles to challenge grit in their everyday practices. As Mahoney in Chapter 7 highlights, peer communities are essential for African American/Black students to successfully navigate and graduate with STEM majors. Practitioners can be involved with structuring peer communities and creating partnerships with academic STEM departments and collaborate on activities such as advising, career supports, and panels featuring the voices and experiences of graduates.

Faculty and instructors also play critical roles when they do not adopt a grit logic in the classroom. While we have been socialized to gravitate toward those we identify as "high-achieving" based on traditional metrics of success, we also must strive to consider how to adapt our pedagogy to support students who may need other strategies to thrive. Let us reassess what academic achievement means and think about more flexibility in ways students can demonstrate mastery of course material.

Together, faculty and staff should demonstrate an ethic of care toward all of our students. We must (a) better understand the life circumstances students have experienced that may continue to put stressors on their academic progress and (b) recognize the resilience it already took for our students to show up to our classrooms. A final point regarding higher education practice we would like to make: it is vital for faculty and staff to develop positive, working relationships with each other and respect the work that we do. Similarly, we also must strive to create partnerships across units (e.g., academic departments, student affairs units) so that we are able to make referrals to students when necessary, better understand aspects of the campus community, and generally have a broader understanding of how the campus serves students' needs.

The contributing authors collectively have documented the disproportionate impact of racialized systems and structures on students of color, their families, and communities. Collectively, the chapters also discuss the pernicious ways that our systems—K-12 educational systems, higher education, broader social structural, and our system of knowledge generation—contribute to racial inequality. We each have responsibilities to be reflective about our research, teaching, and practice, as well as to consider how we must critically examine deeply ingrained concepts and perspectives. Our society went through a rapid reconsideration of our practices due to COVID-19, and while some of those changes may not have lasted, others undoubtedly have.

We began the book discussing the context of book bans and political attempts to ban true instruction about the history of this continent. It seems to us that the book banning and the banning of teaching history is an attempt to hide the history that has produced inequality in this country. Political actors want us to ignore the past so that we cannot understand the present in appropriate context. As editors and contributing authors, we believe that by debunking grit as a useful measure of educational achievement, we have situated the concept in appropriate context in order to understand the harms it can cause. We again refer to Love (2019), who stated, "at the heart of grit research ... is the desire to 'fix' marginalized people so that they can participate in and replicate the system that they might have just narrowly survived" (p. 116). As contributing authors, we look to promising practices, emergent theories, and rigorous research to reduce inequality in higher education and support the success of students from a variety of backgrounds.

References

Duckworth, A. L., Peterson, C., Matthews, M. D., & Kelly, D. R. (2007). Grit: Perseverance and passion for long term goals. *Journal of Personality and Social Psychology*, *92*(6), 1087–1101. https://doi.org/10.1037/0022-3514.92.6.1087

Galton, F. (1892). *Finger prints*. Macmillan and Co.

Howard, T. (2022, June 15). *Educating African American students: Issues and challenges for the California State University, University of California, and California Community Colleges*. Keynote Address, The California State University Inaugural Juneteenth Symposium [video]. YouTube. https://youtu.be/8bPbYEmj1OY

Kramer, S., Amos, T. Lazarus, S., & Seedat, M. (2012). The philosophical assumptions and challenges of asset mapping approaches to community engagement. *The Journal of Psychology in Africa*, *22*(4), 537–544. https://doi.org/10.1080/14330237.2012.10820565

Jayakumar, U., Vue, R., & Allen, W. (2013). Pathways to college for young black scholars: A community cultural wealth perspective. *Harvard Educational Review*, *83*(4), 551–579.

Love, B. L. (2019). *We want to do more than survive: Abolitionist teaching and the pursuit of educational freedom*. Beacon Press.

Montagne, R. (2014, March 17). *Does teaching kids to get 'gritty' help them get ahead?* [Radio broadcast]. NPR. https://www.npr.org/transcripts/290089998

Morales, S., Flores, A. I., Gaxiola Serrano, T. J., & Delgado Bernal, D. (2023). Feminist pláticas as methodological disruption: Drawing upon embodied knowledge, vulnerability, healing and resistance. *International Journal of Qualitative Studies in Education*. https://doi.org/10.1080/09518398.2023.2181441

Person, D. R., Kaveh, H., García, Y., & Carsey, T. A. (2021). What leaders believe: Increasing educational attainment among urban youth. *Urban Education*, *56*(3), 355–369.

Ris, E. W. (2015). Grit: A short history of a useful concept. *Journal of Educational Controversy*, *10*(1), article 3.

Yellow Bird, M. (2004). Cowboys and Indians: Toys of genocide, icons of American colonialism. *Wicazo Sa Review*, *19*(2), 33–48.

INDEX

Pages in *italics* refer to figures, pages in **bold** refer to tables, and pages followed by n refer to notes.

Crazy Bull, C. 52
Credé, M. 17, 27; et al. 17–19
Creswell, J., and Plano Clark, V. 119
Critical Qualitative Inquiry (CQI) 200–201
critical race analysis of grit in STEM *see* everyday structural racism (challenging)
Critical Race Pedagogy 42
Critical Race Studies in Education Association (CRSEA), annual conference 42, 45n7
Critical Race Theory (CRT) 5, 33, 36–42; commitment to racial justice 41; Community Cultural Wealth (CCW) 92; and deficit-thinking 40; definition 37; dominant ideology (challenge) 39–40; in education "critical race tools" 38, 45n4–45n5; experiential knowledge (centrality) 40–41; Freirean Critical Pedagogy 38; honesty of tool to examine education 203; intersecting tenets *37*, 37–38, 42, 243–244; legal foundations and tenets 38; medical sciences work 42–43; "modern" era of civil rights 35; Monaghan 36, 38; race, racism, subordination 38–39; recognizing relational history 34–35; transdisciplinary perspective 41–42; University of California, Los Angeles (UCLA) 36–37; white privilege (challenge) 39–40
critiques of grit 17–22; conceptual muddiness 19–20; deficit-thinking 21–22; Duckworth's approach to studying grit 19–20; grit's modest predictive power 17–19; historical origins (debunking grit as "natural" or "universal") 20–22, 26; multiple truths 52; perseverance measurement 18; predictor of GPA claims 17; researchers doubt the validity altogether 26; *see also* grit problem, "rugged individualism"
Cruz, C. 96
cultural capital: advantaged in society 19; Bourdieu's conceptualization 19
"cultural deficit" frame (challenging) 33–34
"culture of poverty" 61, 242

deficit-thinking: African American students in STEM 131; bootstraps mentality (California Community Colleges/grit measurement) 137, 142–143; California Community Colleges (CCCs) 135; community colleges 138; and Critical Race Theory (CRT) 40; faculty/staff 142; grit definition 21–22, 163; and Indigenous feminist theories 53; and Latinx/a/o student challenges/failures 186; racialization of grit for Asian Americans 74–75; SCND student value 171; settler colonialism in U.S. 64; term for student of color 51; upholding 245
degree aspiration model (Carter) 5, 146–147, **149**, 150–152
DigiHunt 214–215
Diné Twin Warriors story 59
Duckworth, A. L. 185, 240; and Eskreis-Winkler, L. 11; et al. 1, 13–16, 73, 91–92, 105–106, 114–115, 122, 186, 199–200, 222, 242; and Gross, J. J. 54–55; *New York Times* interview 16; and Quinn, P. D. 15–16, 54, 63, 74, 182; TED talk 1, 26, 73, 114, 162; use of Galton 241–242; and Yaeger, D. S. 129
duoethnography (Norris) 202

Education Opportunity Program (EOP): counselors 104–105, 107; summer bridge program 102–103
"education survival complex" 2
educational achievement rates, group disparities research 3
educational environments: bias for white upper income students 186; color-neutral approaches 79; Indigenous postsecondary (PSE) graduates "survive" 52, 62; K-12 to community college pipeline 165; Latinx/a/o students 185; "race positive" 25, 27; STEM disciplines (hostile environments) 13, 23–24, 226–227, 234; understanding ways marginalized students navigate 27; *see also* K-12 environment
educational inequities, K-12 environment 136, 220

their lives remain difficult 61, 242; "I'm sorry you've had to be so strong" 64; Indigenous postsecondary (PSE) graduates "survive" education 52, 62; Indigenous students and grit 55–57; indigenous students overcoming a difficult past 50; interrogating terms 51; marginalized first-generation students 63; Melanie (Mohawk) 58–59, 62; Mohawk students removed from campus tour 62–63; myth of extraordinary people as college material 63; Native American higher education literature 55; negative stereotypes/social desirability response bias 54; perseverance indicator 50; role of invisibilization in grit narratives 59; settler colonialism in U.S. 56–57, 62–65; White gaze 63; widening economic inequality today 61; *see also* Indigenous feminist theories

grit problem 1–7; academic achievement 243–244; character education as tools of exclusion 242–243; conceptual linked to white supremacy 240–241; cultivating grit 2; deep contradictions 241; deficit-thinking 245; desire to 'fix' marginalized people 2; eugenics and the frontier 241–242; frontier west *grit* 241; grit as an exclusionary concept 23–24; "grit" historical foundations 4; harming students of color in higher education 243; help poor people by making their lives remain difficult 61, 242; higher education practice 245; implications 244–246; institutional contexts and support 244; "naming social problems not defining students by them" 2–3; overview 1–3; racist foundation 242; "rugged individualism" 241; students' individual talents and resilience strategies 1; "trends and fads" 245; white supremacy 240–246; *see also* critiques of grit

Grit Scale 15–16; Black male students' GPA and grit scores 54, 74; conscientiousness/perseverance

measurement 27; diverse population challenge 18–19; inadequate mark (invalid) 129; K-12 environment 54; postsecondary setting 74; structural/external factors (lack) 127, 129; structure 18

Grit-O 15–16

Grit-S 15–16; West Point cadets 54

"gritty" individual/personality: "long-term stamina" 14; Will Smith as example 11

Gross, J. J., and Duckworth, A. L. 54–55

Guajardo, F.: et al. 212–214; and Guajardo, M. A. 203, 215

Guajardo, M. A., and Guajardo, F. 203, 215

Harper, S. R. 64, 223; Anti-Deficit Achievement Framework 5, 116–119, *117*

Harvard Business Review 114

Haudenosaunee, Indigenous feminist theories 57

health inequality: medical sciences 43; "risk factors" 43

higher education: agenda for traditional students 166–167; applications of grit 7; Black and Latinx low enrollment rates 138; conceptualization of grit 73–75; digital storytelling 214–215; economic development of the nation 22; enrollment rates "post-pandemic" 112–113, 128–129; and "frontier thesis" 22, 26; ideologies of hyper individualism 220; Indigenous men (Poolaw's study) 56; long history of exclusion 220; measuring grit 92; pervasive ways grit appears 4; racialization of grit for Asian Americans 80–82, 243; racial/socioeconomic status hierarchies 242; reciprocal relationship with students 64; State of the Union Address (Obama 2009) 166

Hispanic Association of Colleges and Universities (HACU) 190

Hispanic Serving Institutions (HSIs): "background knowledge" 188–189; broad access to education (lack of